ALEUT IDENTITIES

MCGILL-QUEEN'S NATIVE AND NORTHERN SERIES
(In memory of Bruce G. Trigger)
Sarah Carter and Arthur J. Ray, Editors

Aleut Identities

Tradition and Modernity in an Indigenous Fishery

KATHERINE L. REEDY-MASCHNER

McGill-Queen's University Press
Montreal & Kingston • London • Ithaca

© McGill-Queen's University Press 2010

ISBN 978-0-7735-3682-1 (cloth)
ISBN 978-0-7735-3748-4 (paper)

Legal deposit second quarter 2010
Bibliothèque nationale du Québec

Printed in Canada on acid-free paper that is 100% ancient forest free
(100% post-consumer recycled), processed chlorine free

McGill-Queen's University Press acknowledges the support of the
Canada Council for the Arts for our publishing program. We also
acknowledge the financial support of the Government of Canada
through the Book Publishing Industry Development Program (BPIDP)
for our publishing activities.

Library and Archives Canada Cataloguing in Publication Data

Reedy-Maschner, Katherine L., 1975–
  Aleut identities : tradition and modernity in an indigenous fishery /
Katherine L. Reedy-Maschner. ·

(McGill-Queen's native and northern series) Includes bibliographical
references and index.
ISBN 978-0-7735-3682-1 (bound)
ISBN 978-0-7735-3748-4 (pbk)

  1. Aleuts – Fishing – Alaska – Aleutian Islands. 2. Aleuts – Social
life and customs. 3. Aleuts – Social conditions. 4. Fisheries – Alaska
– Aleutian Islands. I. Title. II. Series: McGill-Queen's native and
northern series.

E99.A34R43 2010305.897'107984   C2010-901043-4

Typeset by Jay Tee Graphics Ltd. in 10.5/13 Sabon

Contents

Contents

Figures and Tables

FIGURES

TABLES

Preface

Cold Bay, North Pacific, 4 June 2002, aboard the F/V *Aleut Kid*

Our Aleut fisherman friend Rick Koso arrived in his boat to collect us at the dock in Cold Bay, Alaska, a long, unprotected deep-water port. There we were faced with the logistics of getting our baby boy from a high dock down a slippery ladder onto a rocking boat with a strong wind blowing. I wanted to turn around and go home. I watched anxiously from the deck of the boat as my husband Herb attached a rope to the baby backpack and lifted the pack onto his back with our ten-month-old Alexander strapped in. Herb's camp manager Russ held the rope on the dock while Herb and Alex descended the ladder.

After we were on board and sipping coffee in the warm dry wheelhouse, I relaxed a bit but clutched my son tightly. The boat seemed to plough through the water rather than rock on the surface, and for the first time I did not reach for the motion-sickness pills. Finally, I relinquished my son to the captain, who held Alex on his lap while steering the boat and cracked the window to let the air and sea spray on his face. Later, I lay down with him on a bunk and let the boat rock him to sleep.

We were on our way to King Cove, my research site of the previous two years, before dropping my husband and two of his crew off at his remote archaeological field camp. For the next six weeks, he was unreachable, only able to call me on his satellite phone at US$5 per minute.

On board with us was an Aleut man named Mike Livingston, who has volunteered his labour on my husband's crew. He was raised in Cold Bay but was not told that he was Aleut until he was a teenager and has spent the last three decades making up for lost time. He is now an expert kayak (baidarka) builder and basket weaver and teaches these crafts at the Alaska Native Heritage Center in Anchorage and at village culture camps. The boat's captain remembered going to their unplumbed, non-electrified house years ago. "There was a dead seal hanging in the kitchen, a big ole bull kelp cooking on the stove that your dad sliced up to eat." He shook his head. "They were eating *old* Aleut food. We don't eat that stuff anymore."

Looking out across the water, we saw land that my husband and I had surveyed for ancient Aleut sites, having plodded over hummocky tundra in rain and wind, mapping hundreds of ancient villages, camps, historical trapping cabins, and World War II debris. For most of our time in the Aleutian region, we have looked out at the sea from the land. At this moment, however, I was struck with the notion that for thousands of years this has been the view of the Aleut: the land from the sea.

This was also the view of my grandfather, the sailor Ralph Croner, from the 1930s to the 1960s. He was a merchant marine navigation officer and served all over the Pacific Rim on a variety of ships, from the Bureau of Indian Affairs ship USS *Pribilof* to the geodetic survey ship the USS *Explorer* to the F/V *Cyrus*, a seagoing tug that had been converted into a crabbing vessel for fishing the Bering Sea, the only ship he ever captained. He also served on Alaska Marine Highway ferries – the M/V *Matanuska* and the M/V *Tustumena*. The latter still serves the Alaska Peninsula and Aleutian chain, based out of Homer. A month and a half before the Cold Bay trip, my husband, our son, and I rode this very ship between King Cove and Cold Bay on our way home to Idaho to prepare for a two-week trip to Japan. The purpose of the trip was to bring back artifacts from an ancient Aleut village in Port Moller on the Bering Sea side of the Alaska Peninsula, which had been excavated by Japanese archaeologists Hiroaki and Atsuko Okada in the 1970s and 1980s. My grandfather also spent a great deal of time on ships that went to Japan, Korea, and the Philippines, where he insisted that the women fell hand over foot for him. He was very vain, and a swarm of "sweet little gals" always seemed to be on hand when he was choosing gifts for my mother and her siblings. He seemed to have a girlfriend in every Pacific port. Though he always said that Filipinas were "the most beautiful people in the world," he came home to the old Croner homestead in Fairfield, Idaho, with a Korean woman and her daughter. My step-grandmother was reportedly a laundress or a prostitute in Korea; the stories were unclear. Her name was Deung Nam, but my grandfather called her Tsunami – after the huge sea wave caused by undersea earthquakes or volcanic eruptions so common on the North Pacific Rim – shortened to Su Nam.

Grandpa Ralph drove a car as if he was steering a ship, making big wide turns. As a navigator, he called himself Celestial Sam, even wrote a novel with himself as protagonist, and sang hilarious sea shanties. For every new endeavour he was always "getting my sea legs." In his younger days, he boxed professionally with the nickname Sailor. We all wondered whether he had had the sense knocked out of him; he used to make us all belts and purses by seamens' square knotting but had a harder time remembering our names.

There is a strong oral tradition in my family; we are storytellers. There is also a thread of maritime language in our family; when the weather changes in our landlocked Idaho, my grandmother says, "The tide's coming in." Most of what I know of Grandpa Ralph comes from the stories of my uncles, aunts, mother, and grandmother, stories repeated hundreds of times with the same gestures, pauses, and punch lines that I now find myself repeating. I wish I had paid closer attention while he was alive. Grandpa Ralph was in the Pribilof Islands, where he squeamishly witnessed a fur seal harvest, and used to tell stories of islands with no trees, just wind. Many Aleut elders in King Cove remembered a few of my grandfather's ships passing through and also a geodetic survey ship that anchored near King Cove for a winter.

When I tell people in the Aleutians that I am from Idaho, often the response is "Ah, inland," followed by a declaration that they could never be away from the coast. I like to think that I inherited some of my grandfather's love of the sea, if not his sea legs. I get seasick, and my grandmother says with heavy emphasis, "So did he." I get homesick for the smells, the harbour, and the boats even though I grew up not just inland but in arid southern Idaho amidst sagebrush, and I never learned to swim.

My interest in the Aleutians began in 1995 when I was an undergraduate at the University of Wisconsin-Madison and volunteered my summers on archaeological field projects on the lower Alaska Peninsula and Unimak Island, the easternmost island in the Aleutian chain. Growing tired of tent life and pining for civilization, I began to focus on the modern Aleut villages.

King Cove instantly became a treasured community for me as life-long friendships were made on the first day I arrived. The notion of being incorporated into a Native family, as so many arctic anthropologists have been (I think somewhat self-indulgently, for example, Briggs 1970:20: "I rather hoped I might discover myself Eskimo at heart"), is not part of the Aleut way. I lived with a few families in several extended households, cared for their children, helped with college applications, and participated fully in household duties. My son Alexander was born in August 2001, and fieldwork continued with baby in tow. A great deal of my time was spent in the household of the most politically active woman in the village and with her extended family. The people of King Cove welcomed my husband and me and liked the way we divided our attention between "studying the living and studying the dead." At the same time, they were "hands off"; they were willing to be interviewed, to tell stories, and to share ideas but did not want to be inconvenienced too much. I did not set out to study the Aleut, but rather to work with them to assess their world and concerns within and beyond the community. Analyzing changes in dependence, interdependence, balances of power, values, and norms underlying behavioural patterns has brought to light the ways in which people comprehend the erosion and strengthening of these processes.

My material is based on twenty months of fieldwork since 2000, with the majority of time spent in King Cove, Alaska, and shorter visits to the nearby villages of False Pass, Nelson Lagoon, and Sand Point. Considerable time was also unavoidably spent in Cold Bay, the bleak airport hub that everyone must pass through to get to and from these villages. Though not an Aleut village, it is home to several Aleut and is the regional headquarters of the US Fish and Wildlife Service. I also spent time in Anchorage at the Alaska Court System, the Aleutians East Borough, Eastern Aleutian Tribes, the Aleut Corporation, and the Aleutian/Pribilof Islands Association offices.

Several kinds of interview were employed: life history and general information-gathering interviews; formal interviews with a cross-section of individuals, families, and professionals; informal visiting with as many people as possible; and discussions in the Harbor House. Structured interviews were conducted with people of all ages, economic status, and reputation in the community, including fishermen and their family members, elders, members of the village corporation, tribal council members, business owners, cannery managers and workers, members of law enforcement, local politicians, and health workers, with most individuals wearing multiple hats. I interviewed boat captains and their wives about their concerns and priorities. I also participated in household and fishing activities as much as possible. Though there was no language barrier, there was an "expression barrier" that needed to be crossed. I also collected genealogical data on more than four thousand individuals, living and deceased.

Different levels of data – for example, how fishing occurs, who participates, and how different levels of participation occur – have allowed me to learn a great deal about social organization on land and at sea. Reputational rankings assessing the community status of an individual (heterogeneously evaluated for social and political status and economic success) were informally employed in the Harbor House, using a variable "panel of judges." The same ten to twelve fishermen were the core of the Harbor House assembly, consisting of the harbourmaster and his alternates, elder fishermen, and maintenance crew, all evaluating others' reputations and statuses. Gossip networks of both men and women were also instrumental in evaluating or deciding a person's status (see also Jorion 1976).

Because of the sensitivity of many of the topics discussed, no individuals are identified in the text, except in a few photo captions with permission. Pseudonyms and false initials are used where it is necessary to distinguish between individuals.

An understanding of the nature of the current problems that Aleuts face calls for an understanding of historical processes, if not necessarily colonial processes. Existing material evaluated in this study includes the ethnographic/ethnohistoric and the subsistence/economic to correlate with the village and crime data. These data supplemented the fieldwork, providing a general sense of community, identity, organization, and the village's economic and social circumstances. Archival data have allowed me to explore the contact history and contrast the recent and distant past with the present, making inferences about change through time. All of these data are problematic: they were collected with different research goals in mind; they may pertain to different villages and people; and they were collected sporadically by different researchers. However, they are evaluated in order to make certain knowledge claims about economic and social circumstances. Part of the research included a critical evaluation of the limitations of these data and is discussed as the data are presented.

Social and economic data (demography, health, mortality, general crime, welfare, business) have been collected and analyzed. The measurement of short-term economic events has allowed for the documentation of changes and correlations of effects with the crime data. The Eastern Aleut economy, and arguably Aleut social life, revolves around the fishing industry. The Alaska Department of Fish & Game's subsistence and commercial fisheries reports contain numbers of species harvested for households and the community, demographics, other economic data, and some interview data. Most data available from bureaus, agencies, services, and others are lumped by village, region, or even the State of Alaska, skewing the data away from the population that I am most interested in. AN/AI (Alaska Native/American Indian) is the standard generic classification.

When I began working in the communities, leaders of the Aleutians East Borough linked the changes and stresses within the fishing industry to the increasing rates of crime in Aleut villages. Studies of crime cannot be restricted to violations of codified laws. Customary ways of dealing with nonconformity were noted by Malinowski (1926) and do not have to correspond to law. Compliance is often required for both means of "social control," but this is not always an easy fit. I have attempted to sort out both influences and to contextualize them for whether they contribute to or account for the behaviours in question. The Aleut have local definitions of crime, but they are also Alaskan and American citizens and participate directly in the American judicial system. It is thus critical that quantitative data collected as a by-product of Aleut interaction with the judicial system be used in comparison with local constructions identified during the village-based study. Crime statistics and interview data were gathered from the King Cove Police Department as well as from court records for criminal and civil cases, which included information on divorces/dissolutions, family disputes, and other conflicts that were resolved legally.

This is a study of the fishing community of the Eastern Aleut, not what happens aboard fishing vessels. As a woman (who was neither married to a fisherman nor the daughter of a fisherman), I only went fishing for leisure between commercial openings. Fishing is heavily gendered at the outset, and I followed these rules. To be legally aboard during commercial fishing, crew licences are required for everyone on board. At the same time, a few offers to take me fishing were simultaneously sexual propositions, which I declined. It is understood that women on board are usually tied to the captain or a crewman as family or in a sexual relationship. One opportunity to ride on a tender for a day was thwarted by the captain's wife shouting, "No girls on *my* boat!" The boat, of course, was not hers, nor was it even owned by her husband, who captains it. Rather, she was asserting her domain, perceiving my presence, however benign, as a threat. Nevertheless, I spent time aboard vessels riding between King Cove, Cold Bay, and Sanak Island, fishing for fun, travelling to the old village of Belkofski, and on boats moored in the harbour. Women who do not usually fish still understand fishing, though perhaps not in the same way as the Aleut men or in ways that women who crew might do.

Taken together, I hope to have told a good story through my own experiences and with the best social data available. Most of all, I want to convey that these Aleut villages are healthy, vibrant, and fun places in which to live and work, and while there are considerable obstacles for the people to overcome within and beyond the villages, they do so in creative, dynamic ways.

Acknowledgments

Fieldwork was supported by the Wyse Fund Fieldwork Grant and the Richards Fund, Department of Social Anthropology; the H.M. Chadwick Fund, Department of Anglo-Saxon, Norse and Celtic; and the Ridgeway-Venn Travel Studentship, all of the University of Cambridge. This material is based upon work supported by the National Science Foundation, Arctic Social Sciences grants OPP-0094826 and OPP-0454734. Any opinions, findings, conclusions, or recommendations expressed in this material are those of the author and do not reflect the views of the National Science Foundation.

In King Cove, I am grateful to everyone at Peter Pan Seafoods, Inc., for their interest and support, and for the free meals in the mess hall. I thank the many residents and transients of King Cove, especially Della and Trisha Trumble, Rick and Theckla Koso, Jim and Kathie Gould, Kathy, Ginger, LeAnna, and Larry Bear, Alex and Mattie Samuelson, Cindy Samuelson, Marvin and Walda Hoff, Lawrence and Frances Larsen, Tommy Dobson, Gordon Berntsen Sr, Vernon and Lisa Wilson, Melvin and Lou Ann Koso, Big Shot Mack, Barney Mack, Liza Mack, Margaret Gould, Leslie Bennett, the entire Mack family, and Eddie, Glen, and the Harbor House crowd for their friendship and generosity. The King Cove Corporation, the Agdaagux Tribal Council, the Aleutians East Borough, especially Bob Juettner, Eastern Aleutian Tribes, and the King Cove Police Department provided invaluable support. The city of False Pass and Lotta Hines were very generous to me. In Sand Point, I thank David and Susie Osterback, Alvin and Marie Osterback, Peggy Osterback, George and Arlene Gundersen, and Melvin and Marilyn Larsen. In Nelson Lagoon, I thank Ray and Katie Johnson, Justine Gundersen,

Theo Chesley, Butch Gundersen, and the health clinic staff. Mike
Livingston, Aleut artist, kayak builder, and former police officer from
the Anchorage Police Department generously guided me through the
Alaska Court System and the Alaska Department of Public Safety.
I also thank Lucinda Neel from Fish & Game in Kodiak. Jane
Trumble, Della Trumble, and Lisa Wilson provided beautiful photos.
Barney Mack and Tommy Dobson graciously dug out pictures to
share, mostly boat after boat. The late beloved Cindy Samuelson
spent many an hour poring over genealogies with me, and Marilyn
Larsen shared her impressive accumulation of family histories,
genealogies, and immigration records from years of her own work.
Julie Hillebrant and Herb Maschner assisted with images, figures,
and maps. Some boat sketches are my freehand adaptations from
ADF&G's pamphlet on commercial boats, and others are my own.

I am forever in the debt of my PHD adviser, Barbara Bodenhorn,
who is equal parts tough and nurturing. The Department of Social
Anthropology and Pembroke College, Cambridge, provided a dream
academic environment. Many thanks to Buck Benson for assist-
ance with the graphics. I am grateful to Idaho State University's
Anthropology Department, especially the late Teri Hall, for granting
me an affiliation and being supportive. Appreciation also goes to Fae
Korsmo, Chris and Ann Chippindale, Loraine Gelsthorpe, Anthony
Webster, Allen McCartney, Bill Simeone, Heidi Helmandollar,
Gillian Wallace, Edward Reedy, Kurt Iverson, Diana Cote, Owen
and Stephanie Mason, Sharon Plager, James Laidlaw, Piers Vitebsky,
David G. Anderson, and fellow students at Cambridge. I must also
express thanks to my husband's dynamic crew of archaeologists,
geomorphologists, and biologists, who occasionally made King Cove
base camp and managed to make themselves notorious during their
stays, especially Garrett Knudsen, Amber Tews, Jim Jordan, and
David Johnson. My wonderful husband Herb Maschner introduced
me to Alaska and has supported me in immeasurable ways; nothing I could say here would adequately describe his love, humour,
and encouragement. Hugs and kisses to my beloved sons Alexander
Beowulf and Augustus Dylan, who both unwittingly act as charming
research assistants.

ALEUT IDENTITIES

Introduction

Indigenous peoples of Alaska are often portrayed as timeless groups who hunt and fish primarily for their own consumption. The narrow definition of this practice, labelled "subsistence," was designed largely by the Alaska state government and has been construed as the foundation of all Alaska Native cultures. Similar views of indigeneity have developed alongside the state's regulatory bodies within the various Alaska Native communities as well as outside them. Anthropologists have likewise used the state's language that cleanly separates subsistence and commercial economic practices, assuming that if money is involved, the practice gets pigeonholed as "Western" and non-traditional.

Within the broader arctic community, however, we find that this trend is largely an American phenomenon. A good deal of Siberian, Canadian, Greenlandic, and Scandinavian work reveals arctic peoples to be embedded in broader productive activities that are also part of social relations. In my experience, rural hunting and fishing peoples of Alaska engage in subsistence and commercial pursuits, often with the same people and equipment, yet may separate them based on the destination of the harvested resource. The result has been a skewed emphasis on subsistence at the deliberate exclusion of multiple economic systems that may or may not intertwine with subsistence. The Aleut have a particular way of engaging in subsistence that is inextricably tangled with commercial fishing, and their identity and relationships are negotiated and affirmed in the process of pursuing both. This has led to a number of problems for the Aleut within the political arena of indigenous representation.

Subsistence absolutism is just one obstacle that the Aleut contend with. When I began working in the Aleutians, popular notions of

Native Aleuts and the Aleutians in general were thrust upon me, and I began actively collecting these representations. Most maps of Alaska cut off the Aleutian Islands and place them floating in the North Pacific or somewhere just north of Hawaii. On the wall of the Aleutians East Borough offices in Anchorage is a poster print of an artistic scene from World War II in which soldiers, charged with ridding the western islands of Japanese forces, are trying to read a map that looks just like that, with the distorted islands cut off and stuck in the Gulf of Alaska. Each soldier has one hand on his chin and is scratching his forehead in bewilderment. Mapmakers still have trouble fitting the Aleutians onto Alaska, though the islands are certainly part of it.

Aleuts feature in some popular fictional writing. Sue Harrison's Storyteller trilogy is in the "prehistoric novel" genre and features intertribal warfare between seventh-century Aleut. These books are popular among Aleuts themselves, and my first exposure to them was when an Aleut friend lent me the first in the trilogy. Anchorage-based writer Dana Stabenow's modern mystery series features Kate Shugak, an Aleut woman who is a tough middle-aged detective-for-hire with a suspiciously Inuit-sounding surname. Kate is a self-righteous teetotaller, who is environmentally conscious and politically liberal, traits that are difficult to find in Aleut villages, much less rolled into one person. She is an Aleutian ex-patriate once removed; her parents were supposed to be from the Aleutians but had relocated to Kodiak and then Cordova. Stabenow describes the "epicanthic folds" around Kate's eyes, which would be a barely pronounced phenotypic trait in someone of her generation, who would certainly have Russian or Scandinavian heritage. Thus far, only one book in the series is actually set in the Aleutians, following an unlikely storyline in which Kate swims from a Bering Sea crab boat (in her Gumby suit, of course) to an unnamed island on which she eventually solves a crime involving missing crewmen and later revisits the island for a romantic tryst with her significant other. Most remarkable is that the weather is pleasant for these scenes. She also meets an Aleut girl who uses a storyknife to illustrate in the sand; these were never used by the Aleut and are not used today. Stabenow's books are fun, and I buy each new release the moment it hits the shelves, but one wonders if she chose her protagonist's identity because of the unlikelihood that she would be challenged in her depictions.

Popular notions aside, *Aleut Identities* focuses on the modern Aleut as they live and work today. The twenty-first-century Aleut of the Alaska Peninsula and eastern Aleutian Islands depend on an indigenous commercial fishery, arguably one of the world's most volatile industries. While continuing to harvest traditional foods, they have translated a long relationship with the sea into a commercial enterprise that permeates every aspect of Aleut life, from family relations to engagement with the global community. The book traces the fisheries as they relate to the expression of individual and community relations and to the development and experience of Aleut identity in the Aleut fishing village of King Cove, Alaska. I argue that the term "identity" itself requires definition within a specific cultural milieu. For the Aleut, commercial fishing has become a cultural system in which participation and success are sources of pride and family connectivity as well as of food and cash. I examine how status structures within the fishing franchise both shape individual and community identity and underpin social relations, and I argue that striving for status forms a foundational aspect of these processes. In this context, I propose alternative explanations for identity development that include the important relationship between status as something that is both an aspect of personal identity and part of the structure of community identity.

As *commercial* fishermen, who are involved not only in market exchange but also in capitalist enterprise, this is an unconventional primary self-definition within the Alaska Native community that affects how they are seen and defined by others. I am thus challenging the assumption that Alaskan indigeneity is inextricably linked to "subsistence," and I am contributing to the ongoing critical discussions about indigeneity within anthropology more generally. These indigenous peoples are highly modernized and are embedded in global processes that negatively affect their access to fisheries. The potential loss of identity tied to a marine ecosystem – through changes in marine productivity, market forces, management plans, and environmental policies – is creating social conflict, economic burdens, and political pressures for the Eastern Aleut. I therefore examine behavioural responses, both positive and negative, to changes of fisheries access, policy, and local systems of status and identity. Aleut communities are struggling to claim an indigenous identity that encompasses their entire way of life, one that is based on progressive commercial interests. Here I explore how the Aleut fight to be recognized as indigenous people and as legitimate commercial fishermen, and how they struggle to combat damaging policies set forth by environmental groups and government agencies. Ultimately, the struggle to preserve local rights to commercial fisheries has become indistinguishable from social and cultural requirements.

In the first chapter, I introduce the region, its people, and the theoretical frames through which I shall argue that culturally and socially defined status forms the foundation of individual identity. Threats to identity and behavioural responses can only be understood in local context, informed by underlying mechanisms of status striving and by inherent inequalities. This analysis first demands data that describes aspects of Aleut social and cultural realities and the fabric of social change. Chapter 2 places Aleut historical identity in context and describes the antecedents of social status and hierarchy, historical expressions of identity, how these have changed through time, and what aspects of the past may be relevant today. Four main time periods have been identified – pre-Russian, Russian, early American, and cannery – where each is analyzed for what identity meant and means through time and how the past is used by living Aleuts.

Chapter 3 places the Aleut at sea, framing subsistence fishing and the commercial fishing franchise, and dissecting the industry in the context of Aleut identity. This chapter elucidates the nature of fishing – how participation and sharing is determined, relevant changes in technology, organization, leadership, the economy, and community involvement – building a "limited entry ethnography," to borrow from the permit policy that determines entrance into the fisheries. Chapter 4 analyzes age and gender constructions, focusing on kin relations and building a story of Aleut identity and status from the bottom up. The sequence in which chapters 3 and 4 appear might seem more logical if they were reversed to follow the standard anthropological order, in which household and village dynamics come before the chapter on fishing. However, during the writing process, the social organization could not be described fully without first understanding the connection to fishing, the work at sea, and the work on land with regard to the sea. I cannot talk about families without continually referring to fisheries dynamics.

Chapter 5 examines Aleut identity from the top down, with emphasis on the interaction between the global perspective and the local reality, linking the people of a seemingly isolated area to regional, national, and global concerns. The global economy consumes fish, while farmed salmon flood the market. Disregard by state, federal, and non-governmental researchers (anthropologists included) has given way to an assault by environmentalists and fisheries bureaucracy. Chapter 6 analyzes the effects of disenfranchisement from the social and cultural ideals and presents crime data in context. Concluding in chapter 7, I summarize the themes and contributions. Ultimately, this is a story of the historical and modern Aleut through the lens of status and identity. The lens is itself the commercial fishing industry.

A brief note on ethnonyms: I use the ethnonym Aleut throughout the book and not Unangan (plural, meaning "the Seasiders"; singular, Unangax), which is gaining momentum as the preferred ethnonym in Aleut communities outside the Aleutians East Borough, because "Aleut" was the only term people used in reference to themselves. The only times that I heard "Unangan" in these communities was when it came from my own lips.

I

Nautical Nation: Indigenous Commercial Fishing in an Eastern Aleut Community

THE EASTERN ALEUT WORLD

A casual visitor to King Cove, Alaska, might at first view it as more of a commercial centre than a rural Aleut village. Massive fishing boats, an industrial cannery, and the politics of gear wars dominate the outward visual and social surroundings. At closer examination, this setting is a backdrop for a reverse image that emerges with equal strength. On a calm evening, with fishing boats cruising in and out of the harbour, fishermen sipping their tenth cup of coffee while playing cribbage in the Harbor House, and meals of salmon shared with extended family and friends, the village seems to fit a quaint romantic ideal. Fishing is the lifeblood of the village, the society, and a culture.

This volume traces the fisheries as they relate to the expression of individual and community relations and identity in the small Aleut (Unangan) fishing village of King Cove. The Eastern Aleut make a living in a particular way: by commercial fishing or in support of commercial fishing. For many Alaska Natives, subsistence is a defining feature, with commercial activities taken up in order to meet the minimum financial requirements for continued subsistence. For the Aleut, on the other hand, commercial fishing is more than a "job" that finances subsistence harvesting. Contemporary Eastern Aleut identity is a product of their intimate relationship with the commercial fishing industry, particularly the salmon industry on which so many rely. This engagement with commercialization is a modern extension of their centuries-long traditional fishing economies, a complex transformation of the ecological, political, and economic, yet also relatively unremarkable in their own words; this is simply what they do. Their self-definition as commercial fishermen in an area where the majority of Alaska Natives define themselves as subsistence societies has negatively affected how others see them. But the development and compatibility of commercial and subsistence patterns are not the dominant sources of concern for the Aleut; rather, it is the continuation of these practices – the future – over which they express anxiety: "The fish are always going to be there. I hope we are too."

Identity has been a prevalent but nebulous focus in anthropological analyses (e.g., Barth 1969; Cohen 1993, 2000; Friedman 1992, 1994)[1] and has been argued as being a valuable concept in studies of social and cultural change in the Arctic (e.g., Anderson 2000; Dombrowski 2001; Nuttall 1992; Pullar 1992), but the concept itself requires further contemplation. What is identity and how do people make meaning through identity? What does it mean to be Aleut? What happens when the hallmarks of being Aleut are challenged? This story is an analytical engagement that moves between the nature of Eastern Aleut identity, outside understandings of their identity, and local responses to social and economic change. Not everyone is able to achieve the role of fisherman because of the institutionalized limited entry system. In particular, I am concerned with what happens to men and women who are shut out of participating in the fisheries at their desired levels and thus the future prospects for the next generation of Aleuts.

Seeking to define identity and status in Aleut terms, I focus on local constructions of identity that hinge on context, and the impact of changes to these contexts, through the lens of individual success and status. Using elements of personal success, status, and societal values, I place these within their cultural contexts and consider the circumstances surrounding relationships between social change, economic change, and social opportunities for individuals, proposing alternative explanations for identity development that include the important relationship between identity and status.

The relative absence of publications and research on the Aleut is conspicuous, a condition that I feel contributes to many contemporary problems that Aleuts face, and hence this volume is presented simultaneously as an ethnography of the Eastern Aleut and a study of the effects of culture change. This research also contributes to the anthropology of fishing in that the Aleut uniquely participate, share, hire relatives, and support their families in a global industry in which they dominate the local fleet. The relationship between subsistence and commercial economies from the individual, household, and fishing fleet levels within "indigenous commercial economies" will give the Aleut a proper context in northern studies. This is a misunderstood part of the world and part of Alaska, where indigenous peoples are highly modernized and embedded in global processes.

The anthropology of fishing is a growing area of interest in the social sciences, tackling the "tragedy of the commons"[2] (Acheson 1981; Gilbertsen 1993; Hardin 1968; McCay and Acheson 1987), fishing strategies (e.g., Durrenberger and Pálsson 1986; Gatewood 1983, 1984; Poggie and Pollnac 1988), applied aspects of fisheries management (Maurstad 2000; C. Smith 1981), calls to save diminishing fish stocks and the societies that exploit them (McGoodwin 1990; Playfair 2003; Sider 1986), and aquaculture[3] (e.g., Lewis, Wood, and Gregory 1996; Tango-Lowy and Robertson 2002). Most fish are managed using biological data, and although "traditional ecological knowledge" (TEK) of localized or indigenous fishing peoples is a growing emphasis in management systems (e.g., King 1997; McDaniel 1997; Menzies 2006), this work still often separates TEK from more scientific knowledge practices and vice versa (Durrenberger and King 2000:10).

What is lacking from many fishing society studies, particularly in the northern context, is an analysis of the land and sea connection, the social organization intimately tied between them, economic implications, the effects of policy on resource claims, and the ramifications of change. Acheson's (1981) call for "shore-based studies of fishing communities" has scarcely been heeded; notable exceptions include, but are not limited to, Pálsson's Icelandic community studies (1988, 1991, 1993); Nadel-Klein's (2003) study of Scottish fishing villages; Mishler and Mason's (1996) "Alutiiq Vikings" study on kinship and community; and Taylor's (1981) study of an Irish fishing community. The "tragedy of the commons" has been a debate about property and ownership, but these discussions often stop short of tackling cultural claims to resources.

In many coastal indigenous communities, their survival and the ability to earn a living often depend upon the strength of the fisheries. The collapse of fisheries is a global trend that cannot be ignored; coastal communities, particularly indigenous peripheral ones, are especially vulnerable and have much to teach us about sur-

vival and integrity against global forces.[4] In the Aleutians, villages
are reliant on commercial exploitation of marine resources and have
few prospects of economic diversification, which places the Aleut in
a precarious position where changes in marine productivity, global
markets, and state and federal management have both short- and
long-term repercussions at sea and on land.

Thus, this study presents the story of the relationship between
Aleut identity, society, economy, and the commercial fishing industry. It seeks to identify the connection between the negative impact
of changes in the commercial fishing industry on status, identity,
social problems, and social relationships in the context of a global
sphere of changes that are being felt at the individual and community levels.

The Eastern Aleut

Inhabiting the Western Alaska Peninsula, the Aleutian Islands, and
the Pribilof Islands, the Aleut are fishermen, hunters, trappers, politicians, business owners, and health workers, among many other
roles. The overwhelming majority are oriented towards the sea and
its resources as the source of sustenance, income, and life. The Aleut
draw upon an archaeological record that reveals a 10,000-year relationship to a marine ecosystem (Laughlin 1963, 1980; Laughlin and
Aigner 1975; Maschner et al. 1997; Maschner 1999a, 1999b, 2000;
Maschner and Reedy-Maschner 2005; McCartney 1974, 1984), from
which the Aleut link their present maritime sociocultural identity
directly to the past, positing a recent history with the depth of many
millennia. Today, there are thirteen communities in the Aleutian and
Pribilof Islands.[5] The Aleut are a heterogeneous population: those
of the Pribilof Islands (St Paul and St George) are primarily fur seal
hunters, birders, and commercial and subsistence fishermen; those of
the western Aleutian communities of Atka and Nikolski are subsistence hunters and fishermen who participate in commercial fishing
at a reduced level and are dabbling in tourism. Unalaska is a town
of about 4,000 residents and home of Dutch Harbor, a large ship-
ping and fishing port. Adak is a former military base in the process
of being recolonized as an Aleut fishing community. The Aleut who
fall within the Aleutians East Borough, the "Eastern Aleut," whose
boundaries form a distinct cultural zone both historically and today,
occupy six communities (Sand Point, King Cove, Nelson Lagoon,

False Pass, Akutan, Cold Bay), with a total permanent population of about 2,600 (Census 2000). This number increases threefold during peak fishing seasons. The majority rely on the sea as subsistence hunters and fishermen, seiners, gillnetters, longliners, trawlers, and pot fishermen.[6]

The Western Alaska Peninsula can also be considered an island environment because of the relatively few land animals, the predominately marine orientation, and the isolated nature of the region. No one passes through these villages accidentally. The sheer expense and difficulty of getting in and out of the villages gives every new face an inherent purpose for being there.

The Eastern Aleut are an indigenous people who are also Western and industrialized. They are linked politically through membership in the Aleutians East Borough, economically through commercial fisheries and transportation, and socially and culturally through education, shared histories, intercommunity kinship bonds, and common ethnicity. Most Aleut claim a mixed Aleut, Russian, Scandinavian and/or other European heritage, although most identify themselves as Aleut and Native Alaskan first.

The Evocative King Cove

In the 1880s, English immigrant Robert King married an Aleut woman from Belkofski and moved his family to the nearby cove to trap and hunt sea otters. A few years later, King was lost at sea, but his name stayed with the cove. The present-day village was founded in 1911 when Pacific American Fisheries built a cannery on the sand spit. Many of its founding families consisted of a European husband and an Aleut wife. Western influences on cultural, economic, and social structures have continuously been felt.

King Cove is located on the south side of the Alaska Peninsula at the head of an embayment facing the Pacific Ocean (figure 1.2). It is nestled between high mountain ridges 28 air kilometres southeast of Cold Bay, the government town with the only major regional airport that everyone must necessarily pass through, which is 1,000 kilometres southwest of Anchorage. Snow-patched mountain slopes end at the water's edge and are incised by numerous small streams. In King Cove, you have the sense of being perched on the edge of the world, because in fact you are.

Facing the North Pacific on the southern edge of the Alaska Peninsula but only 20 kilometres south of the tempestuous Bering

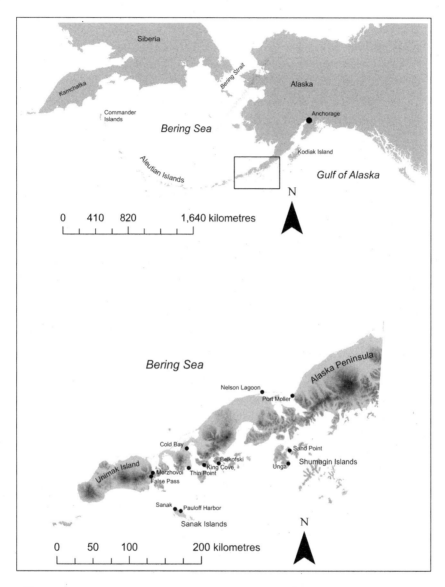

Figure 1.1
Map of the Eastern Aleutian region (provided by Herb Maschner)

Sea and rolling Pacific Ocean, two major weather systems collide over this landscape. Although King Cove claims a maritime climate with temperate winters (20–30°F, –6–0°C) and cool summers (30–65°F, 0–18°C), the environment is anything but mild. Extremely high winds of greater than 150 km/h are commonplace, often blowing

Figure 1.2
King Cove, Alaska, summer 2002 (photo by Jane Trumble)

rain or snow horizontally – and removing the roofs of houses I was living in. The streets puddle up, form huge potholes, and sometimes flood. When it is not raining, the winds dry out the dirt streets and turn the village into a dustbowl.

The Pacific Plate subducting under the North American Plate has created an active volcano complex that includes seven volcanoes within 30 kilometres of King Cove. Tectonics produce frequent earthquakes and the occasional tsunami. Tucked in the back of the cannery's library is an "earthquake meter", as the librarian called it, which was installed in 1988 after they experienced 200 earthquakes in one day. The seismograph registered activity in the few minutes that she and I stood in front of it.

Accessible only by air and sea, King Cove has a 1,500-metre gravel runway outside town. Air access depends on weather, and only small planes can use the strip. The airport "terminal" was a small shack built by high school students that brown bears (*Ursus arctos*) used as a chew toy. This was replaced in 2007 with a more secure one-room building. All flights are VFR (visual flight rules; that is, fly by sight and only in daylight), based on ceiling and visibility data from

Cold Bay. Airfare to all Aleutian communities is expensive; in 2008 the round trip to King Cove cost US$948 from Anchorage via Cold Bay. There is frequent fog, as well as hazardous winds, making travel a challenge. The village is supplied by the cargo shippers Western Pioneer, Coastal Transport, and Sampson Tug, which carry high freight prices. The state ferry M/V *Tustumena* runs once a month from Homer to Dutch Harbor between April and October, stopping in King Cove once each way. The seaward approach to King Cove is not prone to forming sea ice and is often the only route in and out of the village in the winter months, but only if a fisherman is willing to risk it with his vessel and if he is licensed for passengers and carries enough survival suits.

King Cove is a long thin coastal village, with a downtown on the low bay and with two housing subdivisions (Old Rams and New Rams) stretching eastward on higher ground. The Aleutian Housing Authority, which serves ten Aleut villages, applies to the federal Housing and Urban Development (HUD) program for funding, builds single-family homes, and sells them to qualified Native families. All the homeowners have gone to great lengths to personalize these cookie-cutter houses with paint, additions, or repositioning walls. A few have hauled topsoil into their yards to grow lawns on the unforgiving tundra.

Communications technologies are relatively recent. The cannery had a wireless operation for most of the past century. This system was replaced by radiophones and finally satellite telephones. Connection with the outside world is possible via telephone, RATNET (the single channel of the Rural Alaska Television Network), the fourteen channels of the Mount Dutton Cable Company, satellite television, and the scratchy KSDB-Sand Point/Dillingham radio station. The *Dutch Harbor Fisherman* is a bimonthly newspaper, produced 320 kilometres farther down the Aleutian chain, which arrives in King Cove at least one week late; and week-old Sunday editions of the *Anchorage Daily News* can sometimes be found at the King Cove Corporation-owned store. The most important news, such as the price of fish, who is fishing what and where, the state politics, local politics, regulation changes, and gossip can be heard over the VHF radio and at the Harbor House.

In the summer months, King Cove is as timeless as the arctic sunlight. At midnight, children are still riding their bicycles and playing in the streets, the Harbor House is buzzing with caffeine and conversation, salmon boats are moving in and out of their slips, the VHF radio is crackling with chatter, people are driving out to the airport looking for bears, and the bar's jukebox is vibrating its walls. Autumn is a time for the brief but frenzied inundation of crab fishermen, clam digging, stocking the last space in the freezer, and awaiting Permanent Fund Dividend cheques.[7] Winter months are cold, windy, dark, and isolating, but extremely active as the peak of fishing for cod and pollock takes over. Spring is long, slow, and muddy, and a small herring fishery offers a welcome interruption. The boat harbour is the focal point of King Cove, and with its many docks, slips, a boat lift, upland boat storage, stacks of crab pots, warehouses, and 24-hour harbourmaster service, there is continual activity at all hours of the day and night.

The Political King Cove

Life in King Cove is also about a complex political atmosphere, and residents engage daily with institutional and governmental processes. The Aleut, as situated in the greater Aleut world, find themselves under layers of bureaucracy stacked high and overlapping. Each is part of a community in the Aleutians East Borough, a village corporation, a tribal council, and the regional corporation. The Aleut Corporation (TAC) is the for-profit Native corporation that was formed as part of the Alaska Native Claims Settlement Act (ANCSA) of 1971.[8] Village corporations, of which the King Cove Corporation is one, are often organized based on former Indian Reorganization Act (IRA) villages and own the surface rights to the land, while regional corporations own the subsurface rights. The Aleutian Pribilof Islands Association (APIA) is the regional non-profit social service corporation.[9] Eastern Aleutian Tribes (EATS) is the health organization, and regional village councils have passed resolutions giving EATS control of health care.[10] The Agdaagux Tribal Council is the King Cove tribal council. Most former residents of Belkofski now live in King Cove and are part of the Belkofski Corporation and Tribal Council. This list of organizations is not exhaustive, and it is common for one individual to act as a board member for more than one.

The commercial fishing industry provides half of private-sector jobs in Alaska. Ninety-five percent of all commercially caught salmon in the United States is harvested in Alaska, with an average annual catch of 175 million salmon. Alaska produces 80 percent of the world's supply of wild, high-value sockeye, coho, and king salmon, and is home to approximately 17,000 salmon fishermen. The Eastern Aleut represent a small portion of this vast industry, so why are they special? They are important in northern studies because the Eastern Aleut are one of the few indigenous peoples to successfully translate traditional patterns of resource harvesting into a contemporary commercial economy through both active and passive participation, creating an unusual cultural continuity and a social system dependent on participation in the industry.

Given these political and economic conditions, a 10,000-year maritime history, and the current global political climate that shapes participation in fishing, I began thinking about their lives in terms of an "indigenous commercial economy," through which knowledge and practice have been reproduced and revised – and avoiding, as the Aleut do, an imaginary balance of traditions past and disruption by state-level systems in the present. I entered the field assuming a connection between the erosion of identity, defined here in particular ways in relation to the fishing system, and community-defined social problems. The potential disruption of the powerful relationship to fishing resulting from imposed policies, resource depletion, and market displacement is currently blamed by the Eastern Aleut for the social conflict, economic burdens, and political pressures they suffer. Facing social and economic catastrophe, Aleut communities are struggling to redefine an indigenous local identity that encompasses their entire way of life, one that is based on progressive commercial interests. The thrust of this volume is to substantiate and analyze the grounds on which such a connection between identity and social conflict can be made and to explore what seems to be strong implications for the anthropology of fishing as a subdiscipline and delicate issues of identity and status.

TWENTY-FIRST-CENTURY FISHERMEN

To the northernmost extent of the Aleut homeland, anthropologists have presented commercial fishing as something alien to the world of the Pribilof Islands Aleut, arguing that realignment to the fishing business is causing community and cultural disintegration (Corbett and Swibold 2000). In the Aleut chapter of *Endangered Peoples of the Arctic* (Freeman, ed. 2000), which focuses solely on Pribilof Aleuts,

Corbett and Swibold wrote, "Aleuts have become their own agents of assimilation and modernization through their participation in the fishing industry" (2000:14). This Aleut population was relocated from the Aleutians to these two small Bering Sea islands in the late eighteenth century to hunt the northern fur seal where three-quarters of its total population breed each year. Despite beginning as hunters for Russian fur merchants, within the span of a few generations the Pribilof Aleuts were hailing the commercial fur seal hunt as the key to their survival, and when the US government took over the industry after the purchase of Alaska in 1867, the Aleut continued as hunters for another century. Pressure from animal rights activists and budget concerns under the Reagan administration led to its abandonment in 1985 and to a withdrawal of the US government along with its millions of dollars, the economic mainstay of the islands. Subsistence hunting of fur seals by Aleuts has continued, but a slate of social problems increased with the end of the commercial industry.

In the mid-1980s, as the fur seal industry was being dismantled, crab and groundfish fisheries boomed in the Bering Sea, to the benefit of most Aleutian communities. The Pribilof villages of St Paul and St George expanded their harbours and facilities to become regional service centres for fishing vessels and floating processors, a move which Corbett and Swibold suggest would never have happened if the commercial fur seal harvest had continued (2000:8). Pribilof Aleuts also partake in these fisheries as fishermen, and St George is part of a Community Development Quota (CDQ) program that receives percentages of the Bering Sea groundfish allocations. Corbett and Swibold admit that Pribilof Aleuts are successful commercial fishermen with busy harbours, processors, and vessel supply operations, bringing "new prosperity" to the villages. They also state, however, that the marine fishing economy has brought socioeconomic disruption in the way of increased traffic on the roads, transient fishermen transforming the "small village atmosphere," and processors (which require freshwater to operate) that are "straining" the aquifer (2000:13). "The insecure future, increasing loss of cultural identity associated with the seal, and lack of respect from urban populations evidenced by attacks on the traditional Aleut sealing practices, all led to rapid social disintegration," they write. "In the first years after the government pullout, there were unprecedented numbers of suicides and murders, and an increase in drug and alcohol abuse and violent behavior" (2000:8). The local government, tribal council, and village corporation were divided, "intensified by a heritage of oppression and the fact that two institutions were patterned after the dominant society (a municipal government and a for-profit corporation) and the third represented tribal functions" (2000:8).

After reviewing Russian enslavement and American hegemony, Corbett and Swibold list a prosperous fishing industry as the "third major wave" of assimilation and acculturation, since the fisheries are volatile, driven by a global market economy and environmental forces over which the Aleut have no control. Restoring nostalgia over a golden past and asserting that there is something that needs to be reclaimed to bring everyone back into harmony, these researchers talk of "cultural recovery" and "counteract[ing] the loss of Aleut identity" (2000:8, 14).

Why the diatribe on the plight of Pribilovians? I question their analysis because I question their starting point, which replicates a romanticism of the past and a salvage-style anthropology surrounding contact's destructive impact (e.g., "Now is the time to record" Haddon 1898:xxiii; also Bank and Williams n.d.), which has persisted (examined in Rosaldo 1979). Pribilof Aleuts are often described as representative of the entire Aleut population, passively accepting new developments that are negatively altering their culture and their attitude towards the environment. This, I believe, is partly due to a paucity of contemporary Aleutian anthropology in print. But it is also unclear whether Pribilof Aleuts share the views of the anthropologists; it appears instead that these authors are echoing the sentiments of a few. The reality today is that no arctic society can live exclusively on subsistence hunting and fishing.[11] Nor do they want to. A cash income is indispensable for health care, transportation, taxes, heating, clothing, food, and other basic necessities, not to mention satellite dishes, vacations, SUVs, and computers. If, as Corbett and Swibold state, increases in traffic, transients, and stress to the aquifer are the main problems, then I argue that these commercial fisheries are a success. Much like the Pribilof Aleut, the Eastern Aleut have thoroughly embraced the commercial fishing economy and engage daily in processes that link them to a vast industry and global market forces. They regard their livelihood as the modern extension of a customary marine orientation. While the trials of modernity are upon us all, and there can be an uneasy fit for indigenous peoples, these are twenty-first-century hunters and fishermen engaged in twenty-first-century processes, and I intend to keep them there.

Situated not only within a broad literature on the noble savage,
Corbett and Swibold's assertions fit within the dated, yet unfortu-
nately most up-to-date, literature on the modern Aleut (Jones and
Wood 1975). The living Aleut were given up for lost by anthropologists in the 1950s (who considered them a branch of Eskimo, see
also Quimby 1944). "It is a picture all too familiar to anthropologists: a once-thriving, independent people, admirably disciplined
for life in a rigorous environment, now impoverished, diseased and
spiritually weakened, its ancient culture all but destroyed. The story
might serve as a lesson to us. But it is probably too late to save the
southernmost of our Eskimos," lamented Bank (1958:120). In the
anthropological discourse of the 1960s, the Aleut were "continuing to disintegrate at a rapid rate" (Rubel 1961:70). Sociological
research by Jones (1969a, 1969b, 1972, 1973a, 1973b, 1976) again
found little to be optimistic about. Her *Aleuts in Transition* (1976) is
a comparison of "Aleut adaptations to white contacts" between two
Aleut villages, King Cove and Unalaska.[12] King Cove, she argued,
was successful at adapting under the hegemony of American politics
and economy, lacking a chief system, community banya, fish camps,
Orthodox Church organizations,[13] and speakers of Aleut, whereas
Unalaska failed to make a smooth transition in refusing to shed elements of its "traditional culture." For Unalaska, Jones argued that
a study of deviance was irrelevant because one must deviate from
sociocultural norms, and the village had been so dishevelled by foreign control that norms were indeterminate (Jones 1969a:xx). This
assessment was met with resentment by the people of Unalaska, and
it is still fresh in many minds. Though Jones believed she was putting a positive face on King Cove, the people were (and still are) not
impressed with her acculturative suppositions.

Jones related her perceived problems in Aleut communities with
white impositions destroying traditional culture – that they were
"pawns in someone else's game" (1976:68) – which was a fashion-
able standpoint in late-1970s social science. Ethnographic writings
on the Aleut ground to a halt while these types of depiction were
dominant, and thus ideas on the Aleut remain fixed there. Today,
an imagined composition of Aleut villages and their activities has
replaced these former assessments. The State of Alaska has contributed to the problem of misrepresentation by effectively dehuman-
izing and "bleaching" the region white. In debates over fishing rights
involving Eastern Aleutian fishermen and Yup'ik and Iñupiaq fisher-

men of the Yukon-Kuskokwim Delta and Norton Sound, Alaska's former governor Tony Knowles and natural resource agents referred to the Eastern Aleutian region and its people solely as "Area M," the Alaska Board of Fisheries designation for these fisheries. Area M is believed by many to consist of "Seattle boats" and wealthy part-time fishermen from outside Alaska.

One of the leading problems in giving the Aleut a more global image is that there is no ethnography on living Aleuts. Most arctic (and hunter-gatherer) volumes refer to the Aleut in footnotes or conflate Inuit (or Eskimo) and Aleut while really only discussing the Inuit.[14] More recently, the new term Alutiit (Alutiiq, adj.), which refers to Pacific Yupiit, has been erroneously used to describe everyone from Prince William Sound through the Kodiak Archipelago and along the Aleutian chain (recent example in Nuttall 1998:2). This study is a contemporary ethnography of Eastern Aleutian society, one that introduces the people as they live and work today.

Hunter-Gatherer-Fishermen

Anthropologists have long deliberated the definition and position of hunter-gatherer peoples, using terms such as "Fourth World" and "encapsulated" in search of an appropriate classification (e.g., Dyck 1985; Lee 1988; Myers 1988; Swift 1978; Woodburn 1988). Indigenous peoples have also adopted these terms as political tools with which to locally (or even transnationally) unite geographically peripheral peoples and make political claims collectively.[15] Strong themes in hunter-gatherer literature emphasize relativism, unique beliefs and practices on their traditional lands, and unique ways of relating to the environment (debated in Burch and Ellanna 1994; Kelly 1995; Leacock and Lee 1982; Myers 1988), which tend to treat hunter-gatherers as existing outside global economic and social processes. Bettinger (1991:7) notes that hunter-gatherer research is often dictated by a larger theoretical agenda rather than focusing on the hunter-gatherers themselves.

The modern Aleut do not fit any tidy definition of indigenous or hunter-gatherer people. Like other Native Alaskans, the Aleut have multiple political and economic statuses. They maintain some autonomy but also enjoy certain governmental privileges. They are kin-based. They continue to reside in their homeland and use wild resources to their fullest, inextricably for home use and commercial

Figure 1.3
Aleut Dancers with ABC's *Good Morning America* camera crew, June 2002. King Cove
was featured as part of a larger story on Alaska for its successful telemedicine program.
Dancers donned costumes for the filming event, but since the boys, who are customarily
the drummers, were all out fishing, the older girls stepped in to drum.

sale. The Aleut are wealthy relative to most of North America's and
the world's indigenous peoples (many earn more than anthropology
professors). They eat salmon and halibut, but also pizza and fried
chicken. Mayonnaise and Worchester Sauce are key ingredients in
some "traditionally" prepared foods. Few speak the Aleut language,
and there is no everyday traditional dress or adornment, unless you
count fishermen's rubber boots and Helly Hansen raingear. They
also wear Tommy Hilfiger and Ralph Lauren clothes and watch HBO
and MTV. Aleut leaders have dined in the homes of senators and
have travelled to meetings as far away as Washington, DC, Japan,
and Iceland to protect access to fishing. Most, however, have never
been out of the country, and many have never left Alaska. They pilot
boats through the Pacific Ocean and Bering Sea's dangerous waters,
yet many are uncomfortable with cities or the potential dangers of
the outside world.

Hunter-gatherer-fisher societies have exhibited greater social complexity than mobile foragers for much of human history (Ames and
Maschner 1999; Price and Brown 1985; Renouf 1984), and the same

could be said of these contemporary marine-based societies. For all the weight that so many indigenous Alaskans place on subsistence,[16] together with sustenance, social relations, knowledge systems of the environment and human relations within it, often to the exclusion of commercial economies,[17] Eastern Aleuts place *commercial* activities at the heart of sociocultural relations and identity, which makes them stand out amongst indigenous Alaskans. Many Native Alaskans sell their fish, pelts, or basketry, for example, as commoditization of goods, but this often remains short of going into business. The Aleut, however, are part of a for-profit capitalist enterprise and are not just individual fishermen selling fish.

They are caught in a kind of "culture trap," in which outside critics expect them to behave in certain ways and are disappointed when they do not. For example, several non-Native cannery employees found this dual use of tradition and modernity to be disappointing and decided that it was too late for me to study Aleut culture in King Cove. They recommended that I move farther along the Aleutian chain, particularly to Akutan, where the people were "pure blooded" and "more traditional." The small population, lack of political representation, turbulent history, lack of material cultural display or ritual, small number of Aleut speakers, geographic remoteness, expense of travel, and full participation in an industry that has traditionally been associated with white men has made it easy to overlook the fact that the Aleut are a living indigenous people. These factors have direct consequences concerning fishing rights and in their ability to earn a living. The battle over salmon rights involving the Yupiit, Iñupiat, and Aleut (discussed in detail in chapter 5), is also a debate over different representations of traditional lifeways.

EXPLORING IDENTITY AND STATUS

Indigeneity and Identity

Being commercial fishermen greatly affects the politics of (mis)recognition and representation. Hodgson (2002) describes a trend amongst indigenous peoples (and anthropologists' roles within it) to adjust their identities, formerly based upon ethnicity or occupation, to "indigenous" identities and rights of self-determination. Hensel (1996) found that the Yupiit are concerned with identity and ethnicity at the village level as a matter of degree through discourse and practice; that is,

how a Yup'ik is perceived can be based on what he or she says and
does. The Aleut, on the other hand, are not concerned with degree of
ethnicity; one is not seen as more or less Aleut based on fishing practices, but one can be seen as more or less of a fisherman. The dominant
concern for the Aleut in relation to ethnicity is to be recognized collectively as an indigenous people who are commercialized.

In Abner Cohen's (1974, 1981) volumes on the political elite of
West Africa, he sensibly separates cultural identity – in its variety of
collective representations, manifested in individual behaviour – from
ethnic identity, which is relational and political, marked out by symbols and elements of culture. The urban elites claim legitimacy on
their ethnicity and use the language of identity in struggles to maintain it. Cohen concludes that ethnicity does not count until it counts;
that is, in politicized contexts, ethnic identity is used to present a
united front. The Aleut are amongst the trend Hodgson and Cohen
illustrate: their indigeneity has become a political tool, but only in
outward contexts, and anthropology has played a large role in that
(a subject I shall return to in chapter 5).

Identity has been argued as being rooted in both fixed (for the
modernists) and fluid (for the postmodernists) psychic realms, found
both in oneself and in the shared essential characteristics of one's
group (Erikson 1980; Foucault 1979b; Lévi-Strauss 1966, 1969;
Sökefeld 1999:417). How individuals forge identities in contemporary society (e.g., Giddens 1979, 1984) and how individuals choose
membership to group identities based on their views and social
practices (Cohen 2000) have been explored. Friedman argues that
history makes identity, that people need a history to identify themselves for others, and they choose meaningful historical events to
construct a relevant contemporary identity (1992:837). Marcus contends that "local identity emerges as a compromise between a mix
of elements of resistance to incorporation into a larger whole and of
elements of accommodation to this larger order" (1998:61). Thus,
"what was once called 'identity' in the sense of social, shared same-
ness is today often discussed with reference to *difference*" (Sökefeld
1999:417–18).

Definitional efforts have been scarcely substantiated by ethnographic example, and it appears that there are no dominant definitions, theories, or rules about identity in anthropology. Erikson
wrote that "the more one writes about this subject, the more the
word becomes a term for something as unfathomable as it is all-

pervasive" (1968:9). Cohen (1993) suggested that we might be trying to do too much with one term when identity is an all-encompassing gloss for many behaviours and beliefs.

The question here is not which definition or approach to identity is correct but which is most useful in our understanding of Aleut social and cultural change. What does it mean to be Aleut? Many Aleuts say that fishing, living on the coast, and eating fish constitutes who they are. Young boys describe themselves as fishermen, both for what they are now as crewmen and for what they will be (ideally) as boat captains. The act of fishing in turbulent waters and unpredictable weather is extremely difficult, and fishermen derive a great deal of status from overcoming these obstacles. Living and working in this harsh environment takes great skill and ingenuity, and surviving the everyday is an empowering validation that Aleuts can continue to live in their homeland.

Coupled with studies of identity is the notion of agency. In Sökefeld's (1999) study of identity in northern Pakistan, he contends that continually pointing out shared elements of identity overlooks the individual aspects. In a multi-ethnic town where there were "plural and contradicting identities related to social conflict," he found that the individual was constantly trying to "present oneself as a consistent self," which took different forms depending on the circumstances (1999:419). The primacy that anthropology bestows upon culture "reduce[es] the self to a product of culture and often remain[s] blind to individual motivations, aims, and struggles" (1999:430).

Agency also features in Barth's study of group identities among the Pathan in Afghanistan, revealing that group boundedness and identity depend less on a large aggregation of beliefs and practices and more on its members, who select "only certain cultural traits and make these the unambiguous criteria for ascription to the ethnic group" (Barth 1969:119). He argues that when life's circumstances make these criteria difficult to satisfy, "it is to the advantage of the actors themselves to change their label so as to avoid the costs of failure; and so where there is an alternative identity within reach the effect is a flow of personnel from one identity to another and *no* change in the conventional characteristics of the status" (1969:133). However, in some cases, if no alternative identities are accessible and if diverging from a key criterion is not very costly to the group's coherence, then the "basic contents or characteristics of the identity start being modified" over time by individual members of the group (1969:134). But what if there are no alternative identities for an individual to subscribe to?

Aleut fishermen strive for an impressive catch record. There is a profound sense of pride in filling the fish holds of their boats. The most successful are called "highliners," who often, but not always, have the largest boats, better equipment, a seasoned crew, and more money.[18] Most fishermen boast of their innate ability to fish. They frequently talk of the history of fishing in their families as being "in my blood." In the current era of uncertainty, they also talk of their lack of interest in – as well as the ability to fulfill – any other type of job and how devastating it would be to have to leave their village. Part of identity is to have a future. The fisheries are a forward-looking enterprise. Fishermen are always thinking about what is on the horizon – the next opening, the next season, and the next year. The future, I argue, is a way in which identity is renewed. Fishing as "in my blood" implies continuity, where this identity is renewed seasonally as well as generationally.

Fishing Societies and Status

The ethnographic record reveals humans placing a great deal of value on an intangible social resource: status. "Status" refers to one's relative standing among peers and competitors in a social or cultural group. Discussions of status range from the evolutionary biological (e.g., Barkow, Cosmides, and Tooby 1992) to the structural (e.g., Leach 1954) to the symbolic (e.g., Geertz 1973) and beyond.

Goldschmidt believes that competitiveness and status striving have strong cultural components and that all societies have mechanisms of aggrandizement; whether it is the best hunter, most talented orator, best soldier, or becoming chair of an academic department, the underlying mechanism is cross-cultural (1991:240–1). In all societies there are individuals who strive for the highest ideal of what that society considers important, which can result in differential access to success as defined by that society. For example, traditionally on the Northwest Coast of North America, rank and status were associated with a man's ability to lead successful wars and hold potlatches (Ames and Maschner 1999; Drucker and Heizer 1967; Rosman and Rubel 1971). The evolutionary anthropologists found that having status has consistently contributed to reproductive success in many societies, where men of high status have more wives, access to more mates, have more children, and their children live longer (Borgerhoff Mulder 1987; Chagnon 1988; Daly and Wilson 1988; Irons 1979; Ortner 1981).

Specific to the ethnography of coastal fishing communities, in which this study is situated, the stereotypical image of hardy weather-beaten sailors exists because there is a basis of truth in it. Renouf (1984) recognized that the institutionalization of status differences was often associated with maritime hunter-gatherers, and this is very much in evidence in the Eastern Aleutian communities. This was also recognized in some of the early classics of anthropology engaged with fishing societies and status amongst fishermen (e.g., Firth 1939; Malinowski 1922). Fraser noted that the Malaysian "Good Man," who "exemplif[ies] adult values which parents strive to instill in their children," is a status more easily achieved for the boat owner or "steerer" with higher economic status in fishing (Fraser 1966:40). Conversely, a "low prestige status" associated with meagre earnings was a primary reason which many Italian fishermen gave for young people leaving the occupation (Cattarinussi 1973:34–7). These references mirror the Aleut situation where, as will be shown, early historic Aleut society was highly stratified, and individual male identity was based on success as sea mammal hunters, fishermen, and warriors. Status-seeking activities follow similar criteria today. As fishing boats replaced labrets as social status markers among the Alutiiq (Mishler and Mason 1996:268), fishing boats have likewise emerged as status indicators among the Aleut. Thus, "men go to sea because of the rewards they receive for doing so" (Fricke 1973:4).

If we consider "ship-as-community," as Fricke (1973) does, status differences are stark. Technological development, for Fricke, created a division of labour at sea in which an "achieved status system" develops. This is manifested in the quality of the living quarters, where "carpeting, a recognized status symbol," is found in the master's large cabin, and his crew are stratified into other accommodation (1973:5). These divisions resonate on shore as well. Fricke states that "the division of labour at sea has effectively changed the density of community links because few homogeneous groups are involved in the seafaring occupations which are large enough to retain an identity within the context of shore society" (1973:5). The terms "seafarer" and fisherman mask many different skills and status levels.

The identity of people within these fishing cultures, therefore, is often related to their role as fishermen, or in connection with fishing. This phenomenon is never truer than in King Cove, where fishermen and their families do not form an occupational subgroup of a larger community; rather, they are the community.

In Geertz's (1973) classic description of identity in Bali, men involved in the cockfights and gambling are caught up in "esteem, honor, dignity, respect ... and status" (Geertz 1973:433), but Geertz asserts that "no one's status is actually altered by the outcome of a cockfight; it is only, and that momentarily, affirmed or insulted" (1973:433). Geertz presents this culturally defined status system as a complex system involving art, emotion, play, competition, pride, and temperament, but with specific rules about what is important and appropriate conduct. Matches between near status equals are more about status rivalry; matches between individuals of unequal status are less so. Those who are in it for the money, the "status gamblers," are dismissed as not being true cockfighters (see also Barkow 1989:162–3). In this regard, status struggles are ritually acted out in a gaming arena in a relatively peaceful manner. For high-status members of the community, the cockfight represents something different than it does for low-status members. In this manner, fishermen fishing an opener alongside one another are in a different relationship with each other than they are with someone who sets a subsistence fishing net.

Fishing is a status marker for the Eastern Aleut, though there are many levels within it. The status, honour, and the prestige of being a fisherman is in many ways representative of what it means to be Aleut for men and for women, but skill in fishing does not affect ethnicity. Thus, people strive for status within the rules of their culture, but the ways in which they do so is indicative of what constitutes identity in that society.

As something achieved, status is an important aspect of personal identity. As something to be striven for, status is also part of the structure. The salmon fishery itself has status, but it is the community that gives it status. Post-structuralists, who use tenets of structuralism while adding agency and intentionality, have given us practice theory, in which practice is a socially recognized form of activity requiring adherence to rules. Practice theory, for Ortner, "seeks to explain the relationship(s) that obtain between human action, on the one hand, and some global entity which we call 'the system' on the other" (1984:148). There is no level playing field in practice. In the Aleutians there are asymmetries and inequalities on land and at sea. The interplay between people who appear to be fully within the fishing franchise as fishing captains and their families and those who participate at different levels, as crew or in support of fishing, experience fishing and life on land quite differently.

Cultural symbols are also controlled by individuals to legitimize representations of themselves and their behaviour (Earle 1997; Layton 1997:99). For example, the Tlingit elite wore Chilkat blankets and various hats to indicate their prestige; conical hats were viewed as holding a higher status then beaded or frontal hats (Jonaitis 1991).[19] Leaders also displayed their wealth within the lineage house: the more crest objects a lineage owned, the more prestigious it was. The Aleut also have recognized cultural symbols that indicate elevated status across the communities (set out in chapters 3 and 4).

Status differences in themselves do not imply inequality. Foraging societies are often non-materialistic and egalitarian where hunters' kills are shared and cooperation is a distinguishing cultural attribute. For many of these societies, striving for status is systematically discouraged; status and authority are usually identified with sex and age (Lee 1969, 1988; Peterson 1993; Woodburn 1982). Among the !Kung, a kind of "constructive machismo" between men arises from belittling success and affecting modesty: "Modesty is bragging and insults are praise. The more somebody insults your meat, the better you know it is" (Lee 1988:266). This fits with the status model in that the discouragement of aggrandizement is what culturally constitutes the ideal.

Identity can be linked to gendered behaviours or symbols (MacCormack and Strathern 1981; Ortner and Whitehead 1981; Strathern 1988; Woodward 1997, 2000). This has implications for the Aleut, among whom the central activity is a male activity, and the dominant female activity is in support of the male activity. Ortner and Whitehead (1981) explore the notion of prestige as a cross-cultural feature shaping cultural notions of gender and sexuality. They contend that in the process of "becoming," there are criteria that one must fulfill, which then alter one's perceptions of self and society.

Status is a contested topic in gender studies (Ortner and Whitehead 1981; Sacks 1979), but it is generally accepted that women and men have different status structures, where different forms of femininity and masculinity are locally constructed and culturally exalted. Men in hunter-gatherer societies, in which hunting is the major source of male prestige, often define themselves by their skill as hunters. For instance, the literal translation of the Yup'ik term for male human (*angun*) means device or machine for hunting (Fienup-Riordan 1983b:34). Aleut men define themselves as fishermen, and women define themselves as wives, mothers, aunts, nieces, and daughters of fishermen, but these categories are experienced heterogeneously.

Status plays a strong role in mate preferences. Buss concluded that the "single best predictor of the physical attractiveness of the man a woman actually marries is his occupational status" (1997:192). By this model, women form relationships with high-status men, protecting themselves and enhancing their reproductive potential, enhancing their own status, and ensuring access to nutritional, economic, and social resources. Female attraction to men is affected by male status (control of resources as both an indication and a reward of status) or the recognized potential to gain status (Ellis 1992:268–9).

Masculine ideals vary cross-culturally. Aggression has been shown to often play an important role in male status. Jankowski (1991) shows that people join gangs for a variety of reasons, involving honour, respect, and access to drugs and women. This is similar to Chagnon's interpretation of the Yanomamö *unokais* (men who have killed), who are socially rewarded and have more wives and offspring, meaning that cultural success can lead to biological success (1992:205). The situation does not always call for dominance displays or aggrandizement. Benedict wrote that among the Zuni, the "ideal man" is one who does not seek status, does not try to lead, and is a "nice polite man" (Benedict 1934:99 in Wright 1994:260). That there is such a thing as an "ideal man" is significant; he just happens to come in a subtler form, striving to be polite.

These examples indicate cross-cultural variation in customary ideals of the masculine self. A widespread phenomena is the struggle of young men to define their roles and achieve status, however it is defined (Brown 1991; Wilson and Daly 1985). It is critical, then, to define the manifestation of this in the Aleutian context and the relationship between an individual's status, his or her behaviour, and the availability of alternative outlets to locally defined routes to status and prestige.

Local constructions of female power and hierarchies are equally important, though they tend to be more problematic because of lack of research. Some researchers have found conflicting evidence for what drives women's behaviour among the same population. For example, Friedl (in her reading of Spencer's 1959 material) argued that Iñupiaq women only gain self-esteem from their household skills, their children, and "vicariously from their husbands' standing in the community" (Friedl 1975:45). This has been challenged by Bodenhorn (1989), who, based on her primary ethnographic material, argues that since wives ritually attract animals, they themselves are regarded as hunters in an interdependent relationship with their husbands, not a dependent one.

Women's roles in foraging societies tend to be more crucial to the economic life of the family than the domestic role of women in Western society, because the domestic circle is the locus where all food (often hunted by men) is brought and prepared and where all gather to socialize. In fishing societies, especially where fishing is industrialized, there is a strong sexual division of labour (Acheson 1981:298; Nadel-Klein 2003:88–91). However, Nadel-Klein and Davis (1988) show that women's roles and social status in fishing communities is highly variable (also Fiske 1987). Aleut women cannot be reduced to fishermen's wives, but their role must be seen as complex and very much tied to fishing.

Status as a Limited Entry System

Weber (1947, 1948) explored the possible connections between power, prestige, and unequal access to resources. He argued that an understanding of whatever are considered valuable resources within that society (e.g., money, knowledge, land, power) must first be mapped out. He further suggested that social inequality tends to develop when people have unequal access to the culturally defined criteria. People are entitled to different degrees of prestige, depending on criteria such as descent, wealth, ethnicity, education, or perhaps Westernization. Society ensures the appropriate behaviour of its members by rules about social stratification, especially through status, role, and prestige.

In *Darwin, Sex and Status,* Barkow's model of prestige "involves an ongoing comparison of the self-representation with the representation of others" and the higher ranking of one's representation over others (1989:180). We choose different symbolic "prestige allocation criteria" (our social identity), depending on where we can excel. The choice of a social identity is important and often includes specialization so that one can become the best at one thing, and there are multiple paths to high status from which one can choose (1989:188). Choices are limited for the Aleut, who live in a "single social-identity/skill area," where men compete "in terms of a shared set of evaluation criteria" (1989:189). Thus, the quest for social status is itself a limited entry system.

Anthropologists, therefore, have analyzed the degree of variation in the definition, strength, permeability, or loss of individual and social group identities in different settings and over time. Identity could be said to be a kaleidoscope, which changes with context. A good deal of identity discussion, from gender (Strathern 1988) to ethnicity (Baumann 1996), has been about agency and practice, mutually constitutive and continually shifting. The languages of indigeneity and culture, however, are often fixed. I propose an unconventional definition of identity that requires process and stasis to be thought of theoretically together. Defining culture or authenticity as unchanging prevents people from shaping their own identity.

Thus, identity and status are inextricably linked; the ways in which individuals strive for status is indicative of how identity will be measured in that society. This, in turn, indicates what that society considers to be important, such as what the people talk about, worry over, and do most of the time. What do the Aleut consider to be markers of status? Who has access to these markers and who does not? And what are the dynamics surrounding this system?

What does it mean to be Aleut? And, more specifically, what does it mean to be a "good" Aleut? And what happens to those individuals who may not meet some or all of the recognized criteria for being a "good" Aleut? Part of the process of identity construction taking place now is characterized and influenced by conflict and crisis within these socially constructed definitions.

CULTURE CHANGE AND CONFLICT

Research on the nature of social problems within arctic communities has centred on colonial processes. Researchers have also used non-Native categories of meaning to investigate unrest, which is

Figure 1.4
F/V *Aleutian Star* makes a set in rough seas.

often an extension of colonial framing. Loss or replacement of "old ways" or traditional roles has been held liable for so many societal problems worldwide that it would be impossible to cite them here. In Alaska, Shinkwin and Pete (1983) attribute the rise in domestic violence in the Central Yup'ik area to changes in residence and concomitant shifts in gender relations forced by missionary policy. Traditionally, men and women lived in separate dwellings in a weak marital bond: men and boys lived, worked, ate, and slept in a men's house (*qasgiq*); women, their daughters, and very young sons lived in individual households. They shared dwellings when travelling or in a temporary camp but still maintained sexual separation in their work patterns. These residence patterns changed at the insistence of priests, who compelled men to live with their wives in nuclear family arrangements, which were common by the 1930s. The altering of an important male institution and the decrease in social control by elders created new social problems.

Others have made direct links between acculturation and social conflict in the Arctic by emphasizing the role of alcoholism, unemployment, modernization, and lack of education (Lee 1995; Marenin 1992; Palinkas 1987; Wood 1997; for the Aleut, see also MacLeish 1997; Merculieff 1994, 1997). But these authors ascribe social categories of analysis that may be less important to the societies they are describing than factors linked to specific systems of status and identity, and thus attempts to explain "Native" crime rely on categories that may be appropriate only to white, industrialized society (Lee 1995, 2000; Marenin 1992). Wood (1997), in his study of Canadian Arctic Inuit, found no relationship between violent crime and Western-defined social and economic underdevelopment. Believing underdevelopment to be a consequence of the "colonization process," he statistically measured employment, income, education, and housing density and found no connection between "colonization," as he defined it socioeconomically, and violent crime. Nor did he find a relationship between crime and the negative effects of external market forces on income, such as the European Economic Community's ban on the importation of sealskins. He also found that a high per capita consumption of alcohol is not a predictor of violent crime; "dry" villages do not always have less crime. Thus, what are often considered to be correlates and predictors of crime in mainstream American/Canadian society may not indicate the same things in indigenous villages. A sense of "wellbeing" has been argued to be a crucial measure of community health among the Iñupiat (Reimer 1999), and McNabb states that "possession of higher education, a good salary, and ample savings doesn't guarantee a rosy future in rural Alaska. Household economic well-being is therefore better explained in terms of political economy and the Native cultural idiom – harvest, sharing, consumption of wild resources – than by factors relating to individual attainment in a Western competitive mode" (1988:121).

Some have tried to explain problems in arctic communities through the strength or erosion of Native identity, which also contain colonial threads. Fienup-Riordan notes that Yup'ik "elders passionately believe that if contemporary young people understood and became aware of the relevance of their traditional ways, they would not be confused about their Yup'ik identity. They point out that this understanding can effect positive change among all people" (2002). Hensel (1996) argued for Yup'ik society that ethnicity and identity are constantly constructed through subsistence practices, and change in subsistence is a primary factor affecting cultural identity and thus social health. Basso (1996) and Kari and Fall (2003) approach identity through the construction of particular localities, rendering places meaningful, which has implications for the portability of identity, since many Alaska Natives are emigrating from their villages in search of work, education, or mates and are finding it difficult to succeed in the new context.

Still others have examined "proper behaviour" to know when certain values can be threatened, an approach that also contains a sense that change and contact are threatening. Hennigh reported that the Iñupiat preferred "a quiet man" and any man who crossed their social boundary was subject to sanctions (1972:104–7). Briggs's (1970, 1982, 1985) studies of within-household family management and the emotional patterning of Canadian Inuit explored these relationships through vignettes about interpersonal interactions. Through intimate living arrangements, she elucidated ways in which Inuit expressed and controlled their emotions and how they controlled what was considered "improper" expressions in themselves and others. She chose to illustrate this using those who deviated from the "ideal" and the ways others controlled these "undesirable tendencies" (1970:7).

Palinkas (1987), who examined problems of psychosocial stress related to integrating modern commercial industries with traditional subsistence practices in the Bristol Bay region of Alaska, argues that social conflict occurs among disenfranchised residents who have been lost in the attempt to merge these two systems. Many individuals who have not been able to participate in either the old or the new economy resort to deviant behaviour. There is a surplus of people with nothing to do, and traditional practices are so intertwined with social identity that exclusion from them leads to dramatic shifts in behaviour, since these people have no alternatives to social success. On the other hand, when an individual has an opportunity to engage in alternative forms of competition – such as Native arts, hunting, or, in Alaska, village basketball games – many of the same accolades given to successful warriors prior to the twentieth century are now given to the accomplished artists or sports stars.

In the Canadian Arctic, for example, hockey has become an "essential therapeutic stage for attaining social status and self-esteem" (Collings and Condon 1996:260). Rapid social, economic, and political change has contributed to a "prolongation of adolescence"

(Collings and Condon 1996:261; Condon 1990). Inuit youth no longer transition smoothly into adulthood, but instead spend years in a liminal stage where they neither learn hunting and fishing from their elders nor acquire any education or job training. Hockey has become so popular that it fills this liminality with a tangible identity. The competitive and physical nature of the sport also provides a "venue which the frustrations and uncertainties of many young people are expressed and, in some cases, amplified" (Collings and Condon 1996:262). Thus, youths delay their rites of passage but create an alternative identity within which to strive for success. Hockey, then, is a kind of double-edged sword, providing young people with an identity and a place where they can work out frustrations but also where conflict can escalate.[20]

The above approaches are largely unsatisfying when applied to the Aleut case, which is why this ethnography is so important, but the comparative cases also raise the issue of searching for culturally specific categories of meaning for the Aleut. In the Aleutians, all change is not threatening, and all conflict is not a function of change. There is a great deal of conflict that may have little to do with the colonial process (see also Burch and Correll 1972). Recent research among the Iñupiat challenges the notion that contact brings cultural collapse and instead indicates flexibility, resilience, creativity, and resistant determination in the face of the colonial process (Bodenhorn 2000/2001). Culture is constantly being modified and adapted by individuals.

The Aleut are Western, industrialized, indigenous marine harvesters for whom the last two hundred years have been about change, adaptation, resilience, and survival. Flexibility characterizes their outward dynamics because it has been their most successful strategy. The factors that affect social stability are a combination of contemporary processes: external bureaucracies and environmentalism, low subsistence harvests from natural disasters or restrictions on harvests, regulatory changes in the commercial fishery, a Native corporation's failed or successful enterprises, family difficulties, and changes in leadership – factors that affect the Aleut every day.

ALEUT IDENTITY

Eastern Aleut culture and society is so intimately coupled with a commercial fishing socioeconomic system that the two cannot be separated. Commercial fishing is so integrated into every aspect of being Aleut – family, politics, education, religion, material culture, diet, and economy – that a major disruption in this system is tantamount to sociocultural disaster. On the surface, fishing is a commercial industry driven by profit margins and the world market. Locally, success or failure in fishing has become synonymous with a system of status for all Aleuts. In common with many northern peoples, a major facet of Eastern Aleutian culture is the ability to change from within and adapt to external realities. However, threats to commercial fishing threaten cultural stability and the behavioural health of individuals, the family, and the community. In this context, the Eastern Aleut are in a global struggle as they fight to be identified as Aleut, to be recognized as legitimate commercial fishermen, and to combat dehumanization and peripheralization by environmental groups and government agencies. These struggles are explored through the lens of identity, emblematic displays of identity, and cultural persistence as defined by the Aleut.

2

Identity, Status, and the Structure of Traditional Aleutian Society

HISTORICAL IDENTITY

There is a growing sense among Eastern Aleuts that they must recapture their historical identity in order to combat contemporary political, economic, and social trends. This identity is emerging as a valuable position for debate in disputes over indigenous rights and commercial fisheries, and undoubtedly history will be revised by present circumstances. What might be defined as "traditional" is beginning to be used as an ideological resource in negotiating access to socioeconomic resources, but concepts of "the traditional" may be biased. Fienup-Riordan noted that for southwest Alaska, "current testimony by the Yupiit themselves on their history is also often biased – an ideal view framing their past in an effort to affect the present" (1990a:123). A historical identity is still developing in the Eastern Aleutians and may emerge to reflect the strategies of other Alaska Natives, who seem to "know" their history and traditions.

Historical processes are critical to an examination of social concerns among the Eastern Aleut, where history and tradition are imagined in different ways. Although linear histories are seen among academic historians as suspect (Foucault 1972), a relevant reconstruction of aspects of Aleutian history that contribute to an appreciation of the present is, in fact, linear and gives formal context to what the Aleut implicitly "know." I have asked specific questions of historical material that I believe relate directly to contemporary circumstances: What constituted rank, identity, and status? How did these structures change through time? How is present-day Aleutian society linked to the pre-Russian, Russian, and early American periods of authority? How did Eastern Aleutian society become intertwined with a commercial economy? How have their experiences under two different empires shaped contemporary life?

This chapter explores the history of rank, status, and identity through ethnohistorical documentation in order to identify traditional avenues for success and to ask how they have changed through recent Aleut history. Four main time periods – pre-Russian, Russian, American, and cannery – are used to document changing relationships between identity in the economic, social, and political world of the Aleut. These time periods also form a type of inverted pyramid in which the discussions of prehistory and the Russian era are pan-Aleutian, the American period discussion is oriented towards the Eastern Aleutians, and the discussion of the cannery period is specific to the Alaska Peninsula. As I hone in on the specific region of study, historical works become harder to find. In the following sections, I review the history of exploration, a vast literature resulting from that era, and build an ethnohistorical construct of pre-Russian-period Aleut social and cultural complexity, status, individual roles, and community expectations, tracing significant aspects of continuity and change through the turbulent histories of Russian and American authority, and ending with the modern Aleut society intertwined with a commercial economy. Although the particular economic foci changed, identity associated with status and marine harvesting remained constant.

THROUGH RUSSIAN SPY GLASSES AND INTO ALEUTIAN HISTORY: INCESTUOUS SOURCING AND HISTORIOGRAPHICAL ISSUES

I begin with a well-established timeline of explorers, hunters, military personnel, missionaries, and diseases, bringing us rapidly from Russian contact to American control. Early waves of mid-eighteenth-century Russian explorers were officially commissioned to search out new lands and economic opportunities. Their arrival on the Aleutian Islands in 1741 swiftly transformed these expeditions into hot pursuits of sea mammal skins, creating a lucrative fur trade. The Russian government established sovereignty by dispatching government representatives and conscripting indigenous hunters. The Russian-American mercantile company was established in 1799, which developed into a monopoly. At the beginning of the nineteenth century, Orthodox missionaries began arriving at some settlements and commercial posts, and the church was rapidly established as the organizing moral force. American and British merchants also travelled to Alaska, trading from their ships, but the Russians were the first to build permanent settlements throughout the territory. In 1818 the Russian navy assumed authority and banned foreign ships from Alaska's waters. Nevertheless, in 1835 the Americans and British obtained trading rights with them. By the 1840s, however, seals and sea otters were depleted and the Russian-American Company was losing its raison d'être. At home, Russia was embroiled in the Crimean War (1854–56), and a decade later it sold the territory of Alaska (and its people) to the United States.[1]

This timeline becomes more muddled with reference to the Aleut. Given the following summary of historiographical issues, it is not surprising that our understanding of traditional Aleut life is fragmentary and incomplete. To understand contextual problems, the observers of the observed must become the subjects of analyses. Most voyages were officially sponsored and oriented towards acquiring wealth in furs. Cruikshank warns that explorers' impressions are "valuable to historians but ... usually tell us more about Victorian values than about the indigenous peoples described. Yet these very observations became authorizing statements, the foundation on which policy decisions were made by colonial institutions" (1998:5). The literature on geography, climate, and natural resources is more trustworthy, but with regard to people, fact and fancy are mixed in indeterminable ways.

In 1741 two vessels of Vitus Bering's Second Kamchatka Expedition,[2] commissioned by the tsar to determine the relationship between Asia and America, sailed from Kamchatka (e.g., Frost 1992). The *St Peter*, commanded by Bering, landed on the Shumagin Islands, where crew members Waxell and Steller described the first encounter with Aleuts (Steller 1743/1988; Waxell 1743/1952). The *St Paul*, commanded by Alexei Chirikov, arrived near Adak Island and was approached by Aleuts in baidarkas (kayaks). These voyages were marked by scurvy and death (Ford 1966). Steller, a naturalist and physician, described the Aleuts' appearance and material culture as similar to that of the Kamchadals, trying to place them in the world order as he knew it (1743/1988). Explorers at this time, however, mostly took note of an abundance of fur-bearing sea mammals. News of these events (and samples of skins) spread quickly back across Siberia. The tsar wished to secure rights to these new lands and commissioned additional voyages. Floods of hunters ensued for decades,[3] and the journals from this time describe tense and sometimes bloody encounters with the Aleut. In 1764, St Petersburg financed an expedition led by Pyotr Krenitsyn and Mikhail Levashev, which resulted in a detailed map and sketches of the Aleut (Glushankov 1973). A second government expedition, of Joseph Billings and Gavril Sarychev (1785–93), bound for the Bering Strait, again resulted in contact with the Aleut (Black 1984; Merck 1980; Sauer 1802/1972; see also Bergsland 1998). This first wave of eighteenth-century voyages consisted of entrepreneurs relentlessly expanding into the region to find new areas to exploit. The explorers were not all Russians: Captain James Cook's third voyage (1776–80) stopped briefly in the Aleutians while in search of the Northwest Passage.

Many published reports of these early expeditions are abridgements or translations of translations, further alienating the story. The majority of ships' logs and journals have been lost to fires in Russian depositories (Black 1984). Some memoranda were housed in the Bol'sheretsk office in Kamchatka (Liapunova 1996), and it is from these sources that many Aleutian treatises were written. Most, however, are from secondary sources and consist thereafter of people citing each other. A typical paper trail, for example, finds Berkh (1823/1974) citing Davydov's account of his 1802–07 voyage (Davydov 1977), as well as the journals of Cook, Coxe, and others. Berkh's account was then used by Polonskii, who gave no references in his still unpublished 1850s–60s works, which were then heavily (but selectively) cited by Makarova (Black 1984:9–12; Makarova 1975). Coxe (1787) published material based on Müller's journals (Müller never actually visited the islands or saw an Aleut) and journals from the Krenitsyn-Levashev expedition in English. Pallas, who incorrectly posited a single ethnic group throughout the Aleutian and Kodiak Islands, edited and translated Coxe's English translations of Russian documents into German (1787; Masterson and Brower 1948). Waxell's (1952/1743) narrative of Bering's second expedition was translated into English from a Danish version of the German original. Both Jochelson (1933), who spent several months in the Aleutians and produced primary data on the early twentieth-century Aleut (see also Bergsland and Dirks 1990), and

Bancroft (1886), who did no primary research, published excerpts from Tolstykh, Korovin, Stæhlin (1774), J.L.S. (1776), Coxe, Pallas, Berkh, and others, adding their own interpretations.

Soon after the initial voyages, Catherine II, who ascended the Russian throne in 1762, ordered explorers to record indigenous peoples' food, clothing, customs, population, and faith; and to ascertain whether they made war and traded with other groups, and whether they were taxable subjects of another authority (Berkh 1823/1974:26–8). Early visitors made wild estimates about the Aleut simply by eyeing the shorelines (e.g., Shelikhov 1981). Natives were portrayed as "treacherous Aleuts" and "bloodthirsty savages," compared with "brave Russians" (Berkh 1823/1974:33, 41), though Golovin described how "lawless Russian *promyshlenniks* [fur hunters] exploited the meekness and naiveté of the Aleuts for evil purposes" (1983:107). The voyages continued in the Russian period (1799–1867), and although Russian-American Company records mostly contain data on economic activities and ships' logs, the occasional ethnographic description seeped in.[4] The journals of merchants and *promyshlenniki* during some seventy voyages describe many encounters with both sides, showing hospitality but also bloody feuds (O'Leary 2002).

At the beginning of the nineteenth century, after Russian sovereignty was established by imperial decree and economic self-interest became the only catalyst for expansion, there was a blurred line between official and commercial activities. The colony was only superficially administered from St Petersburg and thus was governed by local elites, which later included Aleut elites. Russian fur hunters baptized the Aleut en masse to make them imperial citizens. Government officials and missionaries sent reports on the conditions in Russian-Aleut settlements, pressuring Tsar Alexander I to issue a ukase in 1821 for protection of the Native people, entitling them to an education and a pension, for example (Porter 1890).

Between 1824 and 1834, the Orthodox priest Ioann Veniaminov, "a self-taught ethnographer, linguist, and biologist" (Liapunova 1996:31), carried out religious duties on Unalaska, all the while concerning himself with Aleut origins, language, and culture. In *Notes on the Islands of the Unalashka District*, he criticized the explorers' accounts because of their brief visits, their ignorance of the language, and their emphasis on economic exploits (1840/1984:113). Despite its 1840 date (published in English in 1984), *Notes* remains the

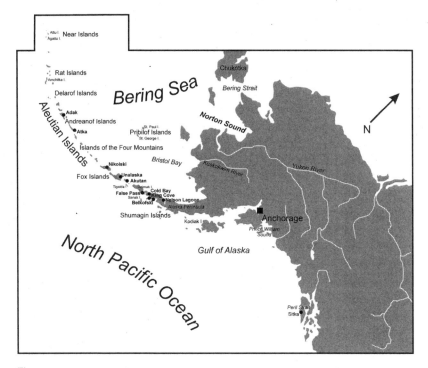

Figure 2.1
Historic place names

most comprehensive ethnographic description of Aleut life to date. Knowledge of language and customs was crucial in order to communicate the gospel, but the moral obligation to save the people's souls turned into mutual esteem and affection. When the Russian monk Makarii arrived on Unalaska in 1795, most Aleuts had already been baptized by the *promyshlenniki* (see also Netsvetov 1980 on Atka). Thus, Veniaminov arrived to find an already Orthodox society. He created an alphabet, translated the Bible and the Gospels into the Aleut language, and taught writing in the church schools. Veniaminov is still revered: "He gave much more than he received. In return, he knows our ancestors' gratitude and respect. We feel the same about him today" (Alice Petrivelli, in Foreword to Veniaminov 1993).

These early sources, while flawed in many ways, provide the bridge between prehistory and the present. They are the lenses through which archaeological data are interpreted and social information is derived, and through which modern social discourse is evaluated.[5] Field researchers asking about old ways occasionally find that informants cite Veniaminov and his contemporaries back to them, as occasionally occurred with me. There is a disconnect from historical *facts*; one Aleut woman said, after she bought a copy of Venaminov's *Notes* and had read other accounts of twentieth-century events, "We didn't know any of this. Our parents never talked about it." By most accounts, the present is comparatively serene relative to the social disruption in history, and the Aleut recognize that some problems they face today are related to historical processes. The past is not something to overcome but something to understand.

PRE-RUSSIAN PERIOD (PREHISTORY TO AD 1741): SOCIAL COMPLEXITY AND IDENTITY

Having outlined the major sources and the difficulties in using them, I move from this contact history back in time to construct a pre-Russian Aleutian society in terms of social and economic complexity. Aleutian archaeologists debate the origins, settlement timelines, population, warfare, contact with other groups, and social organization.[6] Details of non-material culture, such as social organization, marriage patterns, navigation, knowledge of anatomy and medicinal plants, and basket weaving have all been investigated, with Veniaminov as the main source.[7] Solid attempts have been made to reconstruct sociopolitical organization (Black 1984; Lantis 1970; Townsend 1980), and although I draw upon these works, my reconstruction of the sociopolitical and economic realms is made here in the context of identity, rank, and status.

Tremendous time depth for humanity can be found throughout the chain, and the modern village of Nikolski (population 19 in 1999) on Umnak Island claims continuous occupation for nearly 10,000 years (Hall 1999:28). Archaeological research indicates that at one time the Aleutians supported some of the largest sedentary hunter-gatherer villages on earth (Maschner 1999a, 2000; Maschner et al. 1997). The presence of prehistoric international contacts has been assessed using material evidence of trade and a record of shipwrecks from Japan (Black 1984:40; Hoffman 1999; J.L.S. 1776; Maschner 1999a), arguing against previous notions that Aleutian society was isolated and homogenous (Laughlin 1980); a vast interaction sphere along the North Pacific includes present-day Japan, China, Korea, the Gulf of Alaska, and the Northwest Coast of North America.

Ancestors of the modern-day Aleut arrived in the Aleutian region thousands of years ago as sedentary hunter-gatherers with an almost exclusively marine orientation. The archaeological record shows that whales,[8] sea lions, fur seals, sea otters, and walrus; fish such as salmon, halibut, codfish, and herring; intertidal resources in the way of sea urchins, clams, and mussels; and birds, eggs, and edible plants were (and are) found in abundance and supplied a broad diet (Hoffman 1999; Maschner 1998, 1999a; McCartney 1984). A variety of harvesting techniques included the use of seafaring baidarkas, harpoons, bows and arrows, spears, clubs, weirs, nets and fish hooks (Collins, Clark and Walker 1945:24). While many fish and bird species were available on a seasonal basis only, many marine mammals and groundfish were available year-round. This abundant environment has strong implications for the political economy in that the same resources were available everywhere, and conflict and trade were never about gaining access to food.

Identity, Rank, and Power

Veniaminov reconstructed a ranked society prior to Russian contact based upon his work with the Aleut. The class of "honourable ones" comprised the chief (*tukux*, in Russian *toĭon*), his relatives, and his children; the "common people" were other Aleuts and freed slaves; and the slaves were the lowest class (1840/1984:240). Ascendancy to power could have had some regional differences, since explorers described several means of attaining the rank of chief. It may be that succession in eastern villages was through "customary lineage chiefs," while western village chiefs were found within a "hereditary kin group" (Mousalimas, Introduction to Veniaminov 1993:xxii). Townsend argued that the Near Island villages were the least complex politically and the eastern Fox Islands villages were the most complex (1983:122) (see figure 2.1 for island groupings). She concluded that slavery was an *institution*, not only the incidental capture of war prisoners (1983:121). Slaves were disenfranchised individuals, prisoners, and orphans. The nobility had the power to punish their human property with death, to barter or sell them, and to free them. Slaves were required to care for and defend their owners. Kind owners who supported their slaves and their families also accrued prestige (1983:122).

The number of relatives one could claim played a strong role in a person's rank. Coxe wrote:

> In each village there is a sort of chief called Tookoo; he decides differences by arbitration, and the neighbors enforce the sentence. When he embarks at sea he is exempt from working, and has a servant called Kale, for the purposes of rowing the canoe: this is the only mark of his dignity; at other times he labors like the rest. The office [of chief] is not hereditary; but it is generally conferred on him who is most remarkable for his personal qualities; or who possesses a great influence by the number of his friends. Hence it frequently happens, that the person who has the largest family is chosen. (Coxe 1787:278, c.f. Lantis 1970:250)

Renowned warriors and skilled hunters were eligible for chieftainship if they had a significant following of relatives and slaves (Lantis 1970:242–3; Townsend 1983:122). Veniaminov wrote, "He who has large family ties through marriage is so powerful that no one will dare to offend him" (Veniaminov 1840:II:76, c.f. Lantis 1970:250).

Veniaminov described a paramount chief who was chosen from among all the village chiefs in the polity and who commanded wars, decided punishments, and received shares of any booty and precious goods, such as driftwood or carcasses for construction (1840/1984:242), in addition to having social benefits. Failure as a leader in a war expedition or an inability to live up to the prestige of one's ancestors could result in demotion in rank (Lantis 1970:243). High-ranking individuals had to consult the paramount chief before they could initiate a raid that had the potential to increase their status; thus, the chief could control social mobility (Townsend 1983:123).

Even greater political differentiation could be found between villages within an island group.[9] Warfare was perhaps the surest expression of individual and group identity, occurring between Aleut villages and against the Alutiit and Yupiit (Golder 1963b; Maschner and Reedy-Maschner 1998; Snigaroff 1979). Young boys were trained in the skills of navigation, hunting, and warfare from an early age. A nobleman already renowned for his skill in war and his knowledge of the enemy could assemble a group of warriors (Lantis 1970:263). Warriors took great care in maintaining their honour and that of their kinsmen. They would mark their bodies in certain ways to indicate their achievements in war (Veniaminov 1840/1984:213).

Townsend argues that indigenous warfare was so widespread that it helped facilitate subjugation by the Russians (1983).

Social Processes, Male/Female Relations, and Status

The kinship system in Aleut society is difficult to determine because of sociopolitical heterogeneity throughout the islands and the circumstances of contact. It is possible, based on archaeological data of residence patterns, that there were multiple descent systems (Maschner and Hoffman 2003). Prior to Russian contact, Eastern Aleut households were composed of single families and corporate kin groups inhabiting *barabaras* – semi-subterranean dwellings, with roof entrances, common central rooms, and side rooms believed to cordon off family units (Veniaminov 1840/1984). Veniaminov indicates that cross-cousin marriage was preferable (c.f. Lantis 1970:205–13; Liapunova 1996:145–6) but notes that parallel cousin marriage was a form of incest. There were no marriage ceremonies, though the birth of a child signalled a union; occasionally, children were betrothed (Chamberlain 1951). One's mother's sister and father's brother were called "my other mother and father," and the terms for parallel cousins were the same as for brother and sister, with suffixes (Bergsland 1994, 1997). After Russian contact, Aleut kinship terms changed to reflect their Russian counterparts.

Marriage is often about forming alliances beyond two individuals, and marriages were often between nobility in different villages. The abduction of wives from other villages was also practised. A "strong man" could take a woman from another man at will, often instigating a war (Tolstykh in Jochelson 1933:12). He likewise had the authority to demote a current wife to slave status (1933:12), which likely depended on the relative position of her family. Famed warriors could take concubines from among their captives. Polygamy and polyandry were equally common and seem not to have been linked to particular social conditions. Few men had more than two wives, though a few men whom Veniaminov encountered had more than six wives (1840:77–8). Women with two husbands were admired for being able to take care of both.

Most histories agree that men's and women's roles in Aleutian society were sharply defined, but their roles were not so rigid and mutually interdependent that survival was contingent on the activities of both men and women, as in other arctic societies (see

Robert-Lamblin 1982b:198). Women had special powers from puberty through their reproductive lives that affected men's success in hunting: they were not allowed to hunt; no sexual intercourse was allowed before men went hunting; women were not taught certain songs and stories; and they had to be careful when sewing skins for a kayak lest their hair get caught in the seams and bring bad luck (1982b:200). Menopausal women lost these powers and became exempt from these taboos. Menstruating women had particularly strong powers, which could both harm and heal. These powers were still considered to be important in the 1920s and 1930s. Elders I spoke with from Belkofski village described ritual obligations of a woman at puberty, during menses, and during pregnancy that were still being observed at that time. Robert-Lamblin believed that a woman's status was as important as her husband's in maintaining the group's "equilibrium"; but she noted that "the predominant role and prestige went to the Aleut hunter as supplier of meat, the food held in highest esteem, and skins necessary for clothing" (1982b:201).

Men's Societies and Nomadic Aleuts

Although kin were indispensable, Rubel identified fraternities, with men "depending on" one another in significant ways throughout their lifetimes. These non-kin partnerships existed where a man could expand his social network and ensure sources of economic and social assistance (Rubel 1961:61). A version of this type of relationship continues today in the context of captain-crew relations and sharing networks.

Competition for status between Aleut men is found in numerous texts. Choris[10] wrote about verbal duels between rivals, in which each man was challenged to listen to his competitor without expressing anger (Lantis 1984:177; VanStone 1960:154). Demonstrations of hardiness in the environment could also have been articulations of social standing: "They pass with bare feet over high rocky mountains, sometimes covered with snow, and when the feet or another part of the body are hurt or cut by a sharp rock, they hold the wound by the hand and another man sews it with a bone needle ... The patient himself sits smiling and holds the wound by his hand, as if not feeling pain, and thus demonstrates his strength and valor" (Tolstykh in Jochelson 1933:11). Young boys bathed in the icy sea;

"by that means they are rendered bold, and become fortunate in fishing [hunting]" (J.L.S., Coxe in Lantis 1970:190).

"Outside men"[11] appear in many texts. These are disenfranchised, wayward young men (and possibly women). On the Aleutian chain, they are believed to have been bands of young Aleuts who refused to submit to the Russians (Hudson 1998). These bands are alleged to have attacked young Aleuts and coerced them into joining their nomadic gangs. One Aleut man of Tigalda claimed to have fatally shot one of these nomadic Aleuts in self-defence, for which Veniaminov gave him penance (1993:176). The priest explained: "Along this chain and along the Alaska Peninsula, some nomadic Aleuts wander. They are both local Aleuts and Kodiak Aleuts. They ran off in former times, and they attack young Aleuts and try to lead them off to join the nomads as comrades" (1993:184). The fear of villagers losing their young people to such gangs persists in Unalaska (Hudson 1998:78).

Symbols of Status and Identity

Aleut material culture is distinctive. Adorned bentwood headgear indicated the status and valiant activities of the wearers, whether they were apprenticing hunters, warriors, and/or whalers. These "symbols of power and identity" (Black 1991:15) are best illustrated with a description of a whale hunt. A lone hunter, often toting charms made from human body parts (Lantis 1940:367), would go to sea and, upon striking a whale, would return home, seclude himself, fast, and torture himself until the whale was found dead. Whalers often became chiefs, and whalers' hats became chiefs' hats (Black 1991:80).[12] In the Eastern Aleutians, the right to wear such hats was reserved for chiefs and members of the nobility, and one hat could cost the buyer up to three slaves (Black 1982:136). Successes, rank, and allegiance were advertised on the headgear with artistry and amulets (Black 1982:134–50; 1991). Veniaminov wrote that the Aleuts' most "prized" articles were baidarkas that had been ornamented, decorated bentwood visors, quality spears, and adorned parkas (Lantis 1970:272). Wives of "prominent men" wore parkas made of sea otter fur (Tolstykh in Jochelson 1933:11). "Great men" were mummified wearing their visors; likewise, their skin boats were "killed" and they were interred within them in caves (Lantis 1970:216, 222). Thus, rank is revealed in the material culture.

Rank, Status, and Political Order

Chiefs and nobles exercised complete control over their subordin-
ates. Great offences – murder, slander, theft, treason – were pun-
ished with death by spear, sometimes after a trial before the chief
and nobility (Lantis 1970:255). Murder was often handled by the
victim's relatives, instigating a feud. Criminals remained proud and
boasted of their crimes. "It was not necessary to keep the culprit
under guard or bind him on the way to his execution, because every
criminal endeavored to display the greatest possible coolness and
fearlessness at this death," (Lantis 1970:256, quoting Veniaminov).

Lesser offences by commoners were handled by the chief and
usually resulted in the humiliation of the offender. Slaves, on the
other hand, suffered severe punishments, having body parts severed,
being subjected to beatings, and often put to death (Veniaminov
1984:243). The institution of slavery poses an interesting question
for the transition to the Russian era, where Aleut men are considered
to have been "enslaved" as fur hunters, and indigenous slavery was
outlawed (Lantis 1984:177).

Informal control was done primarily by shaming. Offences
included disrespect and neglect of parents and elders, selfishness,
gossip, showing inhospitality to a visitor, complaining about the
weather, and polluting a body of water thereby driving away fish
and game (Lantis 1970:258–62; Veniaminov 1984:215). It was also
shameful to fear death, beg for mercy, die without killing an enemy,
steal, weaken during a long voyage, betray a secret, boast of someone's misfortune, and display public affection. Women were shamed
for not knowing how to sew, dance, care for their family, or for
being affectionate in public (1984:215).

Veniaminov wrote about men using dramatic performance for ter-
rifying and maintaining control over women and children. This was
called *kúgàn agalik,* "the appearance of the devils":

> When it was thought necessary to impress the women and girls,
> certain of the men left the village on a pretended hunt. At night,
> after they had been gone a few days, the men at home made
> believe some calamity was about to overtake the community,
> and, by pretending great fear, made the women remain in the
> huts. While they were thus frightened, strange noises were heard,
> and the "devils" arrived, against whom the men made the show

of a valiant defence. After the "devils" had been driven away, it was found that one of the villagers was missing, and a woman, previously agreed upon, was carried out as a ransom for him. By and by both were brought back, the man apparently dead. He was gradually revived by being beaten with inflated bladders, addressed with invocations, etc., and was given by his relatives to the woman who had saved him. The lost hunters then came in and expressed surprise at what had occurred. (Chamberlain 1951:305; Golder 1963a:140–2)

It is more than likely that the women were savvy about this scheme, but it is significant that the men found such a dramatic show to be necessary every so often, and that the women played along to help them boost their own alleged status in the community.

Hunting ability and participation in a successful hunting party or military expedition was the means by which a man could improve his social standing. The hallmarks of identity for women were also based upon knowledge and ability, though linked to men's status. Rank and power were advertised through body adornment and negotiated through other symbolic representations of status. This history of rank, status, and social dynamics, though fragmentary, indicates great social and cultural complexity, with some regional variation.

RUSSIAN PERIOD REORGANIZATION (1741–1867)

We have seen that at the time of Russian contact the Aleut were geographically, socially, and linguistically diverse. Political units of unequal size and strength were identified in island groupings.[13] Population estimates for the Aleut range at between 8,000 and 20,000 at the time of contact, numbers that were rapidly reduced to perhaps 2,000 through conflict and disease (Fortuine 1992; Lantis 1970:174; O'Leary 2002; Veniaminov 1840/1984:246). The Aleut were already under stress at the time of Russian contact because of warfare (Townsend 1983), which faded as Russian control became more pervasive. The Russian-American Company required some protection for the Aleut people in its charter, though the lawlessness among fur hunters continued.

Amidst the strife after the Russians first arrived, the Aleut exchanged fish as commodities for Russian goods (Veniaminov 1984:65, 69).

But they were already in possession of foreign goods through extensive trade networks around the North Pacific and Bering Sea.

Even though the Russians had a severe impact on the Aleut, some expression of the pre-Russian life continued, including an altered chief system and use of the Native language (Lantis 1984:177). The Russians established their own system of first, second, and third chiefs over the traditional pattern and defined the chiefs' authority within the Russian-American Company, though the positions remained somewhat hereditary (Lantis 1984:176). The Russians used Aleut chiefs to exert control over other Aleuts, and thus the chiefs often became company clerks, continuing their role as local elites. Berreman's informants reported that at Nikolski the Russians selected the chiefs from the pool of elders and bribed them for control; the first chiefs were the only ones with any significant authority, and they were still remembered in 1950s Nikolski as true leaders (Berreman 1953:133). Second and third chiefs assisted the first chief and acted as his informants. Leadership positions began to require skills in both Native and non-Native ways. For example, "Prospective chiefs are generally given careful training from boyhood on so that they will be fit for the office ... His training in the ways of white men is not being neglected, however, because it is realized that a successful leader must now be proficient in both" (Berreman 1953:133–4).

Diaspora and Disruption

Aleuts moved frequently during the Russian period, and small villages were consolidated into larger ones for easier control over them (Jochelson 1925:119). Families were broken up when the Russian-American Company employed many men. Chiefs and nobility were at a greater disadvantage because the Russians sought them out for recruitment (Lantis 1970:252–3). Aleut men were transported to new hunting territory and established settlements in areas previously uninhabited or at a great distance. Four hundred Aleut men were sent to the Pribilofs alone to harvest fur seals beginning in 1788 (Elliot 1880, 1886; D.K. Jones 1980; Veltre and McCartney 2002). The Russian depredation of fur seals is legendary, and only twenty years after their discovery, erstwhile millions faced extinction. Hundreds more Aleut men were taken to southeast Alaska to hunt seals, so many that there came to be too few in the Aleutians to hunt for their families (Lantis 1984:163). As many as 800 Aleut men were part of the attack on Fort Sitka in 1802,[14] and 200 died from eating poisoned mussels in Peril Strait, southeast Alaska (Lantis 1984:165). Some Attuans were moved east to Unalaska, while other Attuans and Atkans were moved west to the Commander Islands and were cut off from relatives after the purchase of Alaska in 1867.[15] Some Aleuts were even taken as far as Fort Ross in California in 1812 (and later visited by Veniaminov in the 1830s).

In the Eastern Aleutian region, parties of hunters moved from their mainland villages to sea otter hunting grounds, most famously to Sanak Island (Fassett 1890/1960). Belkofski village, from which many residents of King Cove claim ancestry and prior residence, was established in 1823 when the Russian-American Company relocated most of Sanak's population there to hunt sea otters and walrus (Black and Taksami 1999:80–5). The surnames of Belkofski's chiefs and other regional chiefs (1999:86–7) read like a modern list of elite families in the region (as do the Scandinavians of Sanak as we shall see), which has social implications for present-day King Cove.

Aleut Status Expressed through Fur Seal and Sea Otter Hunting

During the Russian period, sea otter hunting was a cooperative task between men, a consequence of Russian intervention. The men surrounded the otter, hurled spears until it died, and skinned it on the water, careful to retain the arrowheads in the skin (Fassett 1890/1960). The sea otter furs were brought back to be inspected by someone at the company post, and the skin's ownership was determined by the embedded points with ownership marks on them; the owner of the point closest to the tail received the skin.[16] Thus, a cooperative task was still a pathway to status through individual success during the kill. The Orthodox Church influenced these activities as well. In 1890, Fassett observed that the Russian leader "reminds the hunters of their duty to the church, and with the unanimous consent of the entire party some skin, usually a small one, is donated to that institution, all the rest of the successful hunters uniting to reimburse the donor to the value of his skin, less his prorate" (1890/1960:134–5). "An otter hunter is a man of importance in the community in which he lives, and socially without a peer. Any tool, weapon or implement not in the possession of his own family, which he may wish to use, is to be obtained by the very simple process of going to the place where it is to be had and helping himself to it, using it as long as he may require" (1890/1960:135). Women also played a role in the hunt: an unfaithful wife of a sea otter hunter was thought to be the cause of a man's inability to kill an otter success-fully (Ransom 1946:620).

Shifting Status Relations

Though men derived a great deal of status from the sea otter hunt, the activity removed them from their villages; they lost control of their homes and families and suffered the seizure of their wives and daughters by the Russians, producing a Creole generation. Creole men became ships' captains and merchants, and held a high degree of authority and autonomy in the Russian colony. After discussions of her female ancestors being Aleut and her male ancestors being Russian and Scandinavian, one Aleut woman asked, "Where did all the Aleut men go?" Smallpox and other diseases took a tremendous toll, but it appears that many Aleut men were replaced by Russians as heads of households and as fathers, and their Creole children became the new leaders.

Further, losing 200 Aleut men to paralytic shellfish poisoning must have been devastating to the population (Lantis 1984:165). Women had long been responsible for testing the shellfish by touching one to their tongue and waiting if it went numb before eating them. In the absence of women, the men did not know that the shellfish were not safe to eat.[17]

Cross-cousin marriage, polygamy, and polyandry were suppressed in the nineteenth century and were replaced by marriages arranged by the village chief or priest, sometimes with people from distant villages. Several marriages occurred between the same families – for example, two sisters of one village might marry two brothers of another[18] (Robert-Lamblin 1982a:114). The reasons listed for a man divorcing his wife were sterility or infidelity (Veniaminov 1984). Church-arranged marriages continued through the twentieth century, as reported by former Belkofski residents. In the Russian period, nuclear family households became the norm. Today, restrictions on marriage and mate choice are less rigid. Non-Aleut husbands and wives from Anchorage or outside Alaska are found in all villages.

The Conversion Process

The Russian Orthodox Church established the Unalashka Parish in the 1830s, which included Belkofski and Sanak, and permission was granted to build chapels in the villages (Black and Taksami 1999:80; Pierce 1978). Belkofski and surrounding villages later became a separate parish (1999:87). By many accounts, the Russian Orthodox was a welcomed but imposing church, bringing decadence and ceremony. Mousalimas links Russian Orthodoxy with politics, arguing that chiefs were empowered by the church, since authority was increased through skill and a knowledge of geography (Introduction to Veniaminov 1993:xxii–xxiv). Almost all chiefs were given Russian surnames or had Russian fathers; most had travelled to Kamchatka on religious expeditions, and all were masters of hunting. In the context of a sermon he delivered, Veniaminov wrote: "The main moral lesson is that we, in imitation of Jesus Christ, should obey without a grumble any superior that has been placed over us – no matter what he is like – and should fulfill his legitimate commands" (Veniaminov 1993:23), an argument used to legitimize Russian control over the Aleut and, in some measure, to legitimize chiefly control.

The Russian Orthodox Church became the moral compass, adding its own list of prohibitions, particularly sexual transgressions, to those of the Aleut. "During my ten years' stay in Unalashka," explained Veniaminov, "not a single case of murder has happened among the Aleutians. Not an attempt to kill, nor fight, nor even a considerable dispute, although I often saw them drunk. It is a remarkable thing, almost unparalleled, that ... there has not occurred a single capital crime! This is the case with the Aleutians since the introduction of Christianity" (Veniaminov in Dall 1870:392).

Thus, there was some measure of mutual acculturation facilitated by Russian Orthodox missionaries and the Creole generations. The church has remained a strong force in the villages since this era.

Reorganization

The 1840s marked a decline of sea otters, a decline in Russian interest in the Aleutians, and an Aleut population ravaged by smallpox (Lantis 1970:177; Sarafin 1977). Early uprisings did not quell the Russian onslaught, and the Aleut realized they could not keep them at bay (O'Leary 2002). It was only when the Russians held themselves in check that the Aleut were saved from certain genocide. Conscription of men into the sea otter hunt and their subsequent removal from their villages and families was initially devastating, but there is evidence that these men adapted to the roles and eventually derived prestige from success in the hunts, as well as a complex commercialized economy. Lantis wrote, "Unwillingly and unwittingly, the Aleuts began to develop a new culture" (1970:284–5), a Russian-Aleut Creole culture, but their new society "was no substitute for the inner fire that had gone out of them" (1970:291). As we shall see, this bleak assessment might better illustrate the decades following the American purchase.

EARLY AMERICAN PERIOD (1867–1950)

Aleuts and Creoles had made great strides in adapting under Russian rule, having transformed into captains and fur hunters for the Russian-American Company and fully integrated into a market economy (Black et al. 1999:14–16). In 1867 Alaska was sold to the United States. Russians were given three years to return home or else to receive automatic citizenship. The treaty excluded Native peoples and made them wards, not citizens, of the US government. Just as the Russians were interested in Aleuts as a labour force, so were the Americans, but with a more Protestant economic vision that separated "primitive" producers from "civilized" industrialists.

After the purchase of Alaska, the territory fell under US military jurisdiction, with its own civil and judicial system under the Organic Act of 1884. Churches (still mainly Russian Orthodox but now also Methodist) provided social and educational services (Black et al. 1999:16). Racial distinctions became pronounced as Protestant missions aimed to "civilize" Natives. The United States was at war with the Plains Indians and considered all Native Americans in need of subduing (Berger 1992; Berkhofer 1978). In the Aleutians, the government demoted Aleut and Creole merchants to fur trade labourers in the employ of unregulated moguls. Influxes of non-Native people seeking gold, fur, and other riches began even before the territory was transferred to the United States.

Social mobility for the Aleut was difficult during the early American period. The Alaska Commercial Company (ACC) took over the trading posts, and the hunt for skins resulted in an intense but brief period of prosperity for Aleut hunters (Black et al. 1999:17). The Belkofski district was one of the richest districts for sea otters, producing 700 skins annually prior to 1888, but dramatically decreasing thereafter (Hooper 1897:8). Described as "the principal means of support" for Aleuts for a century and a half of Russian rule, it was thought that "suffering and even starvation" would befall the Aleut should the animal become extinct (1897:9). Their dependency was likely overstated, since most of these men were paid only a fraction of the market price for the skins (Black et al. 1999:17). By 1891 the sea otters was approaching extinction and fur prices crashed. The Americans revised the statutes regulating sea otter hunting parties for 1898 to allow the animals to be killed only from baidarkas or open canoes (Hooper 1897:15). In 1911 sea otter hunting was banned by international treaty and fur seal hunting became the sole right of the US government, still employing Aleut harvesters. The Alaska Commercial Company closed its trading posts throughout the region, including the one in Belkofski. Consequently, trapping, bear hunting and guiding, fox farming, cattle farming, and commercial fishing grew in importance.

Under American economic conventions, the Aleut had become classified as primitive labourers while Euro-American entrepreneurs became wealthy. In contrast to the Russian era, when Aleuts and Creoles had been local administrators with the Russian-American Company, the supervisors now were Euro-American, and they often imported additional labourers from Asia.

Immigrants from Scandinavia and other European nations had also come to the region beginning in the 1870s, particularly to Sanak Island, to partake in the sea otter hunt and later in the commercial cod fisheries (Shields 2001). In an attempt by the government to regulate the sea otter industry, a rule was instituted by which only Alaska Natives, or men married to Natives, had the right to hunt sea otters. This became an economic incentive to intermarry locally. The intermarriage continued during the cod-fishing era, but since there was no economic enticement at the time, it must have been for love. The men became members of the Native community, and their presence as fishermen shaped the local lifestyle concerning the region's commercial orientation (Bjerkli 1986; Black et al. 1999:17). Native people thus were claiming a mixed heritage of Russian, Scandinavian, and Aleut blood, and although they proudly acknowledge all facets of their history, they call themselves Aleut first.

Leadership, Government, and Men and Women

The title of chief and various levels of chieftaincy are no longer used in Aleut villages, although Aleksei Yatchmeneff of Unalaska is remembered as "the last chief" and as the ancestor of many Eastern Aleutian families. There have been claims to a type of chieftaincy. The Orthodox priest Dmitrii Khotovitskii of Belkofski is remembered as a "benevolent dictator" (Black et al. 1999:94), a man who arranged marriages, ordered school attendance, and ruled from the pulpit. Today, he is remembered with respect, humour, and dread. This type of community control was short-lived, and no one has since attempted to fill his shoes.

Self-government among Alaska Natives was initially rejected by the federal government. Later, the 1934 Indian Reorganization Act (IRA) recognized self-government and encouraged them to manage their own affairs, though the act based tribal institutions on non-Native forms and did not include jurisdiction over criminal or civil matters. The 1936 amendment to the IRA (known as the Alaska Reorganization Act) federally recognized most tribes in Alaska as distinct entities with their own leadership structures. Village councils were formed after the passage of the act as local governing entities and as liaisons for communication with the federal government. The councils consist of elected members, exercising community authority that is now shared with the village government and village corporations.

World War II: Forced Relocation

In 1942 the threat of the Japanese landing in the Aleutians prompted evacuation of those who were at least one-eighth Aleut (Kohlhoff 1995). All Aleuts west of Unimak Island (save for Attu Islanders, who were taken to Otaru prison camp in Japan) were taken to southeast Alaska and housed in abandoned canneries for the duration of the war. There, they endured horrendous conditions with no sanitation, army rations as food, and few medical supplies. Aleuts suffered many deaths, particularly elders and small children. Not everyone returned to their villages after the war and several villages became permanently abandoned; those who did return found that the American servicemen, not the Japanese, had ravaged their homes (Kohlhoff 1995; Madden 1992). Indicative of the US government's priorities, many Aleuts were allowed to return to the Pribilofs before the other evacuees in order to resume the fur seal hunt.

In King Cove, Aleuts dodged forceful relocation, but a military camp was installed in the village, and the cannery was used as a front to receive supplies. Many elders remember this time: the military placed them under martial law, took over buildings, forced them to board up their windows, and buzzed their houses with planes, "just for fun." Several Aleut men from Peninsula villages, including King Cove, joined the military as Army Transport captains or in the Rescue Squadron. Although King Cove experienced the war in a less destructive way than other villages, all Aleuts acknowledge relocation as a defining moment in their history, one from which people are still in recovery. Valuable traditional knowledge, language, and leadership died with the elders. Several King Cove men gained status as officers in the military, but they consider the overall impact on their relatives in other villages to have been atrocious.

The military presence is still strong in the Aleutians, affecting several western islands. Nuclear testing on Amchitka Island in the 1970s (Miller and Buske 1996) is still discussed, and one elder from King Cove remembers being "total panic scared." Several Aleut men were hired as part of the cleanup of Amchitka. Local people blame high cancer rates throughout the chain on these tests, among other reasons.

Late-Twentieth-Century Damage

The latter part of the twentieth century saw the devastating consequences of welfare policy towards Native peoples. Ray Hudson reported on how a state social worker arrived in Unalaska in 1967, and in fifteen months she "emptied the town of its children" (1998:120). The National Indian Child Welfare Act (NICWA) of 1978, which seeks to keep Native children with Native families through community-based, culturally appropriate programs, was passed as a response to these policies of removal.

Berreman, writing in an era when technological advances were seen as threatening to "pure" peoples, blames so much of what he saw as negative in Aleut villages on a single advance in everyday use by the 1920s: the dory (1954). He held the baidarka-to-dory transition responsible for the intensification of subordinate roles of women, decrease in marriage, loss of independence, breakdowns in cooperation, decline of the use of offshore fishing grounds, socialization to goals associated with money, loss of training children for necessary skills, and breakdowns in multigenerational communication. In addition, he wrote: "The position of the village chief himself, traditionally a respected leader of village affairs, is threatened.

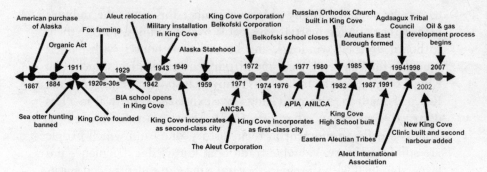

Figure 2.2
Political timeline

His authority is challenged by young people who have been successful in the new economy, and who have won the approval of
the powerful white men in the village" (1954:106). This is a rather
simplistic view of culture change. Not only was the dory never considered a white invention in opposition to the traditional, it is now
standard equipment on even larger fishing boats and indispensable
for salmon fishing. Berreman does not take historical factors of rank
and commercialization into consideration, and he misdiagnoses
problems in terms of white influence. It is remarkable how successful the Aleut have become, since welfare policies grew out of these
types of depiction.

New Political Structures

In 1959 Alaska became a state. Alaska's constitution contained a fish
and game code that granted the state complete control of its natural resources (Case 1984). The Alaska Statehood Act also allowed
the state to select 104 million acres (42 million hectares) of public
lands (out of 362 million acres); predictably, the state chose the best
property, including land that Native Alaskans considered to be theirs
(Burch 1984:657). Large portions of the Aleutian Islands became
the Aleutian Islands National Wildlife Refuge in 1913 (the Alaska
Maritime National Wildlife Refuge since 1980); and portions of the
Alaska Peninsula became Izembek National Wildlife Refuge in the
1940s. Statewide, oil and mineral exploration and military projects,
about which Natives were never consulted, prompted the creation
of the Alaska Federation of Natives (AFN) in 1966. AFN's primary

agenda was to participate effectively in land disputes, and this resulted in the Alaska Native Claims Settlement Act of 1971.

Government recognition and citizenship are recent to Aleuts. Full US citizenship did not come until the passage of the Fur Seal Act by Congress in 1966, seven years after statehood (Merculieff 1997). In 1970 only three Aleut communities were incorporated as cities under Alaskan law, although federal schools, the training of Aleut teachers, and public health-care facilities had surfaced erratically in many villages (Lantis 1984:180–1). Schools built in King Cove are not considered foreign intrusions but are important to the whole community; they employ a number of local Aleut teachers and are administered by the Aleutians East Borough School District,[19] whose school board is made up of local Aleuts.

The Bureau of Indian Affairs (BIA) is the federal bureaucratic arm concerning Native Americans and is based on federal Indian Law. Alaska Natives are subject to these laws, which affect education, health systems, social welfare, and the economy (Case 1984). ANCSA sparked the passage of federal laws that transferred authority for many social services to the state as well as regional and village non-profit corporations. By treaty and other obligations, the BIA still has service relationships with many Alaska Native villages.

With the Americanization of Alaska, Aleuts once again redefined their society. Sea otter hunting continued briefly, but with the loss of this hunt the Aleut also lost positions as hunting leaders and merchants, for which they had been educated and trained under Russian rule. Whereas the Russians had chased the sea otter, the Americans were attracted to the fur seal, and they assumed control over the Pribilof sealing operation and the Aleut labour force. In the Eastern Aleutians, commercial fishing was expanding, and local residents were gaining fishing and processing skills as part of a growing economy. As fur trapping markets declined, commercial fishing became the primary occupation.

THE CANNERY PERIOD

By the twentieth century, the Aleut had a good deal of experience with a monetary economy and commercial enterprise. The cannery period, overlapping with many events discussed above, began almost instantaneously after the American purchase. The region was ripe for commercial development of marine resources in whaling and fishing. American companies built codfish salteries and salmon canneries in the 1880s on the Alaska Peninsula, the Sanak Islands, and Shumagin Islands (Shields 2001). Akutan became a commercial whaling station and Unalaska became a commercial fishing centre. In the early days of salmon fishing, canneries owned fish traps and dories, and hired their own labour or Aleut labour to move the fish from the traps to the plants.

The building of salteries and canneries invited the rise of new villages around them and the eventual abandonment of those villages without commercial companies. The cod industry began apace in the 1870s (Shields 2001). Ships from Bellingham, Seattle, and San Francisco sailed to the cod banks, and men fished from dories using hand lines. Fish were processed aboard the ships and at shore stations, where the salt cod was stored in warehouses, and then the ships returned to their home ports to sell on the market (Shields 2001:20–1). Immigrant Europeans and Scandinavians, whose nations had cod industries as well, came to fish for cod and married locally. Aleut fishermen worked in the cod industry as well, though Scandinavians and Scandinavian Aleuts dominated it. Salmon, herring, and trout were also salted in smaller quantities. Cod fishing slowed during World War I, and large schooner ships had fished it out by the mid-1930s. The presence of cod and an industry for them has gone through major cycles since that time. The Aleut are currently experiencing a cod industry, fishing with long-lining gear and pots. Jacka (1999:226) holds that the shift from Aleut labour to Aleut fishermen's independence from fishing companies is due to Scandinavian influence and the Aleut emulating their entrepreneurial model (see also Mishler and Mason 1996:267 on the "Scandinavian effect" among the Alutiiq, creating a new class of fishermen and a work ethic). These Scandinavian fishermen are now ancestors of many Aleuts, and they take pride in this heritage.[20]

The salmon industry that developed in the late 1800s is the reason for the size and location of most present-day villages. King Cove was established around a Pacific American Fisheries cannery in 1911 from several nearby villages and dwindling cod stations. Belkofski had been a village for a long time, and people were more entrenched there, trapping and fishing, and thus were slow to leave. The last Belkofski family moved to King Cove in the 1980s, bringing the Russian Orthodox icons with them for the new church. Initially, King Cove's cannery depended on company-owned salmon traps. A

Figure 2.3
A fish trap in operation, requiring at least "two people for honesty" (provided by Tommy Dobson)

few privately owned boats began to fish for the cannery, although the fish traps made it difficult for local fishermen to earn a living because the traps were owned by the cannery, requiring little labour to operate. The cannery employed a small fleet of fishermen, both outsiders and Aleuts, to fish other areas where there were no traps. Aleut men chose to be fishermen instead of working in the cannery, where there was a steadier income. The cannery leased boats to Aleut fishermen (and paid them with a percentage of their catch) or financed boat purchases, even though there was no financial advantage to boat ownership because of the high maintenance costs. Those who could not afford the larger boats still made a living by gillnetting or beach seining from small skiffs. Outside fishermen tended to have larger, more efficient boats than local Aleuts. When fish traps were outlawed in 1959 following a territory-wide fisheries crisis,[21] the cannery became dependent on the growing local Aleut fleet.

Canneries diversified into herring packing and crab processing, responding to species abundance and the market while increasing the number of non-Aleuts coming to the region. The canneries hired from such places as the Philippines, China, and Mexico while fishermen came from other parts of America. From the 1940s

Figure 2.4
Early twenty-first-century King Cove and the cannery, with "dolphins," pilings driven
into the water for mooring (provided by Tommy Dobson)

to the 1970s, local Aleut women were the main cannery workers.
As their fishing husbands became more prosperous and their identity as fishermen was at stake, the wives gave up work at the cannery and were replaced by foreign workers, most of them Filipino,
as most still are today. Many of the Filipino workers have been
coming to King Cove for decades, with several generations often
employed at the cannery.

Pacific American Fisheries in King Cove had been the main
regional salmon cannery, requiring fishermen to sell their catch to
them. Other processing vessels came to the region as buyers, but PAF
penalized fishermen who did business with them. Just as sea otter
hunters had been paid in cash or credit in the Russian and American
periods, with the canneries came grocery and supply stores from
which the cannery required its employees to make purchases, paying
them in credit, tokens, or with punch cards indicating the amount
of money the cards were worth. Over time, the village struggled to
become more independent of the cannery's patronage, a process
that is still alive. When the community leaders made attempts to
incorporate King Cove as a second-class city, the cannery blocked
the move for fear that it would carry the tax burden, and it threatened everything from lowering prices paid to fishermen to relocating

Table 2.1
Village populations
Sanak and Pauloff Harbor began as codfish stations. King Cove grew with the abandonment of Belkofski, Sanak, Pauloff Harbor, and smaller fishing stations such as
Thin Point. False Pass arose around two canneries with the abandonment of Ikatan
and Morzhovoi, and included immigrants from Sanak. Most people from Sanak Island
moved to Unga and Sand Point. European immigration and intermarriage seems not to
have had a measurable effect on village size.

	King Cove	Belkofski	Sanak	Pauloff Harbor	False Pass	Morzhovoi
1880	–	268	no data	no data	–	100
1890	–	185	132	no data	–	68
1900	–	147	no data	no data	–	no data
1910	–	no data	no data	no data	–	no data
1920	no data	129	no data	62	no data	60
1930	no data	123	no data	52	59	22
1940	135	140	39	61	88	17
1950	162	119	no data	68	42	0
1960	290	57	no data	77	41	0
1970	283	59	no data	39	62	0
1980	460	10	no data	0	70	0
1990	451	0	no data	0	69	0
2000	792	0	0	0	73	0

Source: US Census, 1970, 1980, 1990, 2000; Braund et al. 1986:3–8

from King Cove (Black and Jacka 1999:106; Jones 1976). The village successfully petitioned again in 1949. The ability to tax allowed
the leaders to start infrastructure projects supplemented with government grants. Tension between the village and the cannery have
waxed and waned over the years. The village eventually compelled
the cannery to allow fishermen and workers to shop at the local
Aleut-owned store instead of tying them to the company store. Peter
Pan Seafoods still extends credit and cash advances on fishing prospects, and supplies fuel, boat repair, and some gear storage. The
relationship with the cannery is still strained at times; for example,
the cannery has threatened to withhold fuel and other amenities if
fishermen strike in protest of low fish prices.

Requiring fish to be caught in boats made the canneries dependent
on a fleet of fishermen. A new harbour and Harbor House were constructed in the late 1970s. The King Cove fleet continued to expand,
despite low salmon runs in the 1960s and early 1970s. Fishermen
also entered the king crab fishery in the late 1940s, a fishery that
boomed for three decades and has fluctuated since. A few King Cove

fishermen started to buy their own crab boats in the 1970s or to crew on larger Bering Sea boats.

An obstacle to the local fishermen came from a fishermen's union in Seattle, which made a deal with the cannery for it to hire a certain number of Seattle fishermen before it could hire locals. The King Cove fishermen attempted to expand their power by joining the Alaska Fishermen's Union in the 1960s, but they left it when they found their needs were not being met, and they joined the United Marketing Association in Kodiak instead. With this membership, they were able to influence the price of fish by striking. Later, in the 1970s, they joined the local Sand Point–based Peninsula Marketing Association (PMA), a non-profit corporation representing the interests of the peninsula's commercial fishermen, reflecting the importance of fishing and the fishermen's politics. Today there are several organizations in addition to PMA: the Alaska Peninsula Coastal Fisherman's Association (APCFA); the Gulf of Alaska Coastal Communities Coalition (GOAC3); and the Concerned Area M Fishermen (CAMF), which is a member of the United Fishermen of Alaska (UFA).

In 1973 much of the cannery was destroyed by fire. Since it was considered an outdated facility, its replacement was double the size of the original; by 1979 the new Peter Pan Seafoods, Inc., was the largest and most diverse cannery in Alaska, moving into processing groundfish and multiple species of crab, and adding freezing capacity and more canning lines. Peter Pan was briefly owned by the Bristol Bay Native Corporation, which sold it to the Japanese Nichiro Corporation (which merged with Maruha Group, Inc., in 2006). Up to the point of the cannery's sale, it owned its own fleet of fishing and tendering vessels.[22] Peter Pan Seafoods had few competitors until Trident Seafoods was established at Sand Point in the 1980s and Bering Pacific Seafoods set up at False Pass in 2001.[23] The new competition has forced Peter Pan to re-evaluate policies towards fishermen in order to keep them loyal.

Following statehood, it became apparent that local fishermen had smaller, older, less efficient fishing boats than non-residents. The proposed solution to this outside advantage (as well as to overfishing) was the Limited Entry Permit Plan of 1973, which will be examined in detail in the following chapters. Limited Entry created exclusive access rights to salmon fishing through the alloca-

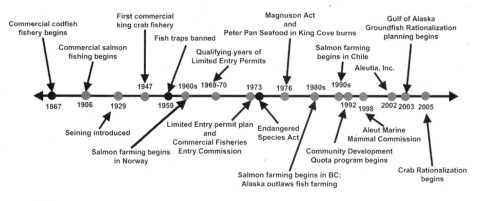

Figure 2.5
Fisheries timeline

tion of permits; thus, the rights to fish were owned by permitted fishermen. In 1976 the United States banned foreign boats from its shores through the Magnuson-Stevens Fishery Conservation and Management Act (PL 94–265), which extended federal waters to 200 miles from US shores as an Exclusive Economic Zone (EEZ). The American fleets swelled both in the number of boats and in industrial power. Engine-powered vessels replaced all others and became equipped with refrigeration systems and sonar. Closings and quotas soon followed these advances, concomitant with harvest intensification. Government loans were extended to fishermen to finance vessels and permits. In 1996 the US Congress enacted the Sustainable Fisheries Act (PL 104–297) aimed at identifying and protecting habitats, but it has been poorly implemented.

Fishing Identity

Since its founding, King Cove has always revolved around its commercial fishing industry. At present, most King Cove Aleuts' concept of history rarely extends back beyond commercial fishing. An open-ended question such as "What was it like out here in the old days?" yielded such answers as "Those old diesels [boat engines] were hard to keep going" or "We used to navigate *without* radar in the fog, rain, you name it." These statements are in large part because King Cove did not exist before commercial fishing. The Russian Orthodox Church is one of the few institutions that spanned the

Figure 2.6
Bumper sticker on a King Cove truck

Russian and American periods, and it contributes to the fishing world. Occasionally, priests will conduct a blessing of the fleet, and many captains carry icons on board.

Fishing in the Aleutians went from bone hooks on woven kelp lines to traps in salmon streams to beach seines operated by entire villages to massive boats operated by small family-based crews, and became the dominant source of male prestige. Socialization of young men evolved from training youths to be "kayak hunters," throwing harpoons with power and accuracy from baidarkas, to running a boat and organizing a crew. The rise of commercial fishing redefined Aleut culture and status once again. The social structure that arose out of commercial sea otter hunting and trade in furs evolved into a social structure that could not be separated from commercial fishing.

RENEWING AN HISTORICAL IDENTITY

Aleut history needs to be a steady, linear story, since this is seen as more relevant to the Aleut. In much of Alaska, waves of foreign intrusions were punctuated by "breathing space" that lasted a generation or longer. This was not the case in the Aleutians. Once contact was made, there ensued relentless waves of people that did not stop well into the twentieth century. Each of these shifting mosaics of people has different implications for the political economy and social relations. Russian and American intentions towards the Aleut seem to have vacillated between paternalism and a kind of self-determination in complex and uneven ways. Recent memory among the Aleut emphasizes the damage as well as the benefits of these contacts – meaning, to paraphrase many Aleuts' assessments of history, that "things weren't always rosy, but they made us who we are today, and that's okay."

Occupation in the Aleutians has continually been made possible by an almost exclusively marine orientation. Prior to Russian contact, Aleut life and identity were based on hunting and warfare. Throughout the Russian occupation, this identity was modified towards select fur-bearing species driven by the monetary economies of distant nations. Aleut men were able to join the ranks within the Russian-American Company and be high-status producers. This was rapidly undermined by overexploitation, as was the American shift in economic relations towards Aleut men. Under the Americans, however, Aleuts went from supporting commercial industries to being primary players. The last century of Eastern Aleutian existence finds an identity based on commercial fishing and political skill. This identity invites re-engagement with language regarding the category of "indigenous."

Through the shifts in government, the roles of men went through transformations, although the core skills were still valued. For Akutan in the 1950s, Spaulding found that "ability, skill, and success in hunting, more than anything else, were the ideals for which men strove" (Spaulding 1955:114). In Nikolski, Berreman described a similar status system, but that a man's prestige formerly gained from baidarka building skills was replaced by the "prestige of possession of a good dory, obtained with money," often by those who had travelled outside the village and had gained greater access to money and material goods (Berreman 1953:106).

The Aleut are a product of cosmopolitanism in which their historical identity has been about incorporating others, not about boundary maintenance. The Eastern Aleut are concerned with heritage and take pride in it but, for the most part, do not spend time trying to grapple with their roots. Many have Russian surnames, such as Shellikoff (from Shelikhov) and Tcheripanoff (from Cherepanov), which connect them with particular figures. They, too, consult Venia-minov to construct their past, and they quote anthropologists such as Laughlin (1980) when describing their culture (www.aleutcorp. com). Many have visited my husband Herbert Maschner's archaeo-logical excavations of ancient Aleut villages, just as eager to learn about the past as we were. Some Aleut cultural heritage programs are surfacing. The Alaska Native Heritage Center in Anchorage fea-tures an Aleut exhibit, but it is blurred with Alutiiq. For example, the reconstruction of an Aleut *barabara* was built as half-Aleut (with a roof entrance) and half-Alutiiq (with a tunnel entrance) in order to satisfy "all Aleuts." In 1999 the Museum of the Aleutians opened in Unalaska, and the same year the Smithsonian Institution opened a permanent exhibit dedicated solely to Aleut culture and developed in collaboration with Aleuts.

The ways Aleuts perceive and negotiate their relations with gov-ernment are constantly changing. Aleuts have not used history as a tool of oppression turned back against the oppressor, except when they negotiated reparations for losses due to wartime relocation. Even in these claims, Aleuts did not invoke culture loss but sim-ply asked that reparations be made for damaged or stolen personal property, church property, loss of lands, and human life (Kirtland 1981; Kohlhoff 1995; Petrivelli 1991). Because many elders died in the removals, some of the government money went to train new leaders "to carry out the traditions of Aleut culture that were tested so severely by the relocation experience" (Aleut man quoted in Kohlhoff 1995:187).

In the current era of rapid social and technological change and increasing political and economic dependency, the emphasis must shift from rehashing histories looking for ancient social phenomena to focusing on contemporary, unbounded Aleut society, life histor-ies, and affairs grounded in everyday life. But we must also recog-nize that many of the most deeply structured roles resurface under changing political systems, such as the relationship between status, identity, and the sea, which has transcended many of the problems faced in the last 250 years. The Aleut thrive on a landscape and at sea, where hardy seafaring explorers could barely survive when ship-wrecked. The current Aleut position is that the political system must allow for structures to be developed that preserve significant local control over marine resources because, as in the past, their status and identity hinges on their access to the sea.

3

Anthropology in the Pelagic Zone

THE FISHING NEXUS

The sociopolitical structures that developed alongside the commercial fishing industry as outlined in the previous chapter suggest that fishing, whether for home use or commercial sale, embodies both practice and knowledge. Chapters 3 and 4 explore the overall importance of the fishing franchise to King Cove and flesh out these structures, illuminating the development of fishing, the socioeconomic organization that is intimately tied to the practice of fishing, and introduce political structures and the current political climate surrounding the fisheries. Here I describe how the Aleut act out both subsistence and commercial economies, how the boundary between these two systems is blurred because the pursuit of both is part of the cultural identity, and how status is negotiated in the integration of these pursuits. A theoretical link between individual, particularly male, disenfranchisement and negative social phenomena is introduced in the first chapter, but a measure of disenfranchisement must begin with what constitutes the franchise and thus precedes the analysis of aspects of social organization taken up in the following chapter. The first half of this chapter considers how status and social identity are embedded within fishing as a set of relations that are inextricably intermixed, and the second half traces the ways in which Aleut fishing intersects with the global economy, all while concerning differential issues of access. Aleuts are not simply participating in commercial fishing; they are managing businesses, and it is this franchise that makes them vulnerable. By and large, the Aleut are fishing for both nutritional reasons and social reasons.

The Eastern Aleut combine two economic forms in unique ways, both heavily regulated in separate bureaucratic systems, in which they weave together subsistence and commercial strategies in an ongoing creation of social relations. It is through these everyday activities and expressions that they create cultural systems, but they are also shaped by them. This is the evolving practice of creating culture through doing, in which individuals structure appropriate behaviour setting the parameters of identity. The technologies, activities, discourses, memories, and institutions responsible for shaping the experiences of the Aleut influence choices and practices, and create a social life. In the Eastern Aleutians, the structure – or, to use my word, the franchise – *is* the practice of fishing, in which identity construction, maintenance, and transformation are interwoven processes. Meaning simultaneously arises from the practice of fishing while also motivating it. As will be shown, fishing-as-practice embodies a "commonsense world endowed with the *objectivity* secured by consensus on the meaning (*sens*) of practices and the world" (Bourdieu 1977:80). This is similar to Geertz's "cultural systems," where symbols and practices are employed together and are mutually reinforcing. In his essay "Common Sense as a Cultural System," he lays out the things that "everyone knows," our presuppositions and conclusions about our world (1983:79), which creates an "authoritative story" more potent than any dogma or philosophy (1983:84).

Within the fishing franchise, external structures also enable and constrain Aleuts' activities and relationships. Access to boats, permits, labour, and revenue are limited by the Limited Entry Permit Plan, which will be analyzed in depth, but Limited Entry also affects access to other resources, both social and political. The interplay between people who appear to be fully within the fishing franchise as captains and their families, and those who participate at different levels as crew or in support of fishing, experience fishing and life on land quite differently. The next two chapters deal with the scope and variability of this franchise. Here I give the distribution before the production in order to ground the reader in on-land dynamics and the demands variably placed upon individuals. Only after this is elucidated does the "business" of fishing accurately correspond to local realities.

In twenty-first-century anthropology, culture is understood to be at once created and experienced. This view originated in part through

Geertz's (1973, 1980) work in Bali, where shared public ceremonies hold symbolic meaning and embody history, myth, society, and
culture. These events are cyclical, formal, restricted in participation,
and facilitated by the state. Meaning, then, is publicly available in
symbols and can be read through semiotic interpretations. In this
sense, fishing is in the public realm of the Aleut, where there are
profoundly ritualized aspects of fishing expressed in repetition and
meaning. Full participation in the commercial aspects is restricted to
a select number of individuals, leaving others in a position of continual negotiation for membership. The material objects necessary
for fishing indicate social positions for the holders and are difficult
to acquire. In contrast to the people of Bali, where the state gave a
forum for these ceremonies in which history and society were acted
out in dramatic form, the Eastern Aleut are struggling to perform
and experience their culture on an oceanic stage with appropriate
props, with a belief system manifested in material form but controlled in large part by government.

POLITICAL STRUCTURES

Simply to go from Monday to Friday, the Aleut have to negotiate
multiple levels of government and "governmentality" (Foucault
1979a, 1979b), especially with regard to economic activities. Alaska's
bureaucracy is such that the state and federal governments regulate similar things in different ways, carving up the ocean and the
land with regard to subsistence and commercial harvesting. Alaskan
Natives can make claims vis-à-vis the federal body, which recognizes
individual tribes, that they cannot make vis-à-vis the state, which
recognizes Native corporations (Case 1984). "Subsistence" itself is a
loaded term with different meanings in different contexts, and it has
a particular yet varied usage in Alaska. Alaska's official definition,
defined in the 1980 Alaska National Interest Lands Conservation
Act (ANILCA) as "the customary and traditional uses by rural
Alaska residents of wild, renewable resources for direct personal or
family consumption" (sec. 801), is at odds with much of the way
Native Alaskans variably embody and practise subsistence. Iñupiat
and Yupiit receive food through a set of social relations, and often
the people are in social relationships with the animals themselves,
encompassing an ideology of sharing as a moral imperative (e.g.,
Bodenhorn 1988, 1989; Chance 1990; Fienup-Riordan 1983a,

1983b). The Aleut, on the other hand, create social relationships through wild species in both commercial and subsistence harvesting and through sharing, and are part of a vast industry as commercial entrepreneurs. Sharing, then, is the enactment of morality but is still considered a choice; it is morally loaded but less of an ideology.

At the institutional level regarding commercial and subsistence harvesting, I have broken down state and federal political structures into relevant regulatory divisions. The state regulators fall within the Alaska Department of Fish & Game (ADF&G), in which a Board of Fisheries and a Board of Game set seasons, harvest limits, methods and means for subsistence take, commercial, sport, and guided hunts, and fisheries on federal and state-owned lands and waters. These are seven-member councils, appointed by Alaska's governor and confirmed by the legislature, which meet several times a year to hear public comment and consider reports. These boards set policy and direction, and the Department of Fish & Game bases management on those decisions. Fish & Game is divided in several ways, but the Division of Commercial Fisheries and the Division of Subsistence are the most important in this discussion. Subsistence fisheries are actually managed by the Division of Commercial Fisheries, whereas the Division of Subsistence is the research branch of Fish & Game that collects and analyzes data on the use of wild resources (www. adfg.state.ak.us). The Commercial Fisheries Entry Commission (CFEC) oversees Limited Entry fishing permits, permit transfers, crew member licences, and vessel registration for the state. The nearest full-time Fish & Game office to King Cove is several hundred kilometres away in Kodiak; however, there is an office staffed in Cold Bay during the summer. This is the only district in the state in which a fisheries manager does not reside permanently.

Federal regulators fall within the National Marine Fisheries Service (NMFS), the US Fish & Wildlife Service, and the US Coast Guard. NMFS is a division of the National Oceanic and Atmospheric Administration (NOAA) of the US Department of Commerce. Its Alaska regional office is home to the North Pacific Fisheries Management Council (NPFMC) that oversees management of fisheries under federal jurisdiction. Input into its management comes from user groups (fishermen), consumers, and environmentalists (www.fakr.noaa.gov). The Sustainable Fisheries Act of 1996 (PL 104–297) mandated management and conservation by NMFS to prevent overfishing and protect fish habitat. NMFS also holds an Office of

Protected Species, which oversees compliance with the Endangered Species Act (ESA) and the Marine Mammal Protection Act (MMPA), among others. An Enforcement Division of NMFS makes vehicle, vessel, and air patrols and inspections, and enforces all federal and state acts. It also deals with harassment of NMFS observers, who are sometimes placed aboard vessels to ensure compliance with various acts and regulations. The nearest NMFS enforcement officers to King Cove are in Kodiak and Dutch Harbor. The US Fish & Wildlife Service maintains an Office of Subsistence Management for the Alaska region and a Federal Subsistence Board. This board receives input from regional advisory councils (RACS). King Cove is a member of the Kodiak-Aleutians Regional Advisory Council. In addition, all fishing boats must be registered with the US Coast Guard[1] (and Fish & Game), which has divisions of Search & Rescue, Aids to Navigations, and Enforcement. They conduct "safety and law enforcement boardings" to inspect for life-saving equipment and vessel safety, or when they suspect illegal activities.

This skeletal list of institutions is far from exhaustive, but those listed tend to be the most relevant to the people of King Cove. These institutions are predominantly *felt* at all times through regulation but only *seen* at particular times during harvest seasons. There are no permanent agency representatives living in King Cove, which affects how the institutions are regarded and the extent to which people follow or knowingly disregard the regulations.

The state and federal governments make legal distinctions between commercial and subsistence harvests where the Aleut do not draw boundaries. The state provides for a subsistence priority, then for sport or commercial uses based on resource availability on its lands and waters (40 percent of Alaska's public lands). The Federal Subsistence Board does not consider any uses other than subsistence on its lands and waters (60 percent of Alaska's public lands). The state recognizes the role of commercial fishing as it relates to subsistences, in that cash income supports subsistence, and the people and equipment are often the same. The Aleut tend to prefer state management because there is at least some acknowledgment of the importance of mixed economies in rural communities, but the state does not allow for protection of Alaska Natives who define themselves as commercial fishermen. Today, the structural relations surrounding commercial and subsistence harvesting are complicated and constantly changing.[2] As will be discussed in chapter 5, the

Aleut struggle to be seen as legitimate commercial fishermen as well as an indigenous society.

Municipal and regional organizations often work together to protect and strengthen their position in the commercial fisheries. Whether it is the King Cove Corporation, the Agdaagux Tribal Council, the city, or the Aleutians East Borough, all political decisions are structured primarily around the fisheries for protection of individual fishermen, the King Cove fleet, and the village ties to fishing.

Foucault's image of power includes structural elements in which those in power control communication and thus knowledge, truth, meaning, and morality (1977, 1979a). Discursive formations, or regimes of knowledge, surround every one of us in our own culture and time, and elements occasionally rise to dominance through privileged ideas of what is "normal." "Free will" conforms to what the discourse allows. Change arises when "counter-discursive" elements begin to receive attention, often linked to the dominant discourse but requiring a means of communication and self-representation. The Alaska Board of Fisheries, for example, controls the flow of knowledge in relation to the fisheries and thus creates a set of rules that the Eastern Aleut must live by but over which they have weak control. Transgressions of behaviour are not simply at the level of ideology but are within larger power structures. Powerful social institutions are analyzed for the credibility they have acquired to legitimize control. The franchise thus demands an understanding of the role of government and regulatory power structures, which direct policies that influence decision-making processes within the village. Enforcement of these policies can be antagonistic; if fishermen do not own or influence the decision-making processes, they may not comply with the rules.

The reader may find the following map (figure 3.1) to be an indecipherable jumble of boundaries. That is exactly what it is. Separating each boundary onto its own map would certainly be easier to digest, but this is how the Aleut must read the map. Every time a fisherman takes his boat out, he must know all boundaries and regulations of lands and waters, in addition to fishing openings, fuel and food needs, gear maintenance, communications, care of his crew, other vessel traffic, tides, wind and weather forecasts, price of fish, and cannery standards, just to name a few. This map is but a portion of the information a fisherman must have in his head at any one time. To include how the lands are carved up between state and

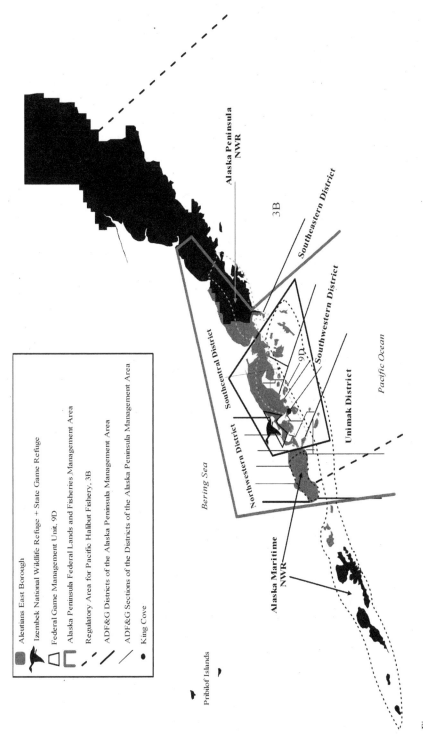

Legend:
- Aleutians East Borough
- Izembek National Wildlife Refuge + State Game Refuge
- Federal Game Management Unit, 9D
- Alaska Peninsula Federal Lands and Fisheries Management Area
- Regulatory Area for Pacific Halibut Fishery, 3B
- ADF&G Districts of the Alaska Peninsula Management Area
- ADF&G Sections of the Districts of the Alaska Peninsula Management Area
- King Cove

Alaska Peninsula NWR

Southeastern District

3B

Southcentral District

Southwestern District

9D

Northwestern District

Unimak District

Bering Sea

Pacific Ocean

Alaska Maritime NWR

Pribilof Islands

Figure 3.1
Map of waters and lands

federal bodies, Native corporations, village corporations, and private ownership would make this map totally unreadable. Within the Aleutians East Borough, eight village corporations plus the Aleut Corporation own lands. There are also surface conflicts between corporations and conflicts with the state over coal-oil-gas under conveyed allotments to the Aleut Corporation. Nor did I include on the map all the bays and lagoons closed to commercial fishing, salmon streams closed to fishing within 200 to 1,000 metres in salt water, and seasonally closed bays.

Limited Entry

Out of the above political structures there developed in 1973 a state law and subsequent federal laws that limit participation in fishing. This law has influenced all subsequent practices and relationships for Alaskan fishermen generally, and Aleuts in particular. The law follows the "tragedy of the commons" economic model of common property resources in which "each man is locked into a system that compels him to increase his (share) without limit – in a world that is limited. Ruin is the destruction toward which all men rush, each pursuing his own best interest in a society that believes in the freedom of the commons" (Hardin 1968:1244). In this model, fishermen are "individualistic profit maximizers," harvesting at a rate exceeding the renewable rate of the resource. The fishermen and local community cannot and will not create institutions to protect the resources, and hence, exploitation can only be curbed by instituting private property or government control (Acheson 1989:357–8; Berkes 1985). This model, however, does not account for actual practices or motivations, and it was criticized by Acheson, among many, who argued that the lack of rules in fishing was not the problem, since customary rules surrounding fishing common resources are well documented (e.g., Acheson 1981:280–1, 1989:358–63; Cordell 1989; Langdon 1989), and the Aleutians are no exception. The problem for Acheson is overcapitalization (1989). The fishermen do not bear the costs of producing fish, only of catching them, and there are too many fishermen fishing. The logic of capitalism demands that fishermen make boat and insurance payments, and meet other obligations within a short window of time. Fisheries economists believe overfishing happens because all the incentives are there for it to happen (Iudicello et al. 1999), and establishing more property rights is the proposed solution through licensing, quotas, boundaries, and taxes.

The Limited Entry Permit Plan of 1973 (Alaska Statute 16.43) is one such "property right," restricting the number of fishermen and fishing operations, with the intention of preventing overfishing. The plan was also a response to the trend that most non-residents had better equipment than residents and were taking over the salmon fisheries. I do not wish to debate the intrinsic worth of the plan, which in all likelihood saved the salmon fisheries from being over-fished during "open" access, but rather to describe the local ramifications of Limited Entry. Limited Entry allocated a certain number of fishing permits in districts across the state which were distributed based on a points system of prior participation in commercial fishing and economic dependence. The original permits were issued free, putting capital in the hands of fishermen. The plan was an attempt to give local fishermen a sense of ownership and control in the industry. While this is true for those Aleut fishermen who were fortunate to receive permits, it has resulted in the exclusion of many Aleut fishermen from their way of life and has created a stratification within the communities into those with access to all, access to some, and access to none of the salmon fisheries.

Limited Entry put a large number of fishermen who could not demonstrate a record of commercial fishing as well as all future generations at a great disadvantage. Those who did not initially fish in the 1970s cannot easily gain entry today. Likewise, if they were crabbing then, they were excluded from receiving salmon permits. When the plan was implemented in 1975, salmon fishing had been in a slump in previous years, and many long-time fishermen had taken land jobs for the few years before the plan went into effect. These turned out to be the qualifying years of 1969–72 (Braund et al. 1986:6. 17; Petterson 1983). Long-time fishermen could not use their prior record of fishing and were excluded. Only forty-three King Cove and Belkofski fishermen received salmon permits, but some received permits for set gillnetting, drift gillnetting, *and* purse seining because of their fishing history. One Aleut elder referred to this system as a "cartel," because those with money and a proven fishing record received permits and often had contacts with the permit agents. Many had fished and could not document it, or they worked as crew (including sons of permitted fishermen) and were ineligible for permits of their own.

Permits are issued to individuals, not corporations, and can be lent to relatives, inherited, or sold. A fisherman may not own more than one permit per gear type per fishing district. Aleutian salmon permits have sold for tens of thousands to hundreds of thousands of dollars. Some Alaskan fishermen have sold permits to outsiders in hard times, but transfer of permits to non-residents is under criticism by residents who do not want to lose control of their fisheries (Langdon 1980). Transfer of permits out of Alaskans' hands is a concern for the Aleut, but an analysis of actual persons receiving permits (see below) shows that this was non-random.

Federal plans modelled on Limited Entry include the Individual Fishing Quota (IFQ), introduced in 1995, in which quota shares are bought and sold, and the Community Development Quota (CDQ) programs developed in the 1990s, in which quotas are allotted to fishermen or communities in poorer parts of Alaska, particularly with regard to groundfish. Thus, state laws and share plans have been created to protect Alaska's seafood industry, but a variety of factors continue to work against the fishermen. This will be elaborated in later sections.

The Fishing Industry

At the level of industry, Alaska's fishermen produce 50 percent of America's seafood (Brown and Thomas 1996:601). A 1913 fisheries business tax (the oldest tax in the state), coupled with the fisheries resource landing tax, make the fishing industry crucial to state revenue (second only to the oil industry). Although seafood harvesting and processing employs 20,000 people, more people than any other Alaska industry, it has been an extremely volatile source of employment (Knapp 2000:20).

Alaska's fishing industry exports to Japan, Canada, and the United Kingdom, with smaller markets in Taiwan, China, and Korea (www. dced.state.ak.us). Japan is the largest importer of Alaska seafood, and the strength of the yen affects its value. Farmed fish from Chile and Norway are also flooding the market, replacing significant sectors of the wild salmon industry. Fish farmers have branched into other species to achieve the same success as they have had with salmon (*Economist* 2003; Knapp 2000:22).

The fishing industry is full of incongruities. It is largely self-regulated; fisheries management councils are set by people with fisheries interests, who will not make decisions against themselves. Fish farms are flooding the markets, driving down the price of wild salmon; but salmon are carnivorous fish, and fish farms still depend on fishmeal produced from wild salmon to feed their fish. Hooked fish are more valued, but the industry has increasingly converted towards netting large schools of fish that are handled roughly. This trend is now being reversed in order to compete with fish farms. The canneries set the prices they will pay per pound of fish, depending on the species and on its condition at the time of delivery, in response to market value.

INDIGENOUS COMMERCIAL ECONOMIES

Alaska's popular media, non-governmental organizations, the state legislature, and many Alaska Native representatives continually treat subsistence as being synonymous with tradition. Some portrayals of commercialization are presented as Native Alaskans responding to unwelcome economic intrusions, with their success being measured on how much of the traditional has been maintained while incorporating new socioeconomic systems (e.g., Jacka 1999:214; Wolfe 1984:160). However, most Alaska Natives have commercialized aspects of their subsistence economy in foods and in crafts such as skin sewing, ivory carving, and weaving, or by being commercial fishermen, while retaining some goods for their own use. There has also been an assumption that progress moves from subsistence to commercial. Many Aleutian anthropologists have conflated shifts in practices with causes and consequences regarding social life. The classic picture of Aleutian fisheries posits that in the span of a few generations, fishermen went from cooperatively harvesting subsistence resources out of skin boats to family-based harvesting of cash resources conducted out of boats costing hundreds of thousands of dollars, and along with that, the loss of control over the resources and reduced participation in traditional activities to the detriment of all (Berreman 1954:103; Jacka 1999; Jones 1969b, 1976). These anthropologists considered the processing plants off-limits as well, although many Aleut men and women had long careers in the canneries: "In contrast to the traditional emphasis on skill, daring, mastery, and fortitude, work in the processing plants does not offer challenge, prestige, self-respect, or even a living wage ... Irregular, unskilled, demeaning factory work fosters family disorganization. To a once vigorous, active, productive people, industrial jobs of this sort mean boredom and idleness, insufficient income and disorderly lives" (Jones 1969b:298). For the Alutiit of Kodiak, wage labour and welfare have been lumped as equally negative substitutes for subsistence, and as responsible for health concerns and social ills (Mulcahy 2001:12).

For the Eastern Aleut, however, I propose an "indigenous commercial economy," through which knowledge and practice are reproduced and revised, thus avoiding an imaginary balance of traditions in the past and corruption by state-level systems in the present. There has been a great deal of work on economies in the Arctic where people engage in commercial whaling, fishing, trapping, and guiding, among many other occupations, yet seem to define themselves by subsistence (Bodenhorn 1989; Burch 1998b; Condon, Collings, and Wenzel 1995; Fienup-Riordan 2000; Langdon 1986; Wheeler 1998; Wolfe and Walker 1987; Wolfe et al. 1984).[3] Subsistence fishing and hunting are crucial cultural markers for the Aleut, but they are defining themselves as commercial fishermen, contending that commercial development has been the "saving grace" of their communities and the sole reason why they still exist today.

The village of King Cove owes its beginnings to a commercial cannery and has grown as a commercial fishing town with all residents tied directly or indirectly to fishing and/or seafood processing. Despite cycles of productivity and decline, the sea has provided a relatively stable economy for the Aleut in harvesting salmon, crab, and groundfish. The industrialization of the Aleutians was not so much an inclusion of its Native people in labour and a progressive industry as it was a concomitant shift in focus regarding the labour market. Aleuts have participated in a monetary economy for much longer than other Native Alaskans. Under the influence of different political systems and through an evolving relationship with state and federal management, they have achieved an important relationship with an industry with which they merge subsistence provisioning and enact social relations.

Commercial Developments

As described in chapter 2, waves of outsiders have come to the Aleutians chasing particular species: the Russians in pursuit of the sea otter and fur seal skins, Scandinavians interested in cod and whales, and Americans in pursuit of fur seals, salmon, and crab. I place the Aleut squarely at the heart of these developments engaging in a wage economy. Though large-scale commercialization of most fisheries occurred under American rule in the 1870s with technological inventions in preservation and transportation, *commercial* industries are *traditional* in the Aleutians.

Industries over time have included fishing for salmon, codfish, halibut, pollock, herring, roe, fish liver and guts for vitamins, salmon "leather" for purses and shoes, fish meal, whaling, sea otter hunting, fur seal hunting, trapping, and fox farming. Aleuts provided major ports of call for whalers in the nineteenth century, "leased" islands for fox trapping in the 1920s and 1930s, participated in government sealing operations, and managed salmon traps and lucrative herring and crab industries (McGowan 1999a; Lantis 1984:182). Sheep, pig, and cattle industries stretched from the Shumagins to Umnak Island between the nineteenth century and the 1970s (Black et al. 1999). Wild horses and cattle remain on Sanak and other islands, and the cattle are harvested annually by Aleuts. Aleuts hunted whales for the Russian-American Company and worked as hunters and processors in the commercial whaling station at Akutan from 1911 to 1942 (Black 1987; McGowan 1999b). Gold was mined on Unga Island, and sulphur and guano were mined on Akun under Russian rule (Black et al. 1999:18; Taksami 1999). Even bears were hunted, skinned, fleshed and salted, and shipped to New York in 55-gallon drums to be mounted and sold in the 1930s and 1940s.

The Eastern Aleut measure their success in new ways, not to the degree in which their historical traditions are still in practice. One Aleut leader stated, "Commercial fishing has become our subsistence. It's the only thing we have. And it's slowly being taken away from us, all of it is. Not slowly, it's being taken away from us fast." His definition is at odds with the official meaning of subsistence and other Native definitions throughout the state. He believes that commercial fishing has grown in importance to such an extent that subsistence is not enough to sustain his village economically, socially, or culturally. Indeed, a disentanglement of the two systems in practice would be difficult, but here I will temporarily disentangle them for description and discussion.

Subsistence: "When the tide is out, the table is set" vs. "Whatever they let us"

The nutrient-rich Bering Sea and North Pacific abound in numerous species of fish, sea mammals, sea birds, shellfish, and other marine species, while the land supports relatively few though valued plants and animals. Environmental changes with respect to the Aleutian Low weather pattern continually change the distribution and abundance of various species. Modern commercialization of wild fish has changed the nature of subsistence acquisition and distribution.

"Eating Native foods is the biggest thing we've held on to," according to one Aleut woman. Subsistence is cited as the constant in a turbulent history and is an important cultural marker. When I asked one woman, "What does it mean to be Aleut?" she simply described her grandson riding his tricycle in the driveway with a strip of *ucela* (dried salmon) hanging over the handlebars as a snack. Unless prompted by the anthropologist, people do not generally talk about subsistence on an abstract level; they simply "do" subsistence by harvesting, storing, eating, and appreciating.

Every King Cove household, Native and non-Native, uses wild foods, though the quantity and variety varies from house to house. The per capita harvest of wild foods was 256 pounds (116 kilograms) in 1992, more than half being salmon; but for Native households only, the average was 325 pounds (147 kilograms) per person (Fall et al. 1993:90–108). The average household uses 15.6 different kinds of wild resources (Fall et al. 1993:90). The people collect *bidarkis* (the local name for black katy chitons, so named because they resemble baidarkas, the skin boats), *petrushki* (wild parsley), *pushki* (wild celery or cow parsnip), cuttlefish (small octopus), seagull eggs, fiddleheads (an edible fern), blueberries, salmonberries, moss berries, and low bush cranberries. They can, jar, freeze, dry, and smoke all types of salmon. They harvest halibut, cod, trout, and several species of crab. They scavenge *ulla* (whale meat and blubber) from beached whales and hunt caribou, geese, and ptarmigan.

Periodically, a few men hunt a seal and divide it up to give to whoever wants the meat, often to close family members but also to those in the community known to like the meat and use the oil. Seal livers are preferred, and seal oil (*chadu*) is desired for dipping *ucela* and *pushki* in. Though sea lions are protected, it is still legal to subsistence hunt them. Most Aleut do not do so, however, because the legality of the hunt is difficult to negotiate owing to the protection of sea lions under the Endangered Species Act.

King Cove residents prefer to eat salmon, crab, caribou, and certain waterfowl over most other species and certainly over store-bought foods. However, at any time of the year, families are just as likely to have lasagna or fried chicken for dinner as they are salmon or caribou, except during the first harvests in each season. At the 2002 annual dinner honouring village elders and celebrating Orthodox Easter, the main course was turkey, ordered from Seattle, while a baking and decorating contest of a sweet Easter bread (*kulich*) happened on the side. Subsistence foods were also served in abundance, but not as the main course. In this manner, there are no strict rules that demand adherence to local food, even on special occasions, yet wild foods, as they become available seasonally, are preferred and shared, and their flavours and textures are mused over at mealtimes.[4]

In an area where one might predict less of a preference for Native foods, I found the strongest enthusiasm: children and teenagers sink their teeth into *chumela*, raw fish heads, eyeballs, and brains, as if they were candy. They fight over crab legs and salmon strips. They scour the beaches for *bidarkis* and slurp them out of their shells. They look forward to eating *chisu*, also called "spawn," which is salmon caviar mixed with diced onion, salt, and pepper. And they love testing the dietary limitations of this white woman from Idaho.

Despite the apparent wealth of food available, there is a sense of both abundance and scarcity in the way people talk. On most occasions, an insistence that there is always plenty to eat and share dominates the discussion. "When the tide is out, the table is set," was echoed many times, often while people were "snacking off the beach." On other occasions, usually in the context of interviews about how much food households receive each year and from where, there is a sense that needs are being unfairly constrained. In response to a question about the different types of gear he employed and the different species he fished for, one fisherman shook his head and replied, "Whatever they let us." This was in part a response to the frustration with changing regulations and the fact that they are limited in how much they can catch, especially when other parts of Native Alaska are not subjected to the same restrictions (see chapter 5).

Kinship, the Division of Labour, and Sharing Networks

Individual economic activities, collective hunting and fishing expeditions, and loosely systematized distributions of wild foods work in concert to ensure that most households are provided for while maintaining individualized aspects of harvesting. A sexual division of labour falls within the larger prestige structures, such that women are not seen in terms of men but in terms of how they are "organized into the base that supports the larger (male) prestige system" (Ortner and Whitehead 1981:19). More detailed analyses of how each gender and age group experiences the fishing franchise follows in chapter 4; however, a general sense of kinship and village demography is required here for the discussion of social organizations surrounding fishing practice.

Kinship in its variety is always founded on biological connections with cultural dimensions that may or may not coincide with biology. Kinship has dominated a greater part of anthropologists' energies and is controversial as an analytical category (e.g., Schweitzer 2000), but it is acknowledged as providing social continuity binding successive and contemporary generations through marriage and alliance. Among many arctic societies, kinship is rejected as being biologically prescribed, yet it remains a critical foundation of social organization and relations (e.g., Bodenhorn 1989, 2000; summary discussion in Nuttall 2000:35–9). A few arctic anthropologists have been included in the kinship structure of the societies they study (Briggs 1970; Fienup-Riordan 1983b), which may be a result of the people needing to classify the anthropologist in their world (Chagnon 1992:139). Whereas Inuit/Iñupiaq/Yup'ik kinship allows for some improvisation, Aleut kinship is a permanent biologically prescribed state that mirrors mainstream America and much of the Western world, made plain during the collection of genealogies, in the discourse, and in the enactment of social relationships.

Genealogical inquiry found that every Aleut member of King Cove (and most non-Aleuts through marriage)[5] fits on the same chart, sharing either an ancestor or a descendant (False Pass, Nelson Lagoon, and Sand Point residents also fit on this one chart).[6] Households are most often coincident with nuclear families. Because of the small overall Aleut population, most people feel that everyone must be related in some way. Occasionally, people deny relatedness, though this does not mean the relationship ceases; these denials are temporary, often because of tensions and are joked about later when tensions have eased. Strained relationships are apparent in the discourse; for example, "There are a couple of kids here running around with my name on 'em."

Aleut kinship terms are no longer used. Modern kinship terms are English terms and reflect the same bilateral kin recognition found in the Western majority. "Cousin," "aunt," and "uncle" are umbrella terms used for a variety of implicit relationships, with "auntie" and "uncle" earning special respect – generally used in reference to genealogical relationships, but also terms for elders. Children are not "adopted out" to other Native families as in Inuit societies, but they can be "borrowed" or "taken." "Adopted out" in King Cove means sent to a non-Native family outside the village, with no more ties to their relatives, an experience that some remember painfully. One man raised his nephew as his own: "They weren't taking care of him when he was a baby so I just took him."

Although King Cove's genealogy is one lengthy continuous chart, to call the community "one big family" is misleading. All Aleuts are related, and they often act upon that relatedness, but not always. While at sea, boat captains override kinship, and everyone on the boat defers to the captain as the ultimate authority, no matter the relationship. At sea, uncles defer to nephews, cousins defer to each other, and grandfathers defer to grandsons while maintaining the appropriate respectful behaviour expected on land. This is not unique to the Aleut; boat captains are found to have the ultimate authority in any seafaring situation, but in a tight-knit community of closely related kin, the phenomenon is distinctive. Kinship plays a strong role in the social organization of the production of fish as a commodity and in subsistence distribution, and fishermen strive to meet family obligations in providing food while remaining competitive. Provisional obligations between women are usually non-competitive, as evidenced by the continual cooperative activities, sharing, childcare, and visiting between households.

All Aleuts participate in subsistence, also called "home pack." A sexual division of labour, though not set in stone, often excludes women from the acquisition of fish and game and from the primary butchering of waterfowl and game. Most subsistence hunting parties for terrestrial foods, such as geese and caribou, are groups of two or three men. Frequently, groups of teenage boys and young men head out of town on four-wheelers in full camouflage, with guns strapped to their backs. Women do most of the processing and storing of fish and waterfowl. In good weather, families head to Belkofski Bay in skiffs to collect foods. Wives often accompany their husbands fishing in order to collect along the beaches, but men also collect on the beaches during fishing downtime in the absence of women. Collecting is not considered "women's work," though it is usually performed by women. On several occasions when I asked where certain meats came from – often as I was sinking my teeth into caribou or geese – I got an answer that suggested it was poached. "It's local, that's all I can tell you," said one man. Thus, some might not be too concerned with legal seasons. The usual schedule of seasonal harvests is illustrated in figure 3.2, but is subject to yearly changes depending on regulations or species availability. On the whole, this illustrates an *expectation* of what is to come, which can result in surprises and disappointments.

Although both men and women fish with rod and reel at Ram's Creek, which has a pink salmon run in July and August, or fish for a multitude of non-salmon species off the docks, most fish taken for subsistence are from commercial catches, with the captain and crew using commercial gear. This is in part because sockeye and king salmon are preferred over pinks and chums in taste and usage, and are usually stored in greater quantities but can be caught only at sea. Fishermen seldom turn prized king salmon in to the cannery because the price is often too low to make it worth their while (25 cents per pound in 2007) and because they would rather eat them. The fishermen bag the salmon while out in their boats and send them back to town with the tenders – the large boats that move fish and supplies from the fishing grounds to the cannery – who leave them in metal containers on the fish dock. The tendermen then call or radio those for whom the fish are intended, and someone picks them up and takes them home or delivers them (see figure 3.3).

Figure 3.3 is but one example of salmon processing and distribution from one fisherman, and it occurs differently depending on who is fishing, with whom he fishes, and the season. The decisions people make regarding the proportion of fish to remove from the commercial catch are based on knowledge of past distribution, assessment of the current needs of the people to whom that individual distributes, his wife's or mother's knowledge of who should get fish and how much, and the price of fish offered by the cannery. The lower the price paid, the more fish people bring home.

Limited Entry restricts the number of boat and permit owners and can greatly affect an individual's ability to provide subsistence resources to his household or to other households that depend on him. Economic status, age, or other circumstances exclude some households from being able to fish, but extended family or friends often include them in their own activities or share a portion of their catches. There were 43 King Cove and Belkofski men issued permits in 1975, compared with 53 permitted salmon fishermen in 2002, but

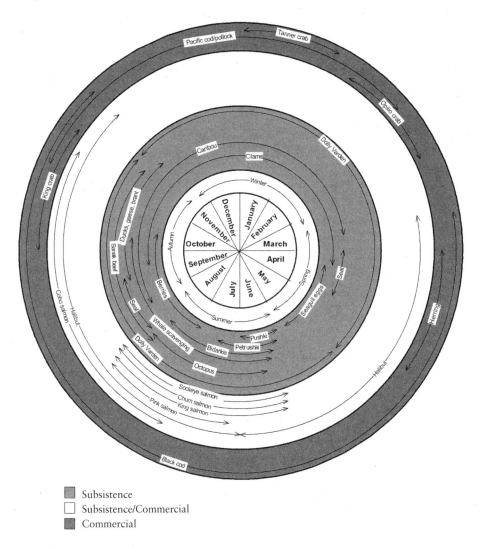

Figure 3.2

Annual cycle of harvesting in King Cove. Harvesting times are approximate and subject to yearly fluctuations in species abundance and regulatory changes. Crab, cod, and herring are also eaten, but there is not a designated subsistence fishery for these species.

fewer total permits (all Belkofski fishermen moved to King Cove by 1980). There are 170 households and therefore approximately one permit for every 3.2 households village-wide. The average household size is 2.9 and average family size is 3.53 persons (Census 2000). This is a good ratio, assuming that all permits are fished (which is becoming more difficult, as we shall see). Men provide most of

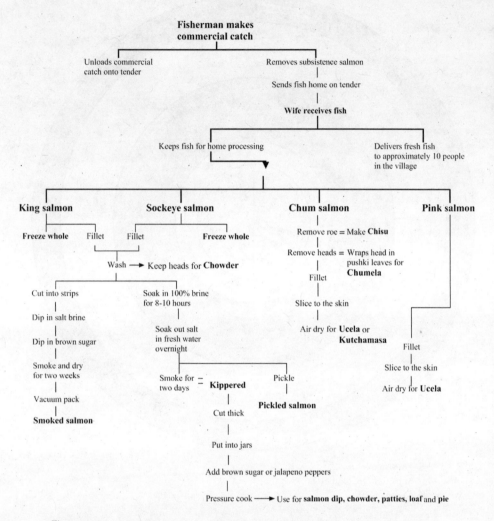

Figure 3.3
Example of salmon from catch to stomach from a single fisherman. Chums, sockeyes,
and kings are often caught together and can all be brought home from one fishing
opener. Pink salmon run later, in July and August, and are caught separately.

the fish, but women are central to provisioning households. For
example, they will tell their husbands, "We need twenty more reds
for Uncle and Auntie, five more for Junior, and fifteen more for us."
They know what is needed, keep track of sharing, and therefore are
crucial to the men's status.

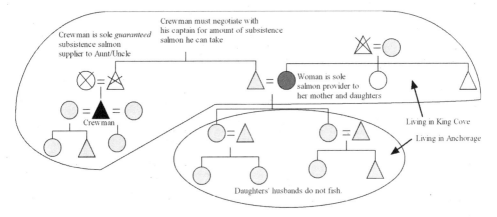

Figure 3.4
Example of one çrewman who must supply two main households, including his own,
from his negotiations with his captain. His aunt must then supply four households,
including hers, from whatever her nephew can bring her. In this case, none of the other
households receive salmon regularly from anyone else. Quantities vary from year to year.

Elders rely on their fishing relatives to stock their freezers; often it
is their sons or grandsons who received their permit from the elder.
Some elders have no reliable assistance because they were outside
or on the fringes of the fishing industry, and now so are their children. For some individuals who are not guaranteed fish, relatives
and friends will give them a portion of their own, saying they "have
too much to deal with" or they "don't feel well enough to jar all this
fish." In one case, an elderly couple who cannot fish and have only
daughters who live in Anchorage, were expecting their nephew to
send fish back in for them. On some occasions, as they were waiting, they were touting how they always had enough fish to last them
all winter, but on other occasions they seemed less certain: "He
[our nephew] better come through for us." Figure 3.4 illustrates an
example of the demands placed on this young crewman in genealogical terms. Crewmen do not automatically have the right to take
fish and must negotiate the right to do so with the captains.

This crewman's parents are both deceased (figure 3.4). His father
had initially received two salmon permits during Limited Entry and
had owned a boat, but all have been sold over the years in circumstances that were not disclosed to me. His aunt, who shares the
burden of supplying her household plus those of her mother and

daughters, uses a broad range of species beyond salmon in the sharing – broader than perhaps in wealthier homes, where salmon is guaranteed in abundance. Her nephew is the sole *guaranteed* source of salmon, and sometimes other foods, such as *bidarkis* is also shared with them from a variety of sources, but this is inconsistent. These other species are often caught and collected by both her (often after a long day's work) and her husband, who has not been employed as a crewman for several years. She holds a full-time job at a local store, pays the bills, and keeps food on the table when subsistence foods are not easily obtained. Their nephew has recently been in trouble with the law, but he was released from jail to fish because he is required to support his children.

Sharing, then, is only partially institutionalized in that surpluses are generally shared with family members first, but portions of fish may go to several different households from one fisherman or crewman. For example, one crewman brought back a dozen chum salmon for his wife, who gave the heads to her aunt. She in turn gave five of those heads to her friend across the street. From the same catch, the crewman also gave me two king salmon, and I gave the roe and heads to my neighbour, who made salmon head chowder and split it with four households, mine included. Thus, I was easily incorporated into the sharing, where expectations abound but there is also room for improvisation. Bringing fish is also a material affirmation of status. Returning from the boat with abundance to share earns prestige for the fishermen, though it can also approximate to showing off. Sharing, however, is expected between some family members and is internalized in practice, creating a sense of satisfaction for the providers and receivers. Without an ideology dictating sharing imperatives, we might expect sharing store-bought foods to mean the same things, but it does not.

Food is also shared with family and friends outside King Cove; families may send seagull eggs or smoked salmon to people in Anchorage with someone on a plane going out. There is less sharing between villages because the same resources are available to each community. However, one woman sent a "home pack" with her sister on the ferry to deliver to her mother, who is in an assisted living home in Unalaska, filled with salmon, *bidarkis*, "pogies" (greenling), *chadu*, *pushki*, and sculpin fillets. Her mother has no one there to gather wild food for her.

Table 3.1
Partial list of cost estimates of subsistence activities, 2002

Item	Estimated average cost (US$)
REGULAR OR REPEATED USAGE	
Rifle or shotgun	350–600
Four-wheeler (optional)	5,000
Boat (range 9–18 m)	35,000–475,000
Skiff with outboard motor	6,500
Outdoor clothing/boots	400
Radios	600 each
SEASONAL OR YEARLY EXPENSES	
Fuel	500
Ammunition	200–400
Subsistence permit	Given by state or federal subsistence board
Hunting licence	Variable

Does not include costs for maintaining the boats. All of these objects have to be shipped, significantly increasing the costs.

Subsistence Costs and Subsistence Harvests

Subsistence harvesting almost entirely requires commercial gear to be affordable and accessible. Capital investments in subsistence have become more intensive, requiring the purchase of skiffs, firearms, and often four-wheelers, in addition to maintaining commercial boats (see table 3.1). Fishing for subsistence is more costly if done as a separate boat trip, and taking fish from commercial catches saves time and money. Fishermen also collect *bidarkis*, scavenge whale meat, hunt birds, dig clams, and gather a range of food while out on their boats between fishing openings. The federal regulation handbook specifies that subsistence-only harvests of salmon cannot be done within 24 hours before and within 12 hours following commercial fishing openings and within a 50-mile (80-kilometre) radius of the area open to commercial fishing; yet it also states that federally qualified subsistence users who are commercial fishermen can retain subsistence fish from commercial catches (Federal Subsistence Board 2001:5, 28). State and federal subsistence regulations both require permits for different areas, but their provisions do not apply to each other. Those who do not fish commercially must wait for appropriate times to subsistence fish. Non-permitted, non-crewing fishermen set their subsistence nets close to the village.

In the early 1990s, subsistence harvests for all of King Cove were found to constitute approximately 60 percent of the total meat, fish, and fowl consumption and 25 percent of the total diet (Fall et al. 1993).[7] The per capita harvest of 256 pounds (116 kilograms) of wild foods in 1992 is slightly higher than the average annual consumption of 222 pounds (101 kilograms) of store-bought meats in the continental United States (Fall et al. 1993:111). Local prices for non-subsistence meats are high, but when factoring in time, effort, and equipment costs for subsistence hunting and fishing, store-bought meats might actually cost less. Braund et al. examined subsistence harvest equivalents and replacement values in dollars in 1984 and found that the estimated replacement costs were US$5,914 per household and US$762,945 for the village, or 14 percent of the total gross income (1986:5.5, 7.54). Though an interesting comparison, giving subsistence food a cash value is problematic for several reasons: not only is it difficult to quantify, but people do not treat it as income, never mind that you cannot buy fuel or travel to Anchorage with subsistence food. Then again, throughout most of the Arctic, as soon as people get access to money, they turn it into subsistence through the purchase of hunting equipment (Bodenhorn 1989:58; Goldsmith 1979; Rasing 1994:171). For the Aleut, cash in itself is not always turned into subsistence, except indirectly through boat improvements, the focus, I believe, being on improving potential commercial exploits. Without fully knowing the nature of the fishing season to come, men and women will pour their resources into preparations for it. The successes and disappointments of the actual seasons are in some ways written off as "that's just the nature of the business," but this also creates an environment of frustration (to be discussed in chapters 5 and 6).

Subsistence permits are issued to all subsistence fishermen by Fish & Game, which then must record the numbers of fish taken on the permits and return them. The permits, however, do not generally include salmon retained by commercial fishermen, and the number of permits issued does not indicate every subsistence harvester. More is taken from commercial harvest than by using other subsistence techniques. Of the 54 subsistence salmon permits issued in 1998 in King Cove, 44 were "successful" and returned to Fish & Game, indicating 146.8 fish harvested per permit (Northern Economics 2000:4.6). A 1992 subsistence survey in King Cove estimated that King Cove's commercial fishermen harvested 37.7 percent of the total wild resources retained for subsistence and, of these harvests, 73 percent were salmon, 21 percent were other fish, and 6 percent were marine invertebrates (Fall et al. 1993:47–8; Northern Economics 2000:4.5). These estimates are probably low as well, since they only include species removed from commercial catches and do not include all the other species collected as a by-product of commercial fishing. Commercial removal was responsible for contributing at least 25 different kinds of resources for subsistence use (Fall et al. 1993:47).

Fish & Game's Division of Commercial Fisheries' Annual Salmon Management Reports (ASMR) do not include the primary way that these households get salmon – from commercial catches[8] – and hence underestimate the connection between the two acquisition systems. Information from the Community Profile Database of Fish & Game's Subsistence Division is likely to be more accurate because it is based on household survey data that included "home pack" estimates. Comparing data from these two divisions' reports, as Northern Economics did in its study for the borough, "it is estimated that the amount of home pack or unreported subsistence harvests is probably as least as much as the amount of reported harvest made with subsistence permits" (2000:4.1). For 1992, the Subsistence Division estimated that 17,136 salmon were harvested for home use in King Cove in 1992 (Fall et al. 1993:50), compared with ASMR's 5,856 salmon harvested for home use for the same year.

These reporting differences were noted by Langdon (1982:175) and Fish & Game (Fall et al. 1993:58–62). However, when the Subsistence Division compared only the salmon caught using "subsistence methods," such as with nets or rod/reel (estimated at 7,036 ± 1,773) with that collected from the subsistence permits, then the average catch per person was quite similar for each database, though the number of salmon estimated during household surveys was slightly higher than reported on the permits, because not every subsistence harvester obtained a permit. Thus, the Aleut are recording on their permits only subsistence salmon that were collected under what the state defines as "subsistence methods." Figure 3.5 provides only the ASMR data because the Subsistence Division does not conduct annual surveys; its most recent for King Cove was in 1992. These data show that it is insufficient to summarize statistics from subsistence permits in order to understand the extent of subsistence use or its relationship to commercial fishing.

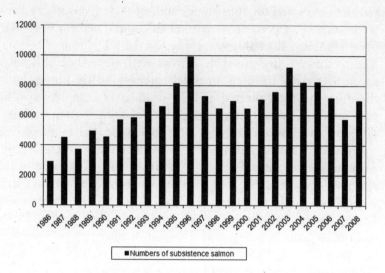

Figure 3.5
Subsistence salmon harvests (numbers of fish) in King Cove per year, 1985–2008
(Annual Salmon Management Reports, Fish & Game, Kodiak). See also appendix A,
table B.

Subsistence and Commercial Economies as Inseparable

Subsistence and commercial integration is continually practised, and
no overt distinctions are made between them. No one, for example,
delineates where commercial activities end and subsistence begins,
and vice versa, unless when asked about them as separate entities.
There is every indication that subsistence uses would be severely curtailed in the absence of commercial fishing, which would have major
social ramifications. As an elder stated, "Kids might eat less [fish] if
there were no commercial fishing. Now, with choices, we still do the
subsistence." Supplying fish to households and sharing raw fish and
finished products affirms roles and responsibilities between friends
and relatives. The status of fisherman, crewman, and the producer of
fish products is negotiated in the mix.

In many ways, Peter Pan Seafoods helps facilitate the distribution
of subsistence fish in King Cove by providing manpower and dock
space for transporting, unloading, and temporarily storing the fish.
Tenders under contract with Peter Pan haul subsistence fish between
individual fishing boats and the cannery dock in King Cove. The use
of tendermen, manpower, and dock space is offered "as a favour to

the fishermen," according to a plant manager. The fish are not always intended for a specific household, and the distributors will take the initiative and deliver fish to elders or those they deem in need.

FISHERMEN AND THE CANNERY:
STRAINED SYMBIOSIS

Most fish for commercial sale are delivered to Peter Pan Seafoods in King Cove. Fishermen and the cannery have a symbiotic relationship: neither one could exist without the other. The cannery pays for boat repairs, parts, and other equipment, and determines the price per pound of fish to pay the permit holders. Fishermen supply the cannery with seafood, sometimes called "product" at the point of delivery. Neither entity fully admits this symbiosis: the fishermen talk of selling their fish to other buyers, and the cannery managers talk of buying their own boats and hiring outsiders to run them.[9]

Peter Pan Seafoods is the third cannery for King Cove (same facility, different ownership), now owned by the Japanese Nichiro Corporation. Its facility operates around the clock during peak seasons, processing black cod, crab, salmon, halibut, Pacific cod, and pollock, producing canned and frozen fish, oil, milt, roe, fishmeal, *ikura, sujiko,* and *surimi*.[10] As many as 500 non-residents are brought in to work in the cannery as needed; 90 percent are Filipino, and the other 10 percent are Latinos, US students, Chinese, and Eastern Europeans, among others. As introduced in chapter 2, local Aleuts, mostly women, gave up wage employment at the cannery when the actual practice of fishing became stable for their husbands. Few local people work in the cannery today.

The standard complaint of cannery managers was that Aleut workers stayed on the job only long enough to make enough money to last the year until the following season. Though in the past some cannery managers tried to indenture Aleuts to the company or to the company store in order to keep them on the job throughout the year, Aleuts have typically worked only as much as was needed for the year. In response to the wavering work behaviour of local people, Peter Pan Seafoods implemented a rule that if you have ever quit or been fired, you can never work for the facility again.

The cannery complex is almost a small village within King Cove, with its own utilities, commissary, library, laundromat, cafeteria, dormitories, and a security guard. Few cannery workers are seen around King Cove, except in the bar or the grocery store. The village used to have a problem with pollution and stench in the waters of the bay, where the cannery was dumping waste, but with pressure from village leaders, Peter Pan installed a fishmeal plant to make a type of fertilizer and fish food with the waste from other types of processing. Peter Pan now sets the standard for harvesting on all boats, since it cannot sell the product unless certain standards are met at every stage between catching and selling.[11] It made refrigerated sea water (RSW) circulation systems for preservation mandatory on all boats in 2002 and will not accept "watermarked"[12] fish. The processing itself is a closed activity, performed by non-local workers. It is the harvesting, rather than the processing, that keeps the village alive.

FISHING VESSELS AND THE HARBOR HOUSE

There is a massive body of shared knowledge regarding fishing boats. Fishing boats have personalities and legacies, and Aleut fishermen remember every boat they ever fished on. On one occasion, I received an invitation to an elder's house to look at old pictures with a friend of his. The man got out his shoebox of pictures and stack of albums, and his friend brought over an old worn suitcase full of loose photographs. Beers were cracked open, and for hours we pored over the pictures, the majority of which were snapshots of boats. Other oldtimers drifted in and out of the house, offering their stories. The F/v *Sacco* triggered stories of a deceased brother; the F/v *Pansy* reminded one man of how much he disliked the captain; the F/v *Catherine J* was the "tippiest boat" they had ever fished on; the F/v *Tempest* was a solid tender; the F/v *Onocos* was run by "two Rudys"; the F/v *Ocean Pride* was run by Norwegians who introduced lutefisk ("How can you make an Aleut sick?" he asked; "Eat lutefisk"); and the F/v *Westerly* burned up just after one of these men got his family to safety. One picture was of a strike decades ago that closed down the East Anchor fishing grounds. There were pictures of False Pass before the cannery burned; boats in the photos burned with it, they remembered sadly. One photograph triggered the memory of a particularly bad winter when 37 boats followed one large boat through the sea ice all the way to Togiak in Bristol Bay. Genealogies of the fishing vessels themselves, in which ships have histories linked to various captains and crews at certain times, are part of the historical legacy of fishing. Vessels alone are sometimes described as singular, living things

Figure 3.6
f/v *Catherine J*, Ernest Mack's boat in the 1960s (photo by Barney Mack)

on which various fishermen have had the privilege or misfortune of working. These retired fishermen were referring to their boats, their experiences on board, and their knowledge of other boats as points of reference in their lives, in the history of the community, and to link them to the current fishing practices.

Fishermen spend the majority of each fishing season on their boats at sea. They also work aboard their vessels between fishing seasons year-round. The captain and his crew form a team on a particular boat in a particular season in which they classify shared experiences, memorable moments, crises, and triumphs. Personal memories are

Figure 3.7
F/V *Ocean Pride* (photo by Barney Mack)

always linked to who one was fishing for, fishing with, and on which boat. The career of a crewman is divided over a long history of different boats and the experiences aboard each. Ownership demands responsibility to maintain the boat, organize a crew to fish, steer the boat, and run the actual fishing operation. But it also offers a measure of freedom to choose one's crew and direct their participation in fishing seasons. Captains and vessels are sometimes identified jointly, the name of the boat identifying the captain. Captains may have T-shirts, hats, or jackets printed with the name of the boat and a sketch of it, for themselves, their crew, and their families to wear. They also display models of their boats in their homes, made by one of a few local expert modellers. Boats are often named after wives, daughters, or other female relatives, but also with reference to being Aleut or in nautical terms. A captain may sell his boat to upgrade to a newer, larger one, in which case he may retain the boat's name or choose a new, more personalized one. The quality and condition of the boat reflects on the captain, as does how close to the main dock he gets to moor it in the harbour.

Figure 3.8
Boat model made by Paul Tcheripanoff, King Cove (photo by Della
Trumble)

Although the Aleut did not have segregated men's houses as found
in many Inuit societies, the Harbor House is a comparable version,
a modern Aleut men's house. The harbourmaster's office is but a
small portion of the Harbor House; the rest is a lounge lined with
chairs where the coffee is always on and the walls are papered with
nautical charts, maps, the American flag, and fisheries news. "If these
walls could talk," said the harbourmaster, "heaven help us all." The
harbourmaster keeps track of boat traffic, use of the boat lift, and the
harbour facilities, and has several employees. Construction on a new
Harbor House was completed halfway through fieldwork, giving
way to new stories, new complaints, and new negotiations. Retired
fishermen still "go to work" (see also Braund et al. 1986:9.58) in
the Harbor House and offer the benefit of their experience to the
younger generations. The Harbor House excludes women (with the
exception of this anthropologist), though not overtly. There is no
similar alternative space in which women congregate.[13]

If the wheelhouse is the office, then the Harbor House is the
boardroom. Most business is conducted in the Harbor House, from
price negotiations to crewman hires to fisheries meetings. Crucial
to this business is VHF radio communication on every boat. Indeed,
every household and business is connected by radio, including Peter
Pan, PenAir, the post office, and the national weather service. Radio

communication is necessary to conduct the everyday business of fishing, but it also provides one's cohort with subtle information on fish
and other boats. The radio passes on knowledge about the weather,
currents, and when and where to fish. Aleuts tease and gossip on
the radio, but also negotiate trust and status. Fishermen carry on
more private conversations on their "secret channels" by directing
one another to "go up a couple on the radio," "go to the other one,"
or simply "go up" to channels which they have prearranged. There
is less formal radio usage than in other parts of the world; fishermen
who are new to the area are immediately distinguishable because
of their radio formality. Those on land scan the channels and know
what is happening on the water at all times: "The radio's been quiet
all day, the guys must be on some fish"; or "The radio's busy, must
be no fish out there." The radio is also used to conduct everyday
business within the village, exchange personal messages, arrange
travel, and talk to those at sea. The flow of information depends
on an understanding of partially coded talk, a language that is not
simply maritime but is unique to this fleet of fishermen.

   The two domains of Harbor House and fishing boat are simultaneously public and private spaces: some activities of the boat
are conducted in public, but onboard dynamics (and some fishing
operations in which they keep their activities a secret) are private.
The Harbor House is a public meeting place in principle, yet it is
understood that it is men's space, fishermen and non-fishermen alike.
Status and sociality are being performed, in which boat ownership
is a public demonstration of wealth, fishing capacity, and often of
the family history in fishing. Fishermen's activities and possessions
are indicative of social class. Identity symbols and expressions are
only significant when they are meaningful to the larger community,
and in a small-scale, intimate, and fairly isolated community, these
expressions convey meanings to each member of the community.
People create their own meanings of these shared symbols, whose
utility and access are described below.

THE KING COVE FLEET: SALMON FISHING, GEAR, AND VESSELS

The different kinds of resource networks that any fisherman needs
to negotiate in order to fish, share, eat, pay his bills, and be recognized as a high-status producer must also be seen through the way

in which commercial fishing demands different kinds of access to resources considered as part of a larger conceptualization of limited entry. Resources such as boats, permits, labour, and revenue are networks that intersect but also form limited entry systems with restricted access. These limits, in turn, are implicated in aspects of social organization, sharing, and gender relations.

Preparations begin in May for the onset of the salmon season. The Alaska Board of Fisheries regulates the fishery such that it cannot begin before a specified day in early June,[14] and there is a frenzy of activity until opening day as the fishermen ready their boats and anticipate the cannery's fish prices. There are three salmon gear types fished in Area M: purse seine, set gillnet, and drift gillnet.[15] The different types of fishing operation can determine success or failure in a season. The proportion of Aleut fishermen who own the different boats and permits and those who crew will be discussed after the general description of the boat and gear types. "Top boat" and "high boat" are the terms for the highest catch in the salmon fleet. These terms can describe fishing performance per opening or for the entire season.

Purse seiners – often called "limit seiners," because these boats are limited to 58 feet (17.7 metres) in length by law – catch salmon by encircling them with a large net and closing the bottom. One end of the net is attached to a power skiff and then laid out in the water in a circle by the boat. Attached to the top of the net are thousands of floats that hold 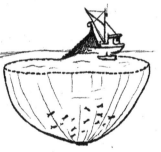 the net at the water's surface while the bottom is weighted and hangs vertically. The bottom is then pursed, or closed, and the bag is lifted alongside the vessel using a hydraulic power block. Fish are dumped from the bag into the boat's hold. A *tender*, or buyer vessel hired by a processor, may lower its fish pump straight into the bag and brail salmon directly into its hold. Tenders deliver the fish to the canneries and bring supplies and messages back to the boats. The tendermen are often non-local white men with a 60-day contract with the cannery during the summer fisheries. Local fishermen will also captain tenders, which are their own boats that they also take crab fishing. Because they are on contract and their earnings are not based on performance, there is very little competition between the tendermen.

Some, however, have better reputations than others for visiting the fishing boats and making personal deliveries to and from King Cove. Purse seiners are generally the largest of the salmon vessels, and their captains and crews typically have higher status than other fishermen because of the expense and value of both the boat and the permit, the larger crew, the potential for greater earnings, and versatility. They can more easily be converted to fish in trawl or pot fisheries or even in crab fisheries for the more daring few. In Area M, purse seines must be between 100 and 250 fathoms in length and less than 375 meshes in depth; the mesh may not be more than 3½ inches (8.9 centimetres), and leads must be between 50 and 150 fathoms.

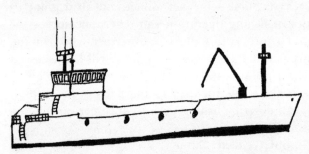

Gillnetters set a curtainlike net perpendicular to the direction in which the salmon are travelling. Vessels are usually between 9 and 12 metres long and have a drum on the stern or bow onto which the net is rolled. Fish are handpicked out of the net as it is reeled back on board. Salmon are typically iced and delivered whole to the processor. The top of the line is kept at the water's surface with corks, and the bottom is weighted with lead. The mesh is large enough to allow the large male fish to get "gilled," or stuck, but the smaller fish, usually female, are not so easily trapped. *Drift gillnetters* set their nets along tidal rips and currents where the salmon tend to migrate,

but do not anchor the net. Area M limits the net lengths to 200 fathoms and the mesh must be at least 5¼ inches (13.3 centimetres) and may not exceed 90 meshes in depth. *Set gillnetters* in Area M anchor both ends of their nets in the water and pick the fish into skiffs. The fish are then offloaded into the holds of the vessels. Set gillnets are limited to 100 fathoms, may be set in no more than two "sites" (designated areas leased by the state to a permit holder), and they must be at least 900 feet (274 metres) away from another set gillnet.

Setnet sites are obtained somewhat competitively; "good sites" are those rumoured to guarantee a decent season. Thin Point and East Anchor are among the "good sites." Purse seining has a more directly competitive element, but even then there are local rules of sharing. If a purse seiner "gets on some fish" and is doing well in a certain area, he may allow certain other seiners to get in line to fish in the same spot, or he may do his best to conceal his success. In fact, taking turns in seining a productive pocket of fish is said to be "mandatory," and each seiner has 30 minutes in which to fish that spot: "As soon as the first boat's net comes up, you are there to drop it. If you are over time, someone will come in and cork you. That means they catch your fish instead of you. They will let their net out inside of your net." It has been said that when some fishermen are doing really well, they may not even call home to their wives for fear of "giving away" their "good spot." Fishermen can be quite protective of their good fortune on the water or quite generous, depending on the circumstances and who is fishing nearby.

The boats themselves are important theoretically because of the variation in gear and fishing capacity, the crew requirements, and the variation in ability to harvest fish, and they have implications for the success or failure in a given season. They are regulated differently, depending on their configuration and permit type. They require constant attention in the harbour as well as at sea. Licences are required, and captains must take extra classes if they want to carry passengers. Boats allow people to move between villages, "get out" to Cold Bay to catch a plane in bad weather, and transport materials. Owners are more easily incorporated into a larger network of sharing labour, such as negotiating with crabbers to haul materials from Seattle or Anchorage, because they are in a better position to reciprocate.

Permit Transfers: A Wealth Transfer System

Permit transfers constitute a wealth transfer system in the anthropological sense, discriminating in favour of sons, then other relatives, then friends, and then strangers. Forty-one King Cove fishermen received salmon permits in 1975 under the Limited Entry program, some receiving more than one permit for different gear types based on their record of fishing (67 total permits, 1.63 permits per fisherman), but the current distribution of permits has changed since that time. In 2005 there were 67 salmon permits for 55 fishermen, 1.22 permits per fisherman (www.cfec.state.ak.us). The permit type is also indicative of the type of boat the permit holder owns. Some fishermen issued multiple permits have sold one permit to finance gear for fishing another permit. Salmon permits for this area are among the most valuable in Alaska and attract new fishermen from out of state, thereby increasing the competition.

At the 2001 annual meeting of the Alaska Anthropological Association in Fairbanks, I presented a paper on Aleut fishermen, putting a human face on the Area M fisheries. Many who commented to me about my presentation – including those from Fish & Game, and the US Fish & Wildlife Service, as well as other anthropologists – were insistent that Area M is comprised largely of "Seattle boats," and many believed that local Aleut fishermen had long ago sold their permits (or at least one of their permits if they were issued more than one) to non-resident strangers. This phenomenon is taken up in chapter 5. Here I show how "resident" versus "non-resident" fishermen is not an appropriate dichotomy for analyzing permit distribution.

To substantiate this claim, I reviewed Area M's permit statistics. In 1975, 100 seine, 98 drift gillnet, and 99 set gillnet transferable permits were issued to Alaska Peninsula/Aleutian local residents (Malecha, Tingley, and Iverson 2000). A total of 25 transferable permits were issued to other Alaskan non-local residents, and 71 transferable permits were issued to non-residents. Changes in permit distribution statewide have been tracked by the Commercial Fisheries Entry Commission (CFEC) since 1980. In the Alaska Peninsula/Aleutian region, of the 214 seine permit transfers from 1980 to 2006, 32 (14.9%) went to a friend/partner, 127 (59.3%) went to an immediate family member, 9 (4.2%) went to another relative, and 46 (21.5%) went to "other." Of the 387 drift permit transfers, 83 (21.4%) went to a friend/partner, 122 (31.5%) went to immediate family, 30 (7.8%) went to another relative, and 152 (39.3%) went to "other". Of the 357 set gillnet permit transfers, 80 (22.4%) went to a friend/partner, 146 (40.9%) went to immediate family, 28 (7.8%) went to another relative, and 103 (28.9%) went to "other" (Free-Sloan and Tide 2007). Figure 3.9 shows the relationship of transferors to transferees for all seine, drift, and set gillnet permit transfers from 1980–2000.

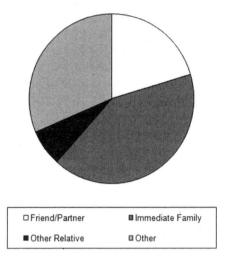

Figure 3.9
Relationship of permit transferors to transferees for all salmon permit types, cumulative 1980–2006 (Free-Sloan and Tide 2007:118–20)

Although many permit holders claim residency outside an Aleut
village or out of Alaska, their status cannot automatically be considered non-Aleut, non-family, or stranger. In reviewing the list of
names and addresses of permit holders for the year 2000 on the
CFEC website, I identified many from Ferndale and Bellingham,
Washington, Anchorage, Kodiak, Palmer, and Kenai as relatives of
Aleutians East Borough residents, but I could not categorize those
whom I do not know of, those from any of the other villages, or
other kinds of relationships. In 2005, 176 permit holders listed King
Cove, False Pass, Sand Point, Nelson Lagoon, or Unalaska as their
primary residence[16] (figure 3.10).

The belief that Area M is composed mostly of wealthy Seattle fishermen who have jobs the other nine months of the year has fuelled
much of the arguments for the closure of the Aleut salmon fishery.
But the above data indicate that not only are a significant number
of local residents holding permits but they did not always sell or
transfer their permits to the highest bidder. Often permits were sold,
traded, or gifted to family and friends, no matter their residency
(Tingley et al. 2001). Statewide, fisheries with lower permit val-

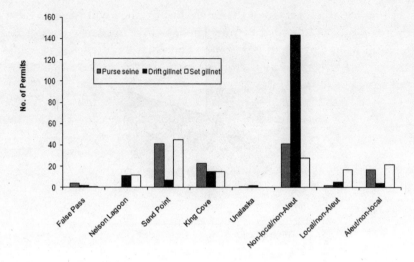

Figure 3.10
Area M permit holders' residence, 2007 (www.cfec.state.ak.us)

ues tended to be gifted more than those with higher values, but an exception to this is the Peninsula/Aleutian seine fishery, with a high percentage of gift transactions and high permit values (Tingley et al. 2001). Before the recent collapse in Area M seine permit values, they were so expensive that no young man could ever hope to buy one, and the most likely way they would change hands was through gift transfer. Setnet permits, however, were cheap enough that a man would be more likely to purchase one, and often they were sold with a boat as a package deal. Driftnet permits were also very expensive, but non-local fishermen sought them out to buy from locals and could adapt most boats to fish this gear.

In 2000 purse seining and setnet permits were predominately locally owned, whereas non-Alaska residents own half of the 163 driftnet permits in Area M. Permit inheritance follows an intrafamily pattern identified in the 1980s (Braund et al. 1986:ch9:38–42). Transfers were most often from father to son, usually with the father fishing the more prestigious seine permit and sons fishing a gillnet permit: "This pattern reflects a predominant commitment among King Cove men to provide their sons access to the community's traditional way of life" (1986:9.40). Permits are typically handed down to sons (and rarely to daughters) who have done well fishing in their fathers' place, and the other children will work on boats fishing for a percentage of the catch. Ideally, they will support their parents off the inherited permit. Though there are fairly large families in King Cove, and one can imagine that children might argue over their father's permit(s), one woman stated, "I have not heard of a big squabble over permits [between siblings]." And neither did I. Often, if the father owned a boat and multiple permits, he might place his son with a permit on another boat that needed a permitted captain, while the father himself fished the remaining permit. This strategy occurs especially if there is only one boat owned by a family. Access to owning a boat and permit by sons of those excluded by Limited Entry is extremely difficult. These young men were and still are forced to work as crew or find alternative employment.

Crews: Shares System, Recruitment, and Kinship

Crews are arguably the most valuable resources for boat captains. Captains cannot fish alone; between one and five crewmen are required, depending on the undertaking. They support the captain's operation and rarely challenge his authority. Captains use their resources, which include kin resources, and their reputation to attract skilled crews. Crewmen will indicate pride in saying "my captain" or "my skipper," or they may grumble about him out of earshot.

Crewmen are not merely plucked from a pool of young men waiting to be hired; rather, they also determine their fate and have greater flexibility than boat and permit owners do. Top crewmen's status depends on certain standards of fishing, and they recognize how valuable they are. If the price of fish is low, many consider such prices an insult to their identity, so even though they receive higher crew shares than those fishing next to them, they will seek other jobs. In the bleak season of 2002, a large number of these top crewmen opted not to go fishing. It is fortunate that this bad season coincided with many land jobs in construction, however temporary, which they snatched up quickly once it was apparent that the price of fish would be low. I believe these men would have abandoned their land jobs in a heartbeat if there had been a sudden turn in fishing success.

Although all crewmen must buy an Alaska Commercial Fishing Crewmember License (issued by Fish & Game), there is little protection for them, since they are often hired with a handshake, and when fishing returns are low they are sometimes only partially paid. Some captains insist on writing contracts in legal language that must be signed and witnessed, specifying expectations on both sides and conditions that would terminate employment, though this formality never occurs between family members. New crewmen are called "greenhorns" or "greenies."[17] Experienced crewmen usually earn more shares than greenhorns; when the price of fish is low, a few captains will seek to employ only greenhorns so that they do not have to pay them as much. This hiring decision is often considered acceptable so that the captain can have a satisfactory income, especially when local crewmen are seeking land jobs for the season. But it can lead to animosity from some in the community, who feel that captains should always hire locally. Hiring greenhorns sometimes backfires, since they rarely bring in as much fish as those with experience. In one instance, a crewman on a crab boat with fifteen years' experience was making the same share as a greenhorn; he was deeply insulted yet he needed the money. "It used to be that guys only hired family and *no girls*, but as things got bad, they started hiring girls too. Seiners need a large crew. They'll hire college students from the Lower 48 because they can pay them a smaller share." Thus, the price of fish offered by the cannery and the conditions at sea play a large role in crew organization.

Most of those who hold commercial fishing permits employ non-permit-holding members of their own family and community. It is virtually impossible to "work your way up" to captain a boat; a crewman must inherit a boat and permit or save money to buy a boat and permit. Crews are more fluid than fixed. Several types of kin relations are found on one boat. For generations, fishermen took their sons (and sometimes daughters) fishing as soon as they were capable. Experience and skill earned them "crewshares," and eventually these young men would lease-to-buy a boat of their own from the cannery. Limited Entry rendered this aspiration infeasible, and kin relations became the primary means by which a non-permitted fisherman could gain access to the fisheries by inheriting a permit or crewing for relatives, and this was therefore the most direct means by which young men could become part of the preferred Aleut way of life. Braund et al. (1986:9.42) reported on crew selection favouring immediate family members first, then other family who are not already employed in fishing, followed by local non-

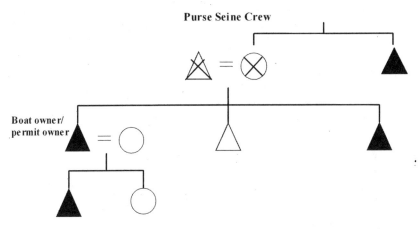

Figure 3.11
Example of a purse seine crew, 2000–01, King Cove salmon fleet

family members, and finally crewmen from out of state, such as college students or family friends. It remains that most crews in the salmon fishery contain one or more individuals who are related to their captain.

When the suggestion was made by an Aleutians East Borough representative that the Aleut hire Yupiit to crew on their boats as part of a solution to the AYK salmon disaster (discussed in detail in chapter 5), the Aleut were offended and showed it with sarcasm and dreadful ethnic jokes in the Harbor House. Never would they hire a Yupiit over a brother, cousin, nephew or friend (nor, I suspect, would any Yupiit accept such an offer). Several said they would prefer to hire an unknown outsider over a Yupiit, because the hire would not be politicized.

Figures 3.11, 3.12, and 3.13 show diagrams of a random selection of captain-crew relationships in the salmon fishery for each gear. These crews tend to remain the same or similar in the cod, pollock, and halibut fisheries. In the crab fisheries (discussed below), crewmen are often young men from these villages and elsewhere and are less likely to be related to the captain or one another.

As noted earlier, a boat captain's authority overrides other kin relations. For example, if a captain employs his uncle as crew, he has ultimate authority over his uncle's activities during the fishing season. On land, the uncle may have more influence because of his age

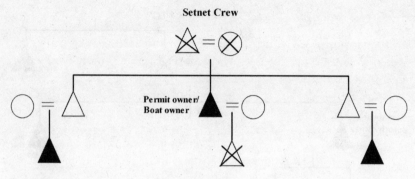

Figure 3.12
Example of set gillnetting crew, 2000–02, King Cove salmon fleet. The captain's nephew was given the option to buy the boat and permit after a trial fishing season when he worked as captain.

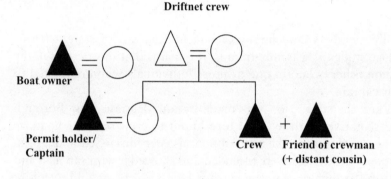

Figure 3.13
Example of drift gillnetting crew, 2002–03, King Cove salmon fleet. The captain in this case lost his boat to a fire at sea in 2001.

and relationship, but in the context of fishing or even of crew duties on land, he is expected to follow the captain's orders.

Thus, crewmen are an important and necessary social category of fishermen and in fact call themselves fishermen. Most young men are committed to living out their lives in King Cove; they are socially connected through family and are totally invested in the lifestyle. Sons of boat and/or permit owners are often automatically in line to take over the operation, and they will invest in it financially and with work before they are due to gain control. Thus, kinship plays a strong role in shaping captain-crew organization as well as in the long-term changes in the distribution of Limited Entry permits.

Fishermen's Codes and Gear Wars

Fishing grounds vary during each season and each year, and are governed by gear type, regulation, and species abundance. King Cove fishermen tend to fish between Pavlof Bay on the Alaska Peninsula and the East/West Anchor area of south Unimak Island in June. In July, they may move to fish the area from Urilia Bay on the north shore of Unimak to Port Moller on the north Alaska Peninsula, all within Area M, with tenders moving to accommodate them. There is a Peter Pan cannery in Port Moller, dubbed the "penal colony" by several tendermen because of its isolation. Fishermen are keenly aware of the conditions throughout the entire area and will move to different areas or change gear (for those holding multiple permits) for a better fishing strategy. Some setnetters hold multiple sites in this regard. In August, boats move closer to King Cove, where it becomes legal to fish, and they set their nets right in front of the town. Many of the locals on land turn out to watch the different boats fish, commenting on technique and the size of fish loads, appraised through binoculars.

The rapid rate in which the technology has developed in just a few decades is astounding. Fathometers, radar, GPS, automatic pilot, hydraulic lifts, refrigeration systems, and sodium lights bedeck almost every boat. The boat attributes have changed over time in terms of gear multiplicity, physical attributes, horsepower, and size. For Area M's purse seine and drift gillnet vessels (which are over 9 metres in length), the average length, net and gross tonnage, horsepower, and fuel capacity have increased significantly since 1978 (Iverson and Malecha 2000; Shirley 1996). There has been a steady annual increase in average vessel length and diversification of gear types per vessel, even though the total number of vessels has decreased during the last decade or more. Regardless of the success or failure of individual or family operations, the King Cove fleet is becoming more efficient.

These trends could be explained by a subtle yet important gear war, in which boat captains strive to expand their individual operations and fish in every type of fishery year-round. This is in large part a response to shorter fishing openers and fewer fish, in which the advantage goes to the more efficient, better-equipped fishermen. This can also be explained by competition in individual status striving and by the need to continually set new standards for attaining prestige.

Non-resident fishermen have often had the upper hand in gear wars; local residents typically own older, smaller fishing vessels with less sophisticated gear, though the gap has closed significantly in the past decade. In the Eastern Aleutians, there is some tension with non-locals "from outside" in all fisheries, "especially if they step out of line," said one woman. There is a "fishermen's code," and if someone breaks the rules "they can blackball people out." For example, she was fishing with her ex-husband in the 1980s and a setnetter came in and set in the way of their drift gillnets. Her ex-husband cut the other fisherman's net. Among seiners, the code of courtesy is that fishermen will take turns setting their nets: "They get in line and rotate. If someone breaks the rules or jumps ahead in line, another boat might drive into the middle of their seines." There were reports of fishermen shooting the buoys of others who violated the code. Most will not leave their nets unattended. One woman who regularly fishes with her husband said fishermen do similar things to locals if they step out of line, but mostly these discipline methods are used on outsiders. While in the Harbor House, one man complained about a fisherman with "Mickey Mouse" gear who was habitually "dumping his gear on everyone else." He added, "Now I'd never dream of cutting another man's nets, but I came pretty close with him." He was angry with the less experienced fisherman but made it clear to others where he drew the line in his own behaviour.

One fisherman, whose usual captain had trouble finding a complete crew and decided to fish with his son instead, sat at home all summer long and scanned the VHF, listening to boats talking to each other. He described to me what he was hearing:

> One guy will get on and say, "I see a couple jumpers over here. I'll take my turn," and then the other guy will say, "Okay, I'm coming over." They *share*. Everybody does. Some boats go co-op. If there's friendship, they cooperate. Everybody shares. That's the way it is around here. They might make a haul and share with another boat that didn't get as much. Seiners are all local. No non-local seiners, and they all cooperate. Non-locals are the tenders. False Pass, Sand Point, and King Cove all stick together. Like glue. Anybody else, you know. Kinda nice, but ...

I, too, scanned the radio channels continually. In my experience, this description was an exaggeration of cooperation on the water. Fishermen can be quite territorial when it comes to the fishing grounds. They chide each other with "You're stealing my spot," but certain fishermen have priority for fishing grounds. Boats crowd into popular fishing spots. Fishermen will rarely give away how many pounds of fish they caught in an opening or where they were successful. To say, "We caught a few fish," means they did really well. "No fish out there" means they could have done better. The above fisherman's insistence that fishermen were all local and the tenders were from elsewhere was meant, I believe, to demonstrate cohesion to an outsider. On a few occasions I overheard tendermen and other fishermen announcing to those in the Harbor House where different fishermen were having the most success. These betraying statements made some uneasy, especially since fish were hard to find that season, making fishing more competitive.

In the following section, I will take the reader through aspects of the "June fishery" – the salmon fishery on which local fishermen depend most. Troubles in this fishery resonate throughout the community and are implicated in most discussions of socioeconomic problems.

THE JUNE FISHERY

Although more detailed aspects of the salmon crisis are discussed in chapter 5, this introduction of the June salmon fishery points to its immediate situation and its rapid decline between 2000 and 2003. In June, fishermen harvest a mixed stock of salmon that are returning to the rivers of the Alaska Peninsula, Asia, and western Alaska. Most people make their "real money" during this month. Days before the opening day, boats from all over the North Pacific stream into the harbour in anticipation. The lines at both grocery stores snake through the aisles. The bar bursts at the seams with patrons drinking and dancing. Hours before the opening, the harbour empties out as boats head for the fishing grounds, and the town falls quiet.

The 2000 June fishery started on the morning of 13 June and continued with added extensions for most of the month. Periodically there are closings of one or a few days, but the fishermen ideally stay out on the fishing grounds, and tenders supply them with groceries and water. The harbour emptied out almost entirely the day

before except for a few fishermen who were waiting for boat parts
or crewmen to fly in once the rain and wind stopped. They "settled for" 85 cents per pound for red salmon. For a week before the
opening, fishermen had hung around the Harbor House in between
readying their boats while they waited for the right test ratio of reds
to chums (they needed a ratio of two to one, set by the Board of
Fisheries). There was a floating "cap," or limit, on the number of
chum salmon they can harvest, from 350,000 to 650,000, and the
2000 chum harvest was capped at 400,000 fish. Fish & Game does
a test fishery to determine the ratio, lest there be too many chums
that have not migrated through that pass and the fishermen reach
this limit and have to stop harvesting altogether before they reach
the limit on reds. Historically, sockeye salmon runs peak between 13
and 22 June and usually decline sharply after 22 June (www.adfg.
state.ak.us), though there is some indication that this peak is shifting
earlier each year.

Peter Pan announced the species' counts by VHF when fishing
closed at 10 PM the first day. Things were "kind of slow," one fisherman assessed. They "had to move [their] boats all over the place
looking for fish." One week into the June fishery in King Cove,
the fishermen in Sand Point and the Shumagin Islands reached
their quota of 363,000 sockeye. Their fishery closed on 18 June.
Consequently, about fifty boats sailed down the peninsula to fish
until the quota for the King Cove area was reached. One King Cove
resident stated, as she watched the other boats cruise across the bay
on their way to the fishing grounds, "I wish they'd stay the hell away.
The guys here need to get their fair share. This happens almost every
year." The tension on the water was felt through the radio and in the
Harbor House.

By 23 June, boats were already heading to Port Moller, where the
July fisheries begin, even though there was no escapement there yet.
This was because there were no fish around False Pass and "so many
boats that there is hardly enough water," according to one fisherman.

The June fishery closes on 1 July, whether the fishermen get their
quota or not. The 2000 fishery closed with only 50 percent of the
South Unimak sockeye allocation harvested. Many fishermen were
not able to make their boat payments or insurance payments for the
year because of this. In 2000, crewmembers were hard to come by.
One man had three girls of less than seventeen years of age working
for him. They could not fish in bad weather because they were so

inexperienced, and hence their total take was seriously low. He was not able to make his payments for the year.

Success rates vary for different types of fishing gear depending on the season. Set gillnetters did well in 2000; even though they are less efficient, there were no closings for them. One friend with a two-man crew was able to get a few thousand pounds of fish each day. Purse seiners were less successful, and driftnetters caught just below their average from previous years. Thus, we saw a slow start to a disappointing season.

In 2001, Area M fishermen were on strike. Peter Pan offered a mere 40 cents per pound for sockeye. There were fewer subsistence fish in circulation as a consequence. One household that depends on a crewman did not get any sockeye, king, or chum salmon in 2001 and instead was reduced to fishing for pinks at Ram's Creek. Only those who could *afford* to take their boats subsistence fishing were able to do so. For 2002 the offer was only 47 cents per pound. One seiner who decided not to fish that summer said, "I'm not giving a fish to Peter Pan. They're getting their fish for free." In 2003 the price was 49 cents per pound for sockeye, but so few fish were being caught that one man called every opening a "practice run" for the real thing. The highliner for one opening got 10,000 pounds (4,530 kilograms), which would be paltry any other year.

Costs and Revenues of the Salmon-Fishing Operations

Area M fishermen own some of the most valuable salmon permits in Alaska, but their value is currently declining. Today, fishermen are still paying off permits they purchased a decade or more ago. Fishermen have said that Fish & Game places higher values on permits than fishermen can sell them for. There is indeed a gap between what the permit brokers list in the advertising sections of the *Anchorage Daily News*, *Pacific Fishing*, and *National Fisherman*, and the CFEC's site indicating values.

Economic Profile

A statistical economic profile of King Cove is difficult to piece together because employment and income data sources for Alaska's coastal communities are incomplete (Northern Economics 2000:11.1 to 11.10). This is due in large part to the non-systematic collection of

Table 3.2
Partial cost estimates for entering Area MS commercial salmon fisheries, 2002

Gear type	Estimate cost range (US$)	Average annual maintenance costs (US$)
PURSE SEINING		
Limited Entry permit and loan payments	30,000 to 40,000	16,000
Vessel 12 to 18 m	120,000 to 475,000	5,000 to 15,000
Purse seine	25,000 to 40,000	2,000 to 3,000
Power skiff with internal engine	25,000 to 50,000	1,000 to 3,000
Hydraulic power and purse blocks	15,000 to 25,000	1,000
Vessel insurance		5,000 to 30,000
Vessel storage and harbour charges		500 to 1,500
Gear storage		500
Fuel (per season)		3,000 to 8,000
DRIFT GILLNETTING		
Limited Entry permit	40,000 to 150,000	
Vessel	95,000 to 130,000	
Gear (200 fathoms)	7,000	
Reel	2,500	
Fuel (per season)		2,000 to 5,000
Insurance		2,000 to 5,000
SET GILLNETTING		
Limited Entry permit	50,000 to 70,000	
Vessel 12 to 14 m	35,000 to 130,000	
Site (leased from the state)	10,000 +	
Nets: up to 300 fathoms	6,000	
Skiff with outboard motor	6,500	
Fuel (per season)		1,500 to 3,000
Insurance		2,000 to 5,000

Costs vary tremendously based on the equipment's condition, its age, length, gear, electronics, hull type, etc. These are conservative estimates based upon interviews with King Cove fishermen. For larger boats, costs are higher. Additional costs include food and supplies for the entire crew, crew licences, radios, and survival kits.

data for the self-employed. All of the state's economic agencies, such as the Department of Labor and Workforce Development and the Department of Community and Economic Development (DCED), have conflicting numbers regarding residents employed in the job category of self-employed commercial fishing, and all indicated too few fishermen. Hence, although King Cove is economically dependent on the fisheries, this fact is hidden by incomplete data. Data provided by the US Census are perhaps the most complete because it gathers individual, household, and community data. It may be significant, however, that the US Census asks for current employment on the date of 15 April for the year the census is taken, and the height of fishing activity in King Cove is from June to September (Northern Economics 2000:11.1 to 11.2). Employment statistics for the village population of age 16 and over (total n=657, female n=263) found only 46 individuals reporting fishing occupations, an obvious error (www.census.gov). For the entire borough, Northern Economics found that the commercial fishing industry employs at least 500 residents and generates $8.7 million in income (2000:11.1).

If a man does not fish, there are limited alternative employment opportunities within the village. Non-fishing jobs include employment at the school, administrative positions, maintenance, seafood processing, municipal jobs, and state and federal employment, which tend to be temporary project-oriented jobs. The median household income in King Cove was averaged at $45,893 for the year 2000 (www.census.gov). Per capita income for 2000 was $17,791. Four families, two of them with a female head of household (no husband present) and 97 individuals reported income below the poverty level in 2000. By and large, households in 2000 were financially secure. However, a fisherman's income depends entirely on the amount of fish caught, the market value, the number and duration of fishing openings, and the regulations affecting fishing.

In 2000 the Internal Revenue Service began taking Permanent Fund Dividends from people indebted to them. Those fishermen whose boats were not making enough to pay insurance, permit payments, or boat payments were stunned. A woman who manages her brothers' finances said, "Last year, the state wouldn't let the feds take dividends. This year, they are taken. It shocked us. People were counting on them … People pay portions of their accounts with dividends usually. Now the feds took them. I'm so upset I can barely talk about it." Credit at local businesses adds another dimension to individual debt. One family business estimated that the town owes it $97,000 in charges. "We are the last ones they pay if they come into money," the owner stated.

Municipal revenues are heavily reliant on the fisheries, so changes in the fisheries result in changes in the community's economic structure. The city budget relies heavily on the 2 percent "raw fish tax," and an additional 2 percent on raw fish is taxed to the Aleutians East Borough. Its budget comes from one-third each of the groundfish,

salmon, and crab fisheries. Of the 2 percent fish tax, 20 percent goes
to the Aleutians East Borough School District. Beyond this 2 percent
are funds from the federal and state governments for schools and
health clinics only. The city also levies a 3 percent sales tax, but
there are no property taxes. In 1984 the fisheries tax constituted
30 percent of the city's budget (Braund et al. 1986:5.4). This was
still true in 2000. Socially, the chief of police at the time predicted
a "trickle-down effect" with the budget problem. "I hope the crime
rate doesn't climb," he said. "It's a lot quieter this year right now. It's
too early to tell yet. This is our first budget crisis ever and we haven't
really seen the results of that yet."

CRABBING AND GROUNDFISH

Local people uphold salmon fishing as the most important community-wide activity, but they fish other species as well, and when
salmon is weak they depend on these other fisheries. Salmon is fished
only approximately four months of the year (June to September).
The other eight months are spent crabbing or in support of crabbing,
which is very important to some, particularly to young crewmen, or
in groundfish fisheries, which have grown to be of critical importance to nearly everyone.

Crabbing: The "Young Man's Game"

Bering Sea crab fishing is often described as the most dangerous
occupation on the planet by both those who take part in it and
those who study it (DHHS 1997; Hodgson 1992: Stoller 2003). The
death rate for commercial fishing is 75 times the national average
for on-the-job deaths (Dillon 1998:8–9). For crabbing, the death
rate is 25 times higher than for the rest of commercial fishing and
9 times that of mining and logging. The Bering Sea is a relatively
shallow (less than 100 fathoms), extremely turbulent body of water,
boiling over an outer continental shelf teeming with marine life.
Earthquakes occur almost daily, active volcanoes line the southern
edge, and islands emerge and disappear in shifting tectonics. Sea
water cycles continuously from top to bottom, stirring up nutrients
and sustaining a variety of species. Finding crab in this tumultu-
ous bathtub is best illustrated by one Aleut elder: "It's like someone
scattered pods of crab like marbles on the ocean floor and you have

to guess where they ended up." It is not uncommon for the fleet to catch nothing at all until the last day of the opening. When I asked if the elder still went crabbing, he said, "No, no. That's a young man's game. I stopped years ago."

Waves can form sharp peaks, often 9 metres high, overwhelm-ing the boats. When the temperature drops suddenly, sea spray forms ice layers over an entire vessels, reaching up to a metre thick and causing it to roll over suddenly. Axes, baseball bats, and sledgehammers to break off the ice are standard equipment on board. In the 38°F/4C° Bering Sea, an unlucky fisherman can be chilled into unconsciousness in minutes. If he is able to clamber into a buoyant insulated survival suit, he may last a few hours. In the event of an accident, it takes several hours for C–130 US Coast Guard Search and Rescue planes or H–3 helicopters based in Kodiak to get to the site.

Crabbing targets several Bering Sea crab species: king, tanner (snow crab), and opilio ("opie"). Crabs are trapped using wire-meshed steel pots. Crab boats typically have long wide decks for stacking crab pots. Smaller boats use pyramid pots that stack inside each other, whereas the larger boats use square pots, each 6 x 6 foot (1.8 x 1.8 metres) that weigh approximately 800 pounds (362 kilograms) empty and cannot be moved without a hydraulic power block. The size of the boat determines the pot limit: boats under 125 feet (38.1 metres) have a 100-pot limit and those over 125 feet have a 125-pot limit. "It used to be that we could fish with whatever the boat would hold," lamented an elder.

Until 2005, when a Crab Rationalization Plan restructured the fishery, giving quotas to both boats and processors, crabbing was a derby fishery with openings that lasted three days or twenty days; following lean seasons, fleets pushed even harder to compensate for the losses of previous years. Once the boats have reached the crabbing grounds, often in a rush, crewmen crawl into the pots to bait them with frozen herring and drop them onto the sea floor, marked only by a line attached to a buoy. There they let them "soak" for a minimum of twelve hours, but often longer, occasionally raising test pots with a power winch to see if there is any crab inside. Once raised, the catch is dumped onto a sorting table, and females

Figure 3.14
Contrasted crab boats heading for the Bering Sea king crab fishery, October 2000

and undersized males are returned to the sea. Legal-sized males are stored in aerated seawater tanks below deck.

The captain stays in the wheelhouse orchestrating the entire operation over an intercom while steering the boat. An experienced deck boss dictates the work of the deckhands. Crab fishermen fish around the clock for the opening, getting little sleep. With the need to stay awake, cocaine and methamphetamine use is rampant. At the closing, crab boats race back to the canneries to deliver their catch; those that are slower must remain out in the bays, where sea water can circulate into their holds and keep the crabs alive, lest they be spoiled by brackish water in the harbour while the boats wait for a space at the cannery dock.

The majority of Bering Sea crab fishermen are non-residents or other Alaskans; it is not a Native fishery. Younger Aleut men may participate as crew. Those Aleuts who do fish for crab typically have smaller boats than their non-Native counterparts. Where the other captains run boats for absentee owners and are somewhat itinerant, Aleut crab fishermen usually own their boats. In one case where an Aleut tried to be an absentee owner and hired a man to run his boat, the hired captain came back to the harbour with too many undersized crabs. He was heavily fined and was found to be dealing drugs in the bar after the ordeal. Figure 3.14 above illustrates the difference in size of local (left) and non-local (right) crab boats. The dangers of the Bering Sea are heightened in the smaller boats and are exacerbated even more by fishermen who feel the need to overstack the decks with pots in order to compete with the larger boats. For one family, another observing fisherman shuddered over how overloaded their boat was and the dangers they faced: "They're so desperate they're taking their 58 foot boat king crabbing." King Cove's main position in the crab fleet is as a support centre. Crab fishermen stated that they prefer to deliver their catch in King Cove because it is more "subdued" than the main port of Dutch Harbor. King Cove has grown as an important support base for these fishermen.

In October 2000 the king crab fleet swamped King Cove for its yearly fishery in the rush to catch as many legal-sized crabs as possible in a three-day period. Crab boats from all over the North Pacific entered the harbour, with captains and crew ready to load crab pots, purchase groceries and alcohol, reconnect with local friends and lovers, chat up the cannery management, and drink at the bar. In 2000 an average of only fourteen crab permits were held by local fishermen, and approximately eleven King Cove captains actually participated in this fishery (www.cfec.state.ak.us; Northern Economics 2001). I expected hostilities between local fishermen and this seeming invasion of haughty white men from "outside." Instead, this was an exciting time for the local people.

Bering Sea crab fishermen are considered an elite group in the world of fishing, both by residents of King Cove and amongst themselves. Where "highliner" is a term rarely used among Aleut salmon fishermen, crab fishermen regularly use it to describe themselves or each other. My naively asking, "Who's the highliner?" in a group of crabbers instigated self-aggrandizing and overconfident statements about themselves. Many crab fishermen exaggerate their catch to impress one another and women. Crab fishermen bring a sexually charged atmosphere with them, and local men keep close tabs on their wives, girlfriends, and daughters (and sometimes mothers) during this time.

The crab fisheries are highly volatile; when the king crab fishery crashed in the 1980s and was replaced by the tanner crab fishery, industry marketers renamed tanner crab "snow crab" to make it sound more delectable. It quickly became haute cuisine in fine restaurants at its height in the 1980s. The tanner fishery has been sporadic since then. In 1999 the king crab fishery was cancelled. In 2000

the season lasted only three days. In 1999 huge crab boats that had
arrived for crab began invading other kinds of fishing, such as cod
and pollock, because they could not take crab. Consequently, local
fishermen with smaller boats had to compete with them, and in some
cases local fishermen were excluded altogether. Quotas are set for
cod and pollock, and the huge crab boats were able to reach the
quotas quickly, leaving the smaller boats scrambling.

Groundfish: Cod, Pollock, and Halibut

King Cove fishermen have made strong efforts to participate in the
groundfish fisheries, despite increasing pessimism created by the
need to compete both with factory trawlers and with other better-
equipped enterprises, and the need to accommodate a steady bar-
rage of new restrictions. Groundfish permits now outnumber crab
permits in the borough. Pacific cod and pollock are harvested using
trawls, and only large seine vessels are big enough to be equipped
with trawl gear. Smaller drift gillnet and setnet vessels have fewer
options for diversifying in fishing, but they can fish for cod with pots
and jigs and may be able to use longline gear, depending upon the
boat's configuration.

Community development quotas (CDQ)[18] and individual fishing quotas (IFQ) have been hailed as the most sustainable fisheries management plans worldwide. Pacific halibut, formerly a
derby fishery, is now a closed IFQ fishery, with quotas set by the
International Halibut Commission. Individuals own shares of the
total allowable catch, limiting the number of boats and people
who can fish. In 2002, when the June salmon fishery was a dis-
appointment, several fishermen decided to fish their halibut IFQs
right away. Thus, demersal fisheries are gaining in importance
to counter the dramatic fluctuations in the beloved pelagic fisheries. Fishermen are taking advantage of all possible avenues, but
diversification only means entering another fishery. Limitations in
groundfish fisheries and their community impact will be discussed
in detail in chapter 5.

FISHERIES ECONOMICS

The following three charts indicate the poundage harvested, the
value, and the number of permits fished in King Cove from 1981

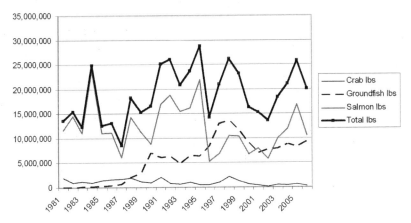

Figure 3.15
Pounds landed for crab, groundfish, and salmon in King Cove, 1981–2006

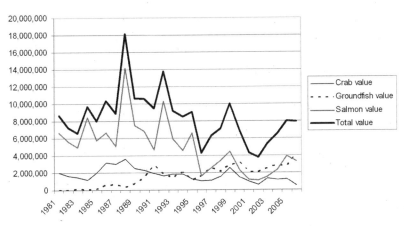

Figure 3.16
Ex-vessel value to King Cove fishermen for crab, groundfish, and salmon, 1981–2006

to 2006. Salmon used to account for most of the total poundage of seafood harvested, but groundfish is gaining in importance. There has been a steady decline in the number of salmon permits held, while groundfish permits have become more widespread, as has the poundage harvested. There are variations in individual earnings, masked statistically by averages. Salmon fishing still drives the total value. Breaking even and falling short can lead to catching more fish to compensate in subsequent fishery seasons.

Number of Permits per Year and Type of Fishery

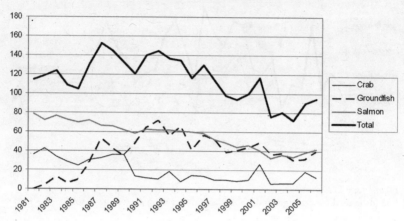

Figure 3.17
Number of permits fished by King Cove fishermen, 1981–2006

POLITICS AT SEA AND THE PASSION FOR PISCARY

I have shown aspects of how the fishing nexus works through social organization, gender relations, and status in the production and distribution of wild resources. Descriptions of vessels, permits, crews, and revenue have elucidated issues of access, not just to these recognized assets but also to a whole host of cultural and social resources. Subsistence and commercial economies are separated in bureaucratic processes, indicating an either/or of traditionalism versus industrial development. Yet Eastern Aleuts do not separate subsistence and commercial fishing; instead, the majority feel that they are able to get the maximum out of their traditional economy to better their lives. Salmon fishing has been the primary Aleut fishery, and almost all boats and fishermen are "salmon boats" or "salmon fishermen." The salmon fishery itself has status. Groundfish, however, are becoming so important that many say they are dependent on these fisheries. There is a schedule to life that is cyclic and repetitive, a ritualized practice in which a commonsense world emerges.

The intersection between cultural identity and commercial fishing has strong implications for Alaskan anthropology: the Aleut have not faded away as many have suggested; a good deal of Alaskan anthropology shows that subsistence and money must be separated, but the Aleut are part of a *franchise,* a for-profit business that is the driving force of the community. In this context, the Aleut propose an alternative definition of *subsistence* and highlight profound variability among Alaska Natives.

Paul Bohannan has argued that culture is the by-product of stories of material things, events, and behaviour (1995:149–58). He wrote that icons are necessary in the creation of stories, that they create contexts for culture. Fishing vessels are both iconic and functional. Houses contain sea memorabilia in the way of paintings, boat models, and photographs. Fishing, and all aspects surrounding its practice and organization, is the dominant discourse.

Hierarchies on the water depend on the status of boat captains, not necessarily in economic terms of success. The highest-ranking group at sea is the boat captains, with "top boat" and "high boat" referring to the highest catch in the fleet. These terms generally refer to the captain and his crew, but while crews may change, the reputation as "top boat" stays with the captain and the boat. "Highliners," a term generally used by non-Aleut fishermen, are the most monetarily successful captains with the most sophisticated vessels and gear, and they typically have no trouble finding an eager crew. The gear types (that is, the permit) used in each fishery somewhat determine highliners and distinguish them from other fishermen in the same fishery. Individuals and families may hold more than one type of permit and use them strategically to enhance their performance. "Highliner" can also be a temporary status from day to day, fishery to fishery, and year to year.

Family members serve on boats, or the crew can be recruited from outside the village or even outside the state. Crew must muscle the gear, run the skiffs, and follow the captain's orders. Crew composition can change frequently, sometimes several times in a season, though some are permanent. Crews receive percentages of the boat's take, which are determined by level of experience or relationship to the captain. Crew will sometimes include a captain's relative who is perhaps not the ideal crewman and cannot get a job on anyone else's boat; other captains in the same family may rotate him between their boats. No one wants to be left "sitting on the beach," unable to fish. Household interconnectivity between families and non-family households is often maintained by the resource potential of crewmen. Captains need crew, and therefore they will keep loose networks alive that will allow them easier access to crew members, and hence access to fishing and ultimate success. Likewise, crewmen will keep a variety of relationships and loyalties alive with prospective captains, often independent of kinship. Throwing kinship into the mix intensifies these relationships.

Controls of social and material resources are both indicators of social position and self-reinforcing rewards for status. Access to fishing facilitates the performance of social relations, which can then be mediated by strong or weak family ties (shown in the following chapter).

Competition is articulated in subtle ways. Fishermen and their families do not consider themselves to be competitive on the whole, yet after an especially successful fishing opening in 2002 for one seine boat that landed 11,000 kilograms of sockeye in one day, a crewman bragged, "We kicked everyone else's butt this year." With pride, one young woman said, "My dad was high boat last opening. I was so proud of him. He's got such a small boat compared to everyone else's." There is tremendous pride in surviving near-death experiences and keeping everyone on board alive. One retired fisherman boasted, "I lost a few boats, but I never lost a crew member."

Genealogical knowledge is frequently called upon in negotiations between Aleut, suggesting that kin selection provides an important conceptual framework for understanding the structure and practice of fishing. Maynard-Smith (1964) argued that degrees of genetic relatedness dictate or influence the amount of collateral investment; that is, the closer you are related to someone, the more likely you will invest time and energy in supporting that person's activities. For the Eastern Aleut, fishing together and sharing are not restricted to kin, but kin often have priority. Who you fish with, and the prestige that it can bring to the crewman or the captain, can be just as important as who your relatives are (a topic taken up in chapter 4).

4

Limited Entry Systems in an Eastern Aleut Community

Those guys had to paddle all the way to Kodiak, kill a few Eskimos, and then paddle all the way back, just to impress women. Today all you need is a big boat.

Aleut fisherman in King Cove, 2001

LIMITED ENTRY SYSTEMS

Traditional and modern avenues for status and prestige differ by degree and scale, but not substance. On the occasion of the above fisherman's observation, my husband and I were talking to a group of fishermen in the Harbor House about oral histories and historical accounts of Aleut men going on raids as far away as Bristol Bay and Kodiak. This fishermen spontaneously added comments about how hard it had been to impress women "back then" and how one impressed women today. What else were these Aleuts doing on their raids? "Stealing women," they frankly added. And one fisherman, whose wife is from Kodiak, added with a wink and a chuckle, "We *still* do that." In Nelson Lagoon, I was told a story about an elder still living in Herendeen Bay who, in the 1950s, travelled down the coast, around the tip of the Alaska Peninsula to Sanak, in a power dory "just to get himself a woman." Mission accomplished, he brought her back to the village, where they live today. Another man from Nelson Lagoon went on a similar mission but got "weathered in" at False Pass, and there he "found one that would do."

Marriageable women, it seems, were a scarce resource, and men travelled great distances to find wives. This also highlights an interesting observation about ethnicity and lifeways: Nelson Lagoon and Herendeen Bay are closer to many Yup'ik villages of the north

Alaska Peninsula, but these men journeyed long distances to find
Aleut women. They also sought Alutiiq women of Kodiak, who
engage in a similar lifestyle. Women, similarly, prefer Aleut men, but
they seek out men who have filled prestige criteria in relation to
fishing. Fishing, then, is necessary for survival, not just in economic
terms or in terms of sharing and maintaining social networks, but in
terms of men negotiating place in the pecking order of fishing, establishing identity through skill, and attracting women. Fishing is also
necessary for women, who keep track of male prestige and seek out
high-status men, and whose identity is linked to the status of their
fishermen. Although there is evidence to suggest that men seeking
status and attracting mates – and women seeking high-status mates
– are universals,[1] I do not wish to engage in this debate, except to say
that these behaviours are very much in evidence here.

As Dall described more than a century ago, "The most respected
and influential were those who were the most successful in the chase.
The great ambition of the Aleut was to be a great hunter. Those who
were unsuccessful were looked upon with more or less contempt.
The number of wives was not limited, except that the best hunters had the greatest number of wives. This seldom exceeded four"
(1870:388).

The modern Aleut also derive pride from their skill as hunters
and fishermen, from impressing women, and from surviving the
dangers of everyday living in the Aleutians, and less from monetary
wealth. Symbols of empowerment have been adapted to the modern
era as fishing vessels have become symbols of identity and status.
Fishermen exaggerate their catch and the dangers they have survived
when talking to one another or to women they want to impress.
They tell tales of bravery in boating accidents, daring rescues, and
how they have got away with skirting hunting and fishing laws. One
retired elder boasted, "I started smoking and drinking and running
my own boat when I was eight years old. That's why they call me
—. I was the youngest skipper in the whole damned Alaska fleet on
the [name of boat]. I'd fish on Sundays see, get ahead of everyone.
They'd just be getting started and I would be bringing in a load and
hiding out from Fish and Game."

Eight years old seemed early to me, and when I asked other fishermen about this, they said he was at least a teenager and was running a "large skiff" with a few of his friends. However, this elder
repeatedly declared these details to me at every visit, indicating that

captaining in his youth was important for his identity as a fisherman. This man chose particular facts in his life to exaggerate – skill at an early age, assembling a crew, competition in time fishing and catch size, and operating beyond the eyes of the watchdogs – indicating not only what he considered crucial to his identity and status but also informing me of the criteria important for being a man, while goading me to be impressed.

"Cradle of storms," "birthplace of the winds," and "people of the foggy seas" are accurate Aleutian imagery (Bank 1956; Hubbard 1935; Jochelson 1928). In one storm in 2000, a 177 km/h gust tore the roof off the house I was staying in, broke out car windows, and broke the sodium lights off the crab boats waiting out in the bay for their turn at the dock. The weather can be warm and sunny one minute and then fog will slip silently down, erasing the hills, the bay, then the house next door. Aleuts take pride in surviving and thriving in this harsh, unpredictable environment, where fishermen risk their lives every time they go to work. "The stuff you see out there [while fishing] is awesome," said one excited young woman, whose name appears on her father's bowpicker.[2] "Landslides, volcanoes erupting, whales, bears fighting. Sharks rammed our nets once. I thought it was so cool!"

Prestige is highlighted in many fishing societies (e.g., Gatewood 1983; Jorion 1976; Nadel-Klein and Davis 1988; Pálsson 1994; Weibust 1958). Gatewood found an insatiable quest for prestige among seine fishermen in southeast Alaska (1983) in which prestige is always in demand and not subject to the law of diminishing returns as is the demand for cash. The only way to gain prestige is to seine well: "There is no desire to be the richest fisherman, but many would like to be the best fisherman" (1983:355). Wealth does not always mean that one is a prestigious fisherman, but Gatewood found an almost direct correlation between the prestige of the captain and the size of his boat's catch. Because canneries have quotas for how many fish they buy, a speed dimension is added to the competition, in which prestige is gained by catching the quota in the least amount of time. Gatewood found that prestige could also be gained through the condition of one's boat, one's skill in repairing seines, and the boat's equipment. Prestige constitutes a "positive feedback system," where one can attract skilful crew members and mutually reinforce the social and financial benefits. "Ole timers" retain the prestige they held in their heyday but are no longer considered to be players in the competition (1983:356). All this is also true in the Aleutians, where the salmon fisheries are characterized by prestige.

The Aleut live in a "single social-identity/skill area" where men compete "in terms of a shared set of evaluation criteria" (Barkow 1989:189). Though fishing is the only game in town, men have attempted to distinguish themselves from one another in aspects of fishing. They refer to one another or to themselves as "the best skiff man," "the best skiff builder," "the best on-board cook," "the best deckboss," among many other talents.

Changes in leadership, politics, economy, technology, resource needs, beliefs, or a combination of these result in changes in opportunities for individuals and can alter prestige structures connected with these. There is now a generation of young Aleut men and women who were raised to strive for certain ideals which they can no longer realistically attain. The Limited Entry Permit Plan was a defining moment for all modern social relations among the Eastern Aleut, though its future impact was not well understood at the time of its implementation. The plan created more than one limited entry system and possibly exaggerated a system of rank and status already in place. The permits themselves represent not only the right to fish but also a suite of social and political privileges. Here I use the notion of "limited entry" to talk about the social and organizational map of King Cove, the use of which is partly my own perception of relations but clearly stems from the Aleut as well, who refer to imposed limitations as a language of explanation for a variety of circumstances. Limited entry systems in this regard are organizing systems for divisions between the land and sea, gender and generation, and the public and domestic spheres.

In investigating the status of senior men – those men who were in their prime when Limited Entry began – I asked how the plan changed social relations. Those who were excluded from fishing are difficult to study because many left the village and the Aleutians; there are certainly fewer lineages living in King Cove today than in the 1970s and 1980s. Today there is a wide gap between the haves and have-nots in terms of fisheries access and fishing capital. Limited Entry has allowed select individuals to continue to prosper in fishing and has forced most men without permits to sell their boats, many to leave the village permanently and hence lose their identity as fishermen and their immediate relationship to the community. Some have been able to maintain a link with the village through their relatives sending wild foods to them or through "coming home" to crew. Being Aleut in many ways depends upon that link. Limited Entry also changed the obligations involved in family relationships, particularly with regard to food distribution, and for many it made the failure to meet their obligations an irreversible reality.

The strategies of gaining status are thus in service of a number of goals and may bring prestige to the individual, the whole family, or the community. This chapter considers relevant demographic factors that influence social relations and examines family organization and status in terms of culturally recognized assets. I described the basic organization of the Limited Entry Permit system in chapter 3. Here I examine some of the implications of that system for Aleut social relations, and consider rank in its modern form through an examination of political and social positions. Generational and gender divisions act as units of analysis in examining identity processes.

LIFE CYCLES, OPPORTUNITIES, AND LIMITATIONS

Individuals experience the fishing franchise differently depending on age, gender, time and place, and expectations. For analysis, generational divisions illuminate the different experiences and expectations placed upon them, which I illustrate in the following sections with representative examples. Elder, adult, and youth are not rigid categories. The title "elder" comes with a responsibility that not every older individual is comfortable with. There are relatively few elders (estimated at 35 men and women), plus an older generation that does not quite qualify as elder or accept the role, but they are still senior adults; then there is a middle generation of adults (approximate ages 30 to 50), young adults (ages 20 to 30), youth (early teens to approximate age 20), and children. In this section, I explore social restrictions and opportunities present for age and gender groups, and consider individualized "senses of reality" (Bourdieu 1977). Levels of involvement in fishing influence the obligations between people.

Demography: A Male Surplus

Germane to an understanding of life cycles is a demographic surplus of men for the Alaska Peninsula and Aleutian Islands. The highest percentage of men and boys statewide has been identified for the Aleutians East Borough resident population, where in an overall

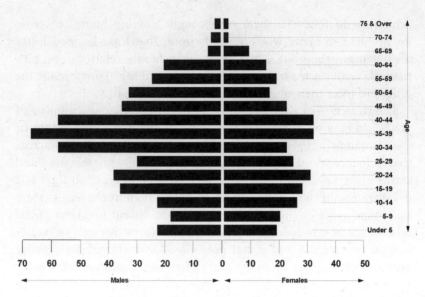

Figure 4.1
Age/sex distribution, King Cove, Alaska, 2000 (www.census.gov)

population of 2,697, 64.9 percent are male and only 35.1 percent are
female (www.alaska.com).[3] Transient non-local fishermen increase
this divide during fishing seasons. The Aleutians West census area
comes in a close second with 64.3 percent males. The 2000 Census
reports a population of 792 in King Cove, 59.6 percent male. For
those age 18 years and older in King Cove (n=623), 389 (49.1 percent) are male and 234 (29.5 percent) are female (figure 4.1).

The excess of men and the scarcity of women have generated factors that influence the prestige structures of both men and women.
There are more men than available female partners, more men than
there are fishing permits, and more men than there are non-fishing
wage jobs. Within this, as will be shown, there is also a scarcity of
the "right kind of man" for women to marry, though this does not
necessarily prevent sexual relationships.

Children and Youth

Ideally, all children today are born in the Alaska Native hospital in
Anchorage. This was not the case just a generation ago, and several
elder women are respected as having supervised most births in the
community. One girl has the distinction of having been born on a

boat en route to Cold Bay, where her mother was to catch a plane to Anchorage. First pregnancies most often occur in a young woman's late teens or early twenties.[4] Because many start having children young, five living generations are not uncommon: in one case, an elder has several great-great-grandchildren and he is only 75 years old. Young parents with children are rarely married and often still live in their parents' homes. These children are primarily raised in their mother's home with the grandparents. This arrangement is not stigmatized, nor does it put the child at an automatic disadvantage in matters of inheritance or social opportunities.

Children enjoy a great deal of play and freedom but are socialized for specific roles. Most young boys aspire to be fishermen and play at being so. In the summer, they build makeshift boats and sail them across the waters of Heart Lake. These are highly detailed models of their father's vessels. One afternoon, I was playing badminton with a six-year-old Aleut boy, knocking the birdie over an imaginary net. His aunt came out of the house, having found the net that goes with the game. As she was stringing it up, the boy said, "Auntie, it's like a fishing net. Can we catch fish in this?" When boys are asked what they are going to do in the future, the overwhelming answer is "fish." When girls are asked what they want to be, a few tend to choose more urban careers, but most often say they do not know. A Sunday school teacher at the non-denominational church said that when they do art projects, *every* boy draws only fishing boats, and they argue over certain features and what the gear should look like. In almost every grandparent's home I visited, the grandsons' drawings of boats were displayed on the refrigerator.

As stated in chapter 2, school is not seen as a foreign institution but is an accepted part of the community. Of course, school is not always considered relevant by students, especially teens, but that is not unusual. The school year ends in late May so that children have time to prepare for salmon fishing. School-age children tend not to fish for groundfish or crab because of school schedules and also because of the dangers present in these fisheries. In school, fishing issues can become part of the curriculum. One school exercise for all age groups was to write letters to the congressional delegation over the sea lion issue and ask for help in matters of fishing (discussed in chapter 5).

When not in school, a great deal of non-fishing time is spent playing, trout fishing, berry picking, *bidarki* picking, exploring on

Figure 4.2
Children's boat model contest, 4 July 2002

four-wheelers, and helping their families. Children learn how to clean, butcher, and process fish and game when they are very young.

Not every Eastern Aleutian child wants to grow up to be a fisherman, but every child has a "limited career perspective apart from some relationship to the fishing industry," according to a health worker. Teenage boys reject opportunities for summer employment, camps, or travel away from King Cove: "I can't. I'll be fishing" is heard at every turn. When one 16-year-old boy was offered an opportunity to work with my husband on his archaeological excavation, his father said, "If he wants to do something other than fish, that's okay with me." However, as the fishing season loomed closer, this boy decided to crew for his brother-in-law and made ten times the amount he would have made with my husband. Parents recognize that fishing has become difficult and their children do not have the same opportunities they had, but they are so entrenched and enthusiasm for fishing is so contagious that they are still reluctant to give it up because it means so much more.

Children often form deep bonds with extended members of their families and may choose to divide their time between two or more households. Few parents contest these arrangements, which are rarely formalized. The reasons for children living with another relative, as temporary as it may be, are often related to disagreements with their parents, or they "just needed a break." In cases where parents are fighting, their children will voluntarily remove themselves from the house for a few days or longer and stay with other relatives, or with this anthropologist.

A few prominent adults in the community are openly critical about how others raise their children. Parents of this "next generation of fishermen," according to one couple with teenage children, "just threw money at them and sent them out of their hair. They were too busy partying and didn't include their kids in their activities." Now the parents are paying the price, they argue. "Children grow up really fast around here" is a statement I heard dozens of times from all segments of the community.

It is often the case that those around age 20 are parents, a fact that launches them into automatic adulthood. Until that age, young people continue to enjoy a great deal of freedom. There are acceptable levels of irresponsibility, and often these behaviours get them into trouble with the law (see chapter 6), but for the most part they are considered to be "acting their age." Most young men and women have leeway in participation in commercial fishing and in subsistence activities. However, in several cases, young men are the sole subsistence providers to their immediate families, or even to several households, as crewmen. Young men spend much of their non-fishing time hunting caribou, geese, and ptarmigan, and honing the necessary skills.

Although there are no ceremonial rites of passage, marriage and/or parenting are key criteria for adulthood, along with responsibility in fishing. Having children at a young age is generally expected. Indeed, when I began research in King Cove childless at the age of 25, this was commented on constantly. During pregnancy and after my son was born, the dynamics of interaction changed, and I felt that I became more of a real person to many people.[5] The community is child-oriented, and young women declare their love for children even when one first meets them.

Postsecondary education is fairly rare, and very few of the youth talk about university; those who do consider it rarely know what they will study. It is difficult to say how many actually leave for larger places, because so many come back and try to leave again.

Most, however, remain in the village and try to find work. Teenage girls are more likely to talk about education than boys are. If they do not fish, there are few local jobs that will get passed around by more girls/women than there are jobs. Girls rarely participate in hunting but may spend a good deal of time trout fishing, picking berries, processing wild foods, and babysitting. A few young men cannot fish because they suffer from severe seasickness; these few are considering attending technical college around Alaska.[6]

An intergenerational awareness of the fisheries impressed me. In late June 2001, when I was home in Idaho and heavily pregnant, I called up to King Cove to check in with a friend. Her 12-year-old daughter answered, and when I asked how things were going, she didn't tell me about her summer plans or a boy crush, she told me about the fishermen on strike. "People are sticking together, though," she said. "Peter Pan offered 42 cents, but they are *not* going for it. Last night they all went out to fish 700,000 pounds for BP [Bering Pacific Seafoods in False Pass]. They're gonna split it equally. It's bad. Peter Pan is threatening to withhold fuel and other stuff if they go elsewhere [to sell their catch]." The young are keenly aware of the plight of the fishermen, in large part because they too are deeply involved in the industry and way of life. "All of us kids around here grew up on boats," stated an elder. One non-Native health worker felt that children do not even get a childhood because of their role in fishing: "There is a blend of desire to just be American kids but they start fishing when they are six or seven." However, I never heard children complain about this!

Becoming a Fisherman

In one salmon-fishing opener, which coincided with a huge storm, a 15-year-old girl was crewing on a seiner. The boat was severely rocking from side to side in the wind and rain. The girl was on deck, pulling the net in, and every time the boat rolled to her side, a sea lion leapt up trying to bite her. It was bitterly cold and the deck was slippery. One crewman had fallen overboard earlier that day but had been rescued right away. The storm raged for the entire opener, forcing most boats to quit early and head for the harbour. When the girl returned, she told her mother, "I'm a fisherman now!"

This young woman knew she had crossed a threshold and had earned the title of fisherman in that one event. It was harsh and frightening, and she did not just get through it but got the work done as well. This also draws attention to a gender matter. As a teenage girl, she was crewing under the captaincy of a friend of her mother's, with her cousin and his friend as other crew. Fishing is certainly not her career choice; she was earning money to attend a basketball camp out of state. She carries the title of fisherman only temporarily. After high school, she is likely to attend college (with perhaps a basketball scholarship) and most likely will never fish again. For the young men on the boat, it is a different story altogether.

For many young men, crewing is a perpetual status, and they strive to get on more successful boats with highliner captains. Becoming a captain is an impossible prospect for many and difficult for others. Here I illustrate the process of becoming a captain with the story of a man in his early twenties for whom circumstances offered a way to the top. He is from a prominent family in that his father owns a boat and two permits and is often a highliner. His father usually hired his own brothers as crew, and his son salmon-fished with an uncle for several years, jumping on outside boats for crabbing and halibut IFQs. Thus, he is already in a prime position for inheriting an entire operation from his father and has the skills to run it. However, his father shows no sign of retiring. His uncle, who has no sons, gave him the opportunity to fish the salmon season using his boat and permit. As captain, the young man organized his crew (two friends of his who are in no position to inherit), and in the first opener they were the highliners. Everyone in town was singing their praises. Women began talking about them, the captain in particular, and took an interest in him in the bars – which, as a shy young man, had been rare for him. At the end of a successful season (relative to the performance of other boats, but still getting low numbers because of few fish), his uncle, who had relocated to another Aleutian community, offered to sell him the operation. Thus he had proven his worth to his uncle, his father, his crew, the village, and to himself.

Being a Fisherman

Being a capable fisherman is the essence of being an Aleut man. Adult men spend the majority of their time working on their boats, both in the harbour and at sea, and must continually demonstrate their abilities as fishermen. Status is maintained through continual hard work and success. Women support their activities by providing supplies on the boat and taking care of in-home responsibilities. Women hold land jobs to provide money for fishing as well as for their families, especially in lean years. Occasionally they will fish with their husbands, but they often wait for him to send them fish to process and distribute. Men and women employ a wide range of hunting, fishing, and processing techniques of most of the available wild foods, which they have learned throughout their lives, and though most of these chores are gender marked, there is some cross-over in activities.

Over several years, men (and women indirectly) have raised and lowered their status through fishing. One couple I met in 2000 went through a profound transformation over three years. In 2000 they fought all the time, and he was often drunk at all hours of the day and night. She held a few part-time jobs to support the family, while he complained most of the time. In 2002, when captains were having difficulty getting crew, he was hired on with a fisherman who has been a highliner intermittently during his career. That season and the season to follow were good for the boat, and with each opening the crewman's demeanour changed. He became friendly, less hostile to his family and others, and quickly got a reputation for "taking care of the whole neighbourhood" by bringing fish to several households between openings. His wife also changed. She smiles more and is often seen taking huge stacks of cakes and casseroles down to the boat for the crew. Her husband still drinks a good deal of beer, but now it is in the spirit of celebration more often than not.

I have seen it go the other way as well. As a seiner, one man had no extended family in King Cove (his brothers had sold out and moved away) and had a difficult time attracting a crew. He could not afford to pay high crew shares, so he hired young women, high school girls, who had no experience and were more of a burden than a support. His wife was extremely ill, and he had to accompany her to Anchorage frequently for extended hospital stays. He eventually turned his operation over to his stepson and had to leave the village. Still, he refused to get a land job, and he became an engineer on barges in Prince William Sound.

In another case, an entire family experienced a downward slide when they overextended themselves just as fishing prices were starting to collapse. Their father passed away in the mid-1990s, and as a tribute to him, the family's corporation bought a seine boat and named it after him. With heavy payments due, large families to support, and poor fishing seasons, they could not cover their bills. To make up for the losses, they took their seiner crab fishing in the Bering Sea for a season – an extremely dangerous undertaking for such a small boat. While I was visiting with an Aleut woman and business manager for her family's fleet, the phone rang, but she was afraid to answer it because she knew it would be more bad news. When she returned to the living room she said, "The Coast Guard wants a stability report now. They are boarding the boat tonight. They may stop the crabbing. We need more licences every year. You never know what stickers or papers you're supposed to have." The bank eventually repossessed the largest of their vessels. While they realized they should not have bought the last boat, they wanted to commemorate their father in an appropriate way and hoped they could build a large family fleet in his honour.

Becoming a captain is extremely difficult now, and often it comes without ownership of the boat and with a temporary permit transfer. One fisherman boasted about finally having his own boat at the start of the season. He was "gonna do it right this time" where he claimed all his previous captains had failed. Later on, I learned that it was not really his boat and the permit was an "emergency transfer" – a distant cousin from Anchorage had transferred it to him for one salmon season only. He hired his son and brother to crew with him, and was fairly successful given the size of the boat and the temporary nature of the operation. Of course, both the permit owner and the boat owner took unknown percentages of his overall income. In this situation, the captain actually "proved himself" and gained more permanence in this arrangement with the boat/permit owners.

Only one family has maintained a successful small business outside fishing as their sole means of support – a grocery store that has been in the same family for generations. They experience ups and downs along with fishing. There are approximately fifty business licences obtained for King Cove, but most of them are small operations providing filler income (e.g., childcare services, salons, taxis, maintenance, bed and breakfasts, bars, eateries, charter services, and fuel sales). Many of these businesses do not advertise and are operated out of private homes on irregular schedules, so you have to be "in the know" to get a haircut or hire someone to watch your children. Women manage the majority of these land businesses.

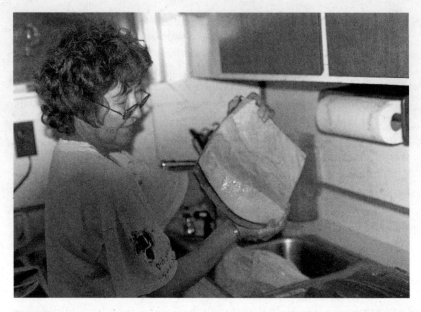

Figure 4.3
Frances Larsen holds up a piece of *ulla*, or whale skin with blubber, while also processing king salmon

Women in Fishing, Women and Fishing

Fishing is a decidedly male activity, but women's knowledge of fishing practices and the requirements surrounding them is extensive,
though they may only occasionally step aboard a boat, and even
less often will they fish. Women crew on a few boats; if they do not
regularly fish, they can fill the roles of crew on a moment's notice if
a crew member quits, gets fired, or is injured. With men gone fishing
for long stretches of time, women control the domestic sphere and
work in politics and community duties. Rarely do they fill jobs at
the harbour. Men maintain some independence from the household
duties, but they must get along with other men on a cramped boat
for long periods and cook and clean for themselves.

Women assume the primary parenting responsibilities. As one
woman stated, "I'm teaching them to be good people. I'm teaching them to take care of what they have, and know how to provide
for themselves." In one case, an elder proudly boasted that he used
to fish out in the Bering Sea almost year-round and missed out on
raising his eldest daughter. "I raised her by myself," his wife said

as a statement of fact, with no guilt implied. Men are often just as involved in raising children, and take great pride in their sons' or daughters' achievements in fishing. While I was watching boats come into the bay with one man, he puffed up when he saw a boat coming in with a full load, riding low in the water. "My son's on that boat," he said.

In the past, female pollution was a major concern in matters of fishing. Menstruating women were prohibited from walking on the beach because they were believed to have the power to deflect fish. One woman told me that perhaps twenty years ago her father would not let women on the boat because it would "jinx it," and he would take his wife and daughters on the boat only on the last day of the fishing season. (After suffering a heart attack later in his life, he took his wife fishing because he felt safer with her there. Practicality wins over taboo). Today, there is no lasting belief that women are polluting and there is no institutionalized segregation, but women still experience difficulties surrounding sex and gender. A non-Native woman mechanic on a crab boat was the topic of much discussion between men, often over lunch in the cannery. They seemed to be trying to convince themselves that she deserved to be on board. I thought the reason was obvious: she is an excellent diesel mechanic. But this was insufficient for most of the men, who debated whether she was a lesbian or whether the captain or crew were really "doing her," but many also acknowledged her skills.

There are no women captains in the King Cove fleet. However, women do fish as fishermen, not as "women fishermen" (see also Allison 1988:231). On board, they function in many capacities: as skiffman, cook, deckhand, among many other roles. Women are usually sexually linked to the captain as family or partners. Entire families may fish their own operation together. Women do not want to be equal to men in fishing, and the social rewards are not the same for them. Ortner and Whitehead (1981) argue that gender is a prestige structure, with women's roles, activities, and the products of their labour generally accorded less prestige than those of their male counterparts. This is true here as well, where men gain or lose status by providing fish and game, and women gain or lose status in food preparation and in the quality of the final products. Black (1998) adds that species hunted by men carried symbolic significance whereas species hunted and gathered by women and children are seen as utilitarian.

Figure 4.4
Jarred salmon, 2002 (photo, and salmon, by Lisa Wilson)

Fishermen's wives are sometimes shore-based managers, similar to Davis's "shore skippers" (1988), in which they balance the books for the boat. Also, following Davis, women who get too involved in men's activities are referred to as "bossy." More often, wives remain separate from the business of fishing and do not involve themselves with crew hires or crewshares, equipment purchases, or fishing itself, but keep to household and family management. They worry over their husbands, sons, and daughters at sea. One woman fretted over her daughter out in a storm, saying, "I'll sleep better when she gets home." One woman told a story about seeing a boat on fire far enough offshore that it looked like her husband's. She told of agonizing moments while she tried to raise her husband on the radio before learning that it was his cousin's boat and not his.

Women also act as a kind of reliability check for men's boasting. There is a great deal of evidence to suggest that men exaggerate the amount of fish caught. One wife told me about her husband bragging to others about his catches, "but I see the fish tickets, so I know better," she said.

Behind Every Successful Fisherman ...

Successful fishermen require two things: a reliable crew and a solid marriage. Captains rarely boast about how many fish they catch because they do not need to; their crews do it for them, so "everybody knows" how well they did. Almost every highliner or successful fisherman has a stable marriage. Staying at home, child rearing, and supporting their husbands are *valued* activities, and women are not pressured to do more than that. Marriage is about working alongside one another. Successful fishermen can attract wives more easily, but they also need wives to be successful.

If his cross-cultural study holds true and "the single best predictor of the physical attractiveness of the man a woman actually marries is his occupational status" (Buss 1997:192), then we can look at non-random mate preferences and determine which characteristics are preferred. In Belkofski in the early to mid-1900s, Father Khodivitskii dictated marriage partners and rules. Choices are made individually today, but there is some family influence. Members of some families consider members of other families to be unsuitable as potential mates, a product of long histories between families. By and large, young women strive to marry successful Aleut fishermen or sons of successful fishermen who are guaranteed a future in the industry. In a few cases, knowing the uncertainties of fishing, several intend to marry outside the Aleutians and move away. For young men, mate choice presents a different set of problems. It is more difficult to bring non-local women to the village and persuade them to stay, so they are often torn between finding a mate or staying in the village. In 2000 the ratio of men to women over the age of 18 was 1.66:1. Thus, there is a kind of scarcity all round; there are fewer women relative to men, but there also are relatively few desirable mate choices for women. Though there is no institutionalized local definition of incest, there is a sense that a few relationships are "too close," and in two cases that I am aware of families tried to block the marriage.

The ideal is to marry or partner with an Aleut, unlike in some parts of Native Alaska, where women are increasingly marrying non-Native men and leaving the villages (Fienup-Riordan 1990a; Hamilton and Seyfrit 1994a, 1994b).[7] Several young women insisted that Aleut men are very well endowed. One woman stopped by to visit with me on her way to the harbour to see her "new honey," a man running a tender for Peter Pan. The first thing she said about him, beaming with pride, was "Kate, you won't believe it! He owns four boats!"

In the nineteenth century, Veniaminov described a type of bride service performed by the prospective husband for his future wife's

Table 4.1
Frequency of marriages in the Aleutians East Borough, 1995–2007

Marriage year	Occurrences	Rate
2007	4	1.4
2006	4	1.5
2005	10	3.8
2004	5	1.9
2003	4	1.5
2002	1	0.4
2001	3	1.2
2000	8	3.0
1999	6	2.8
1998	3	1.4
1997	4	1.8
1996	3	1.4
1995	5	2.2

Source: Alaska Bureau of Vital Statistics, annual reports

family, whereby the bridegroom hunted for a year or two for the bride's family and might perform feats "to show his bravery" (Veniaminov 1840:II:75, in Hrdlicka 1945:167). This form of transaction has modern equivalents. Permit transfers and crew hires have occasionally taken the form of wealth transfer systems, where a man will crew for his prospective/actual father-in-law as a form of groom service, or where a permit transfer may take the form of a bride price and be given to the male's family as a symbolic dowry.

It is common for every able male member of a family to be out salmon fishing during the commercial openings, and sometimes women are out there too. Husbands and wives will fish together for many reasons, including not having to pay a crew, especially if they still owe on their boat or permit, which so many of them do. They send their children to stay with non-fishing relatives (or with the willing anthropologist) if they do not take them on the boat. On the other hand, long fishing openings can serve as a respite for spouses. When men are fishing, women and children seem to have more freedom in household duties and recreation.

In 2000, 86 people (49 of whom were women) reported that they were divorced and 8 reported being separated (Census 2000). These numbers include the cannery population. Reasons given for separation or divorce were infidelity (real or suspected), accusations of laziness, drunkenness, and the inability to find employment or

Table 4.2
Frequency of divorce in the Aleutians East Borough, 1995–2007

Divorce/ dissolution	Resident women	Rate	Resident men	Rate
2007	2	2.2	3	1.6
2006	0	0.0	1	0.6
2005	1	1.1	2	1.1
2004	2	2.2	2	1.1
2003	4	4.4	5	2.8
2002	2	2.2	1	0.6
2001	0	0.0	0	0.0
2000	1	1.1	1	0.6
1999	8	8.3	8	6.8
1998	4	4.2	2	1.7
1997	2	2.0	4	3.3
1996	6	6.0	4	3.3
1995	5	4.9	6	4.9

Source: Alaska Bureau of Vital Statistics, annual reports

gain subsistence foods, initiated by both women and men. A few divorced couples still live together, in part because they share children or because of the housing shortage and the expense of running two households. They may continue to behave as if married or have other relationships. Several women compared their husbands or boyfriends to *bidarkis*, the black katy chitons picked at low tide all summer that are stuck so hard to the rocks that they must be pried off with a sharp knife – a fine simile for their inability to end the relationships or move out of their homes. Many of these relationships were fraught with spouse abuse in the way of beatings, overprotective jealousy, drunken fights, and locking each other out of the home, but all were described in the past tense by the women, even though these men were still living with them.

Some spouses fear bad fishing years because of the potential for spouse abuse. In good fishing years, there is a good deal of hedonistic behaviour. Men may have been chasing women before but are more successful in the catch now. Men may be compelled to travel to Anchorage to party and consequently cheat on their wives. This goes both ways. "Some women pass themselves around when guys are out fishing," one man argued, and I observed a few obvious cases of this. Daniel Pérusse's study of 433 French Canadian men found that social status did not predict the number of children one had, but it did predict the "number of potential conceptions" (1993);

that is, those with power and prestige had greater sexual access to women (in Betzig 1997:8). At the beginning of certain fishing seasons, when there is an influx of fishermen touting themselves as highliners, an already sexually charged atmosphere is heightened. Though it cannot be quantified, the number of potential conceptions undeniably increases.

In lean years, a few entire families, or more often just the male heads of household, will leave the village in search of employment. A few families reside permanently in Anchorage and return to the village to fish and catch up with family. Occasionally, divorced couples with children will find the father leaving the village for other employment, returning only to fish. His ex-wife and children are left in the care of her extended family. The stress of coping with lean fishing years is often blamed for the divorce in the first place.

Elders and Fishing Indemnities

Security in old age is most reliable through one's own children, and possessing a boat and/or permit is a concrete index of a man's ability to meet his family obligations. Elders try to maintain their autonomy for as long as they can by continuing to fish commercially as crew or run their own boat. Having achieved their status (high or other) at an earlier age, elder fishermen are less competitive or daring in fishing and rest on their reputation as running "top boats" or other feats at sea. Elders who no longer fish or hold a job of any kind describe themselves as "pretty dependent" on others to stock their freezers with fish and game. Having a large family and many friends is the best way to ensure that you will be provided for in your later years.

Elders take great pride in the work they did in their youth and may scoff at the younger generations. "I packed water, wood and fish when I was a kid. Oh, I worked hard. Now all these kids have 'push button.' They don't know nothing about that." For hours, this elder told of all the work she was responsible for as a kid. "We made mattresses out of fifty-pound sacks of flour and feathers ... Dolls we made out of men's socks with buttons for eyes for Christmas ... I packed spring water from up the hill in cast-iron buckets as a little girl, and packed alders on my back for the wood stove." Complaining about "kids these days" is a widespread phenomenon, of course, but the complaints here are usually in relation to the automation of fishing today or to village change. Having lost one son in an accident, a woman told me that the other two sons crew with anyone who will take them, but often on top boats. Their father did not receive a permit in 1975. "My husband died of cancer in 1980. I been by myself since that. I been barely making it." Her sons do not assist her financially. She lives in a rundown house with sporadic heat and has no car. She used to work for the cannery and even misses it sometimes, but "there are too many Filipinos now." Her sons are in the "wrong generation," she said. Rubbing her hands together, she described how her more successful nephew stocked her freezer with caribou meat and salmon. "That should last me all winter."

Another elder, who divorced her husband in the 1970s, though he still lives with her, has two sons who had fishing jobs all winter, but when I visited with her in 2003 she had no fuel oil for heat and had been turning on her oven to stay warm. Her ex-husband had left to work the summer in Bristol Bay, and her sons had gone fishing without checking to see that she had enough fuel and food to last.

Though elders may not have the authority or respect that they might have commanded in the past, they are consulted on matters of history, family, and fishing practices. They are honoured with an annual dinner, and the entire community makes concerted efforts to look out for them on matters of health, family, food, and basic needs. Elders tend to form a tight social unit themselves in playing bingo, throwing Polka parties, and taking *banyas* (saunas) together.

"There aren't too many elders around here," lamented one Aleut woman. The number of elders in other communities never fully recovered after World War II, but this does not explain the situation in King Cove. With the prevalence of life-threatening diseases and poor health, most die before their time. A community health provider ranked type 2 diabetes as the primary cause of death, with pneumonia, cancers, and alcohol-related health problems following closely. Death from "drinking too much" or "heart attack drinking" were common causes mentioned. A main concern of community doctors is the lack of physical activity. However, my sense is that physical activity among adults is high: fishing is a demanding occupation and requires great strength and stamina. Many youths begin fishing at a young age and often bear the same physical burdens as the rest of a fishing crew. Like many American young people, they also have aspirations to play professional basketball, and they train for the Native Youth Olympics during the school year to participate in the statewide competitions of seal hopping, knee jumping, and the Eskimo stick pull. At the same time, many people are hampered from taking part in outside activities because of their fear of bears. Some are afraid to pick berries or walk on the beach. This fear is not unfounded. In the mid-1990s, a woman walking home with her baby in her arms and her young son walking next to her late one night were attacked by a bear, which killed the little boy.

The paucity of elders may also have something to do with every-day dangers. One elder lost nine members of her immediate family in the 1940s in a boating accident in the lagoon. Commercial fishing has the highest mortality rate of any occupation in the world, and overturned boats or accidents on the water have claimed many lives. Likewise, the risk involved in travelling to and from these commun-ities is considerable: flying low over freezing waters in small planes and dodging mountains hidden in mist or, if the wind is too high or there is no visibility for air travel, taking boats through choppy seas. Since 1980, there have been 11 deaths related to travel to and from King Cove. These deaths have fuelled a fight for a road between King Cove and Cold Bay, which has the main runway for planes to and from Anchorage.[8]

The causes of death were discovered using genealogical meth-ods tracing back several generations and covering at a minimum the twentieth century. This technique provided a reliability check for official vital statistics and gave a longer time frame in which to evaluate other social and economic fluctuations. Between 2000 and 2007, there have been 64 deaths (known to me), including 3 suicides, in these Eastern Aleut villages. Deaths from unnatural causes such as bear attacks, boating accidents, hit-and-run accidents, and plane crashes were all described to me, though the majority of deaths were health-related. The rate for whites in Alaska is 75.2 years versus the 68.5 years for Alaska Natives (Alaska Bureau of Vital Statistics 1995). There is variation within the Alaska Native population, but the rate is lumped for all Alaska Natives, and modern Aleut life expectancy data do not exist.[9]

This elder generation has survived the booms and busts of multiple commercial industries. The middle generation saw the most prosper-ous years of the salmon industry, and most have always called King Cove home. Young adults are in a generation with great disadvanta-ges. They have seen their parents thrive in the salmon industry, and have seen a constant decline over the years. Their own pockets swell every summer from crewing on boats, but this generation may be running out of opportunities. Marriages seem to stabilize with new-found success in fishing, and those in long-term relationships seem to have better success at fishing.

FAMILY ORGANIZATION

In the 1980s Braund et al. (1986:8.35–7) distinguished between major family lineages in King Cove based on surnames and male heads of household. Braund's study team identified 7 "dominant families" (n=208 people) and 28 other families (n=244 people), the former chosen as dominant because it was their members who occupied formal leadership positions. If we follow this example, today there are 28 family lines in King Cove, 9 of which might be considered core families because of their size and influence. Of the other 19 families, two male heads are white, married to Aleut women. Limited Entry prompted a number of excluded men and their families to leave the village permanently. Though it is difficult to say exactly how many have left since 1974, I can say that in the mid-1980s Braund et al. identified 35 lineages, compared with the 28 that I identified in 2002.

In my own research, it became apparent that many female heads of household, who are also sisters from the largest lineage, were strongly influential community-wide, and their husbands' positions, though highly respected and influential, were enhanced by and maintained with the status of their wives. Thus, male lineages are accurate delineations of some families whereas other male lineages, which vary in size and composition, are better delineated through linking female heads of household who are sisters. Through this "sorority," the families within are organized around fishing and sharing. If we follow the influential sisters, they form the female heads of household (though two are deceased) in five of these nine families. Living members of these five sorority-linked families, including spouses, comprise approximately 25 percent of the village. As King Cove's largest family, this is also the one whose members hold many political positions and command the greatest respect; thus, an extended family's position of rank appears to correlate with size. Members of the nine elite families have tended to marry one another (or to partner with one another) while members of the smaller families also tend to marry (or partner with) one another, with some exceptions. Thus, individuals intentionally or by default maintain and shift their

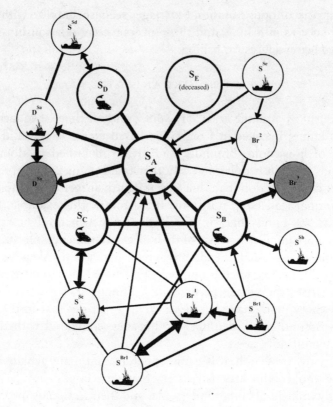

Figure 4.5
Sociogram of a sorority family indicating fishing assets and sharing, winter 2002–03

social positions through marriage. Many people described a kind of competition between two major lineages for numbers of children (18 children from one family and 16 from the other), and joked that they were "enemies," though they have intermarried several times over. They still discuss who won.

Figure 4.5 shows a portion of a sociogram of a family centred around a woman elder and her sisters. S_{A-E} are five sisters, Br^{1-3} are three of their brothers, S^N=son of, D^N=daughter of. Three of these sisters live very near one another in the downtown section of King Cove. The thicker lines show closer relationships and a steady flow of food sharing, care, and communication between them. These often coincide with closer biological relationships, but there are a few exceptions. The thinner lines indicate relatives as well, but as associations with less flow between them. The arrows indicate the flow of actual foods (salmon, *bidarkis*, cuttlefish, crab, for example) but not the social relationship. The sisters receive the majority of fish and redistribute finished products such as kippered salmon or *chisu*.

S_A, in this particular network, is a primary node, with access to almost all of them and their goods and services, though she does not have direct access to fishing through her husband or sons. Her status is ascribed in that she was born into a large lineage, but it is also achieved because she has had a long life as community health provider and is extremely well liked. Others' status is dictated by their connection to the node relative to one another. This does not depend on actual communication; for example, if someone helps work on his cousin's boat, he does not arrange this through the lines of communication but through his relationship.

S_B is a primary node in Anchorage as well, because she and her husband own a house there and spend their winters there. Most relatives who pass through or stay in Anchorage for whatever reason stay in their house, whether they are home or not.

In chapter 3, I showed how King Cove is highly interrelated, but its inhabitants do not always act on this relatedness. Figure 4.5 shows that to get access to someone's labour, material wealth, or sharing, an individual does not simply go from A to B to C to D, but through a node – an individual connecting them to another. Distance from people is not determined by the number of links. While relatedness plays a strong role, it does not decisively determine the social relationship or responsibilities between people. If we were to distribute cousins randomly, this sociogram would look very different, in that some would be entrenched within the network and some would be on the fringes.

Nodes allow people to leap between families; for example, you might have better relations with the in-laws of someone in your network. The shaded circles represent "loose nodes," those who are connected but do not have the opportunity to contribute many goods and services back, and do not allow anyone in the network access to another more distant network.

The above sociogram of sharing can describe a number of lineage-based networks, though in some cases the primary node is male. Inheritance of property is generally transmitted through the patrilineal line, regardless of whether the family is linked by the sorority or is delineated as a male lineage. In two of the main male-organized lineages, corporate kingroups of fathers and sons have formed in which

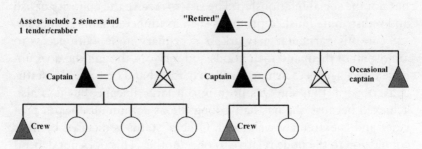

Figure 4.6
Partial genealogy of a corporately organized lineage in which the sons own and fish two seine permits while the father owns the boats. The father was "retired" only in speech. He is still in the Harbor House every day, works on the boat, and helps tender during some openings.

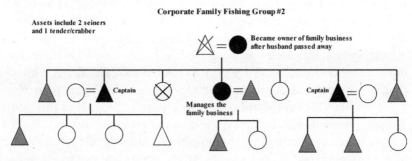

Figure 4.7
Partial genealogy of a corporately organized lineage, in which the family has formed an actual corporation, owned by the mother, managed by the sister, and fished by the brothers and their sons. The family's corporation owns the boats while the brothers own the permits.

they jointly own property, as in boats and permits, and depend on each other on land and on the water. Figures 4.6 and 4.7 illustrate the organization of these two family fishing groups. Families tend to own assets in direct proportion to family size in the village. These are large lineages, and their fishing assets reflect their size.

Family Assets and Limited Entry

Limited Entry put a large number of fishermen who could not demonstrate a record and all future generations at a great disadvantage. As I have said, Limited Entry is arguably the key external structure

Table 4.3
Comparison of numbers of descendants in 2003 for twenty fishermen issued permits in
1973 versus twenty men who were not

	No permit	Permit(s)
Number of children	82	103
	4.1/person	5.15/person
	(44.3%)	(55.7%)
Number of grandchildren	119	236
	5.95/person	11.8/person
	(33.5%)	(66.5%)

that set the stage for future practices and relationships. There is
finality in this plan, and they can never go back to fishing as it was
before Limited Entry.

Permits reflect key differences in life histories between men. For
example, I compared the first and second generations between men
who were issued permits as part of Limited Entry and men who
were not. I cannot incorporate everyone excluded during Limited
Entry because many of them left the village for alternative employment; these numbers, then, only compare those who stayed in King
Cove and raised their families there. I selected 20 men for each
category for whom I had complete genealogical data for at least
two generations. Table 4.3 shows that men who were issued permits
have more children and grandchildren today than those who were
not issued permits.

Are these fishermen simply able to support larger families more
easily? Most of them come from very large families with many children (and sometimes these households have also raised others' neglected children). So are they simply carrying on the tradition? To be
numerous, to have a large family, is a good thing. When one woman
was considering having another child, her friend said, "Sure, you
only have three." An elder who died in June 2002 was praised by
everyone at her funeral for having more than eighty descendants.
Another woman boasted that each of her parents came from the two
largest families at the time of their marriage.

It does appear that for a man who gets a permit, the reproductive
success of his offspring is almost doubled. There is a slight increase
in the number of children, but these children were able to do more
in their adulthood, such as work on their fathers' boats and inherit
boats and permits at a younger age. Several of these fishermen subsequently lost their permits through sale or gifted transfers, but

the trend of larger families still carries through. These data are not meant to show that permits have determined family size, but they do indicate that men who received permits have had very different life histories from those who did not.[10]

In describing how he and his brother lost their right to fish during Limited Entry, an elder stated, "It's a sad story. They were determined to phase people out. I was one of the early guys, just didn't have a record." Entire families were "phased out" of the fisheries during this process, and all of them were the smaller, less influential family lines. It is difficult to quantify this situation because many who did not receive permits had to leave the village, and those who subsequently sold or lost their permits in various ways also left. Many others who did not receive permits stayed on in the village and tried to fill "land jobs."

Comparing the effects of Limited Entry between two men – one given multiple permits and one given no permits – illustrates some of the difficulties and advantages created by the system. The man given multiple permits still owns a purse seine permit, a setnet permit, and a boat, and fishes every season. His only son fishes one of the permits running someone else's boat. He has held multiple political offices within the village and manages a family fishing-support business. The other man was given no permits and says he is "retired," collecting social security. Though he had fished and owned a boat before Limited Entry, he had to hire a lawyer to argue his case for whether he deserved a permit, and he lost the battle. Without a permit, he had to sell his boat. He subsequently held political offices in the 1970s and 1980s.

The experiences of these two men are fairly typical of others with and without permits. There are exceptions, however. One man who was not given a permit was able to overcome the fundamental lack of assets because of his previous reputation and high status within the community and because of his wife's respected position and family size. He was even offered a permit by a state official responsible for their distribution, but he turned it down out of fairness. His primary job for the next two decades was to work for the cannery and run tenders for them. He held long terms in every village political office.

Limited Entry followed the social and status structure in place, rewarding those with clear fishing records who were already well established as fishermen and who were often from the largest families. Those individuals were permitted to continue their activities. Many of the men shut out of fishing were still resentful thirty years after the fact. They emphasize their successes on land in village government, but often their activities in office, or the political victories they accomplished, were entirely connected with reinforcing or facilitating aspects of commercial fishing for the King Cove fleet, such as harbour improvements or forcing the cannery to adhere to certain pollution standards. Thus, these men were disenfranchised from actual fishing but fed back into the system and contributed as if they were fishermen, with all the same things at stake. These men, whether still active in the village in some regard or whether retired or even disabled, continue to take in the weather reports each day and pore over the Blue Sheets, the preliminary commercial fishing numbers released by Fish & Game during the season, as if they have the same things at stake as the fishermen.

Fishing assets and family histories in fishing are exhibited throughout the village. The walls of the King Cove Corporation bar are covered with photographs of boats, many eulogizing fishermen lost at sea. Old photographs of boats and the village are displayed in most homes. Several men have earned reputations for making quality boat models to sell to the captains (fetching approximately $800). These are symbolic representations of capital as well as a source of pride. Two of these modellers have not had stable careers as fishermen and have worked in the cannery or in other support jobs, but they maintain an important role in relation to fishing.

Palinkas (1987) attributes the formation of social classes among the Yupiit in Bristol Bay to unequal access to the salmon fishery, beginning with Limited Entry, the limitations depending on which type of permit the fisherman has and the differences in these technologies. The size of the family with the permit(s), family ties, or even the history of that family's successes or failures also has a significant effect, in that large family networks can help supplement income or alleviate bad years by pooling resources and coming to each other's rescue. In the Eastern Aleutians, however, there is some evidence that Limited Entry did not create social classes but altered a status structure already in place. In the following section I explore rank in its modern form, mapping positions that carry status.

RANK, LEADERSHIP, AND VILLAGE POLITICS BETWEEN THE LAND AND SEA

I enter the discussion of rank by first describing the phenomenon of the village plenipotentiary – the manager, diplomat, and delegate invested with and conferring real power, representing local government at all levels: village government, tribal council, and village corporation. Every Aleut village has what one woman called a "Mama False Pass" or a "Papa Akutan," a leader who holds multiple elected or appointed positions and is highly respected in the village. These individuals are self-taught (usually with some college in business administration), well travelled, hard working, and are often controversial. They tend to occupy elected or appointed positions as administrators at the village, tribal council, or corporation level and command a great deal of status, often as much as the formal leadership positions do. In all but one Eastern Aleutian village, they are women (three of four are Aleut women), and their political authority is both self-possessed and vested by the village fishermen.[11] King Cove has a "Mama King Cove" who sits on at least four separate boards (within the village, borough, federal, and state fisheries-related administrative organizations), holds sway with every administrative body associated with the region, and spearheads development projects in the community.

Women control much of the supporting political structures of King Cove, while men fill the roles of mayor, corporation president, tribal council president, and borough board. Non-natives in the community have noted that it is "matriarchal," often with an adverse tone, but the Aleut population does not have this attitude. Political positions are *tough*, and anyone who takes them on has the village's respect, despite controversies that may come with the roles.

In an eclectic village such as King Cove, where multiple generations from a half-dozen villages have come together in the past hundred years, there is an amazing unity in political pursuits. Tribal councils, Native corporations, city government, and the borough all govern the village, and sometimes their boundaries are blurred. The Aleut enjoy a moderate amount of autonomy in village-based decisions, but they are also beset by a Weberian bureaucratic process. The map of positions that carry status are both political and non-political. The political offices are president of the King Cove Corporation, president of the Agdaagux Tribal Council, mayor, harbourmaster, board members of the corporation and tribal council, city council members, Aleutians East Borough board, and school board. The Belkofski Corporation and Tribal Council based in King Cove are the only enduring leadership structures from the former village, and they were formed after the village was largely abandoned; their combined membership is less than thirty. King Cove's Agdaagux Tribal

Council is not a remnant of past elder leadership, but rather it was created in the early 1990s in response to the national trend granting decision-making power and funds to tribes.

To discover aspects of the ranking system, I spent most mornings in the Harbor House, which is a gathering place of men essentially ranking themselves. This was unsolicited information from men entrenched in fishing, and there tended to be a consensus. Outside this, others often – but not always – came up with the same information.

The relations between personal and positional status work in multiple ways. Some people gain positions because of status; sometimes status is gained because of the position. If we consider Fried's definition of a ranked society "in which positions of valued status are somehow limited so that not all those of sufficient talent to occupy such statuses actually achieve them" (1967:109), then the modern Aleut might be considered ranked. Some families are considered elite, and it is their members who qualify for certain political positions. Elite positions tend to be filled by those who meet certain criteria, and contain elements of both ascribed and achieved status.

Political manoeuvring is a subtle play of negotiation and alliance, and the ability to succeed at this depends in large part upon family size and status, and familiarity with bureaucracy, before education comes into play. However, those in smaller family lineages also are able to access political positions, but through completely different channels. Their methods of gaining credibility are through experience with bureaucracy, education, connection with the outside, and a confrontational style, in part because they do not have the family presence behind them.

Fishermen Politicians

Similar to Rasing's description for Iglulingmiut, where "in the days of subsistence hunting, good hunting abilities had been a *sine qua non* for the political status of a man" (1994:191), being a good fishermen is an important component of an Aleut man's credibility in relation to political issues. Captains and crew are often referred to simply as "the guys" by women. In many fishing societies, fishermen are absent from the political process because they are out fishing for extended periods of time (e.g., Ellis 1977). However, in Alaska, fishermen and hunters engage directly with politicians (for example, as part of the Alaska Eskimo Whaling Commission or with the Board of Fisheries). Successful Aleut fishermen hold many political offices within the village, and decisions are made only between openings when they are present. Increasingly, these Aleut fishermen are expected to strengthen their political positions and adopt the strategies of government politicians in order to continue their livelihood (see chapter 5). For these negotiations, fishing seasons often coincide with critical meetings in Anchorage, such as the Board of Fisheries meeting held every three years, in which fishermen can testify on their behalf and hopefully influence regulations.

City election results are influenced by the state of the fisheries. In good years, voters tend to put community interests at the forefront of their decisions; in bad years, voters tend to choose candidates who are more likely to allow individuals to "get away with the minimum," as one man stated. Before the 2000 city election, the mayor at that time lost popularity because he forced residents to pay their city bills, sometimes by cutting off their utilities. Those in leadership positions found it refreshing that he was balancing the books so that those who did pay their bills were not "supporting the freeloaders." His predecessors (and ultimately his successor) were less strict. Residents could accrue enormous debt with impunity. Thus, a laissez-faire approach is preferred in bad times in order to preserve capital for fishing.

There are hub individuals who wear many hats: they are successful fishermen who simultaneously hold positions in local city or borough government and sit on the boards of all organizations connected with Native concerns and the fisheries. Most fishermen rely on the continued efforts and articulations of these few in order to speak for all. In one instance, a representative from the Aleutians East Borough was recruiting fishermen in the Harbor House to give targeted testimony at the next Board of Fisheries meeting in Anchorage. Only eight fishermen attended the meeting and none would commit to testifying. This reluctance is in part because of a sense of hopelessness, and because this meeting coincided with cod fishing openings, but it was also because of apprehension of the political process.

Family Ranking

A Sand Point family claims a direct line to Finnish royalty. Their grandfather was from Finland and "ended a worldwide tour at Belkofski," where he met their grandmother and moved to Wosnesenski Island

Figure 4.8
King Cove harbour, spring 2002

in the Shumagins. When a granddaughter was married (her first marriage, in the 1970s) the royal family of Finland sent a crown over for her to wear during the ceremony. Her father, this immigrant's son, was in the Alaska legislature. This is hierarchy in the extreme sense, their status fuelled to a large extent by their descendance from Scandinavian immigrant fishermen.

Genealogical distance from the core families described above does not necessarily determine political ranking, but it does determine *access* to certain political positions and influence. Those who do not hold the official positions nevertheless derive privilege from their degree of relatedness. In 2000, city elections were taking place for almost every seat in city government and the school board. In this environment, people were intensely evaluating one another's leadership abilities. However, these deliberations were drawn down family lines, and the election resulted in the entire replacement of one family in control of the city with another, but it was a family whose members were from two of the largest in King Cove. Families typically vote for themselves, so the leadership positions are passed around to the majority. A single lineage may occupy most of the positions on the city council, whereas members of another lineage may occupy most of the positions on the King Cove Corporation board. Major families (unconsciously) rotate control, though different individuals may hold the actual positions. The Agdaagux Tribal Council seems to be more diverse, with members of the larger and smaller lineages equally likely to be members of the council. Control of the Belkofski Corporation and Tribal Council tends to bounce between two of their largest enrolled families. As is common elsewhere, younger people tend to be uninterested or apathetic about politics.

There remains some competition for the administrative positions within the formal community structure because these leadership roles do in fact carry some measure of power. During one term, the mayor and members of the city council tended to be in the same extended family. Despite the relative unity, political disputes can easily form between families over past events. "It's clannish here," said one fisherman/businessman of King Cove. "You have to be careful about who you hire." Nepotism in politics and land jobs is formally and informally suppressed, but is not absent. (Nepotism is expected in fishing and sharing, however). For example, on the King Cove Corporation board, all the members must disclose how they voted and give a legitimate reason for their choice to prevent any partiality. Nepotism still occurs, and there is a significant amount of complaining about it, but little action is taken.

The relations I have just described clearly do not fall easily into a single rank order. Instead, Aleut social organization is much closer to what Ehrenreich, Crumley, and Levy (1995) have called "heterarchical" societies, complex societies where segments within have separate internal hierarchies. Hierarchies are split between the land and sea, but there is also a great deal of crossover. In both realms, however, every political decision is evaluated in terms of how it will affect the fisheries.

STATUS AND MONEY BETWEEN THE LAND AND SEA

"I'm willing to bet billions of dollars have passed through here. Not millions, *billions*," said one Aleut fisherman, drinking at the corporation bar.

"Where did all the money go?" I asked. "There aren't a lot of expensive cars and trucks here, nobody's house is all that spectacular, I haven't heard of people taking exotic trips or anything. So how did all of that get spent?"

He pointed in the direction of the harbour. "Have you seen my boat?" he asked.

To non-Aleuts new to the area, culture is often assumed to be a quantifiable entity and visible only through subsistence activities, Native foods, speaking the language, and displaying distinct cultural items in one's home, such as beaded headdresses, animal skins, and icons. "Culture varies from home to home. It shocks me. I'll visit one house and they'll speak Aleut, and in the next home they can't. In one house everybody will be eating Native foods, and in the next house they won't even touch it," observed a King Cove police officer who had been in the community just sixteen months. In this sense, the display of Aleut items and the use of language do indeed vary from home to home (in my observations, variation in eating Native foods only applies to variety, not quantity). But examination of the household is not necessarily where one should limit one's inquiry. Aleut culture should also be noted by what is absent from the home. Wealthy fishing families by and large do not spend their money on home improvements or material indicators of wealth as found in mainstream America, but on boat improvements or improved replacements. This is not to say that Aleut culture can be quantified by walking the docks at the harbour, but it is to say that boats are visible measures of individual and family status, and what is absent from the home is nearly always present in an unexpected form tied up in the harbour.

Until now, the fisheries have been lucrative enough to allow year-round residence in the village, the lean years being supplemented with "land jobs." Some have found niches for themselves that guarantee an income no matter the state of the salmon industry – for example, renting, storing, and hauling crab pots for the crab fishermen, taking care of boats for non-locals that are stored in the harbour through the winter, chartering their boats, guiding hunts, and renting vehicles, among other things. There is often a tug between participating in both fishing and land jobs. For example, a woman employed by the city was resentful because a mayor would not allow them to leave their city jobs to go fishing, something former mayors apparently had allowed.

The tribal council has coordinated people for training for CDLs (commercial drivers' licences) so that locals, particularly young men, can work on road construction projects and for "six-pack" licences so that fishermen can be contracted to transport state and federal

employees and cannery workers in their boats. Even successful fishermen are hedging their bets with CDLS, though several of them are
perceived by less successful individuals as gaining an unfair advantage. This is an attempt at diversifying the economy and is a form of
"risk management" in the classic hunter-gatherer sense.

"Back in the 1980s, there used to be people camped in the crab
pots looking for a job. Now you can't even get a crew. It started getting hard when the price hit 90 cents. Now it's at 47!" With the price
of salmon being so low, there is a pool of top crewman who became
unwilling to fish. "It's not worth it" is heard continually. "We got
land jobs now. These are a lot harder to get and we're glad to have
them." These fishermen quickly snatched up the temporary land jobs
leaving few potential crewmen for the captains to hire.

On 10 June 2002, as the salmon boats began to trickle out of the
harbour on their way to the fishing grounds, a habitual crewman
paced back and forth in front of his living-room window watching it
all with the VHF radio tuned in. Sporting a belt buckle with a fishing
boat design, he lamented his loyalties: "I should have jumped ship. I
could be fishing right now." The man for whom he had been fishing
for most of his life could not find a full crew of his own, so instead of
running his own boat he decided to go fishing with his son. This left
the crewman stranded. "I should've signed on with another boat,"
he said. Those who considered themselves lucky to have land jobs
looked wistfully out on the water as they worked in construction
and took their breaks in the Harbor House.

Three men working for the Aleutian Housing Authority came to
replace the windows in the house I had rented from a fisherman in
the summer of 2002. Though they were not fishing that summer, and
two had not had fishing jobs in a few years, they spent the entire day
talking about fishing and keeping track of every boat moving in and
out of the harbour.

Land jobs in themselves are considered to be lower in status than
fishing, and though wage employment is necessary, there are no
opportunities to gain prestige. When I asked men with land jobs
what they do, they invariably stated, "I'm a fisherman," even though
in some cases they had not fished for up to five years. Women tend to
see land jobs for men as responsible and good but think they should
be temporary.

Political and economic striving are valued up to a point but can be
discouraged. One man who is relatively wealthy and does not have

a large immediate family to support is often criticized for "getting everything." He wins bids for contracts using his boat, he guides hunters, he is one of the few who has a "six-pack" licence that allows him to transport people by boat, and he ran a local business which he sold in 2001 for a profit. When the CDL program started to train fishermen for a new career, he took the class and became licensed along with those in greater need. This man was criticized as an opportunist, but he has the ability to organize other boats, their owners, and crew to accomplish logistical tasks and has employed at least ten different relatives as crew for a variety of projects in the last few years. Though striving has social penalties, the rewards can far outweigh the social sanctions that may accompany the behaviour, and others benefit from his efforts.

PERFECT DRIFT

During the 2002 horse race at Belmont, a horse called *Perfect Drift* caught the attention of the fisherman watching the televised race with me; his name was reason enough for the fisherman, a drift-netter, to root for him.[12] But it is not simply the impressive fleet in the harbour or the detailed boat models displayed in homes. It is not just that children play at being fishermen or that the weather is referred to in nautical ways, such as a "dory breeze." It is that all sociocultural expressions and relations are intimately tied to fishing, and Eastern Aleut identity is a product of these relationships. A common farewell is not "good luck" or "goodbye," but "good fishing." Fishing is a core metaphor for explaining life's phenomena and embodies commonsense knowledge. For example, "everybody knows a sou'easterly wind blows the fish in" and will make for a healthier, happier season.

Eastern Aleutian society weaves together two economic forms in practice; this coordination exists only as long as it is being continually enacted. The nuclear family provides a basic social unit, but the extended relationships and obligations transcend the household and solidify relationships across the community.

There is a great deal of pressure on men to fish, particularly young men. The majority of these men can never hope to be full participants in fishing, especially those outside the dominant families. The changing structure on the water affects community and familial relations, where Aleut women are finding it more difficult to partner with Aleut fishermen, where subsistence obligations are becoming difficult to fulfill, where politics and leadership are accessible only to fishing families, and where an independence ideal in an occupation dependent on natural resources, state and federal regulations, a Japanese-owned cannery, and fish markets is becoming difficult to realize.

Land jobs safeguard against the vulnerability of the business, as do working spouses. Wives manage the household and the children and mend nets, while husbands fish for days on end, and they may provide additional income if the boat has not been doing well. A male/fishing–female/land job pattern still means that when fishing declines, everyone is affected, not just the men. Women often become the sole consistently employed member of the family, and in the classic hunter-gatherer sense they are keeping their families alive with steady work while the men wait for a fishing opener or other job.

Subsistence practices are often regarded as being loaded with meaning, even embodying culture, while commercial practices are treated as devoid of meaning. The assumptions made about past practices are used to assume things in the present – for example, that the Aleut have lost their culture and are modernized so they do not demand special attention in the present. In defining themselves as commercial fishermen, the Aleut have been treated as being non-Native. An awareness of traditional resource use among the Eastern Aleut has almost dropped from the discourse of state and federal agencies and non-governmental researchers, and has been replaced with references to "Area M," the Board of Fisheries designation for their salmon-fishing district. The following chapter describes external conditions that make the continuance of their livelihood an ongoing daily concern.

5

Fish Wars, Identity, and Dehumanization

Don't people *want* to eat seafood? Don't they realize where it comes from? I just don't understand why they'd want to stop us fishing.

Aleut fisherman in the Harbor House, 2000

GLOBAL PRESSURE

To this point, we have looked at local relations and how they are managed. This chapter turns to processes and relationships on and beyond King Cove. For Aleut fishermen, catching and eating seafood are the pinnacles of experience, and they are astonished that others would not feel the same way. The international political climate of the environmental movement has shifted against commercial fisheries as viable economies, and large-scale fisheries are often presented as environmentally irresponsible, non-sustaining piracy (e.g., Bours, Gianni, and Mather 2001; www.greenpeace.org; Oceana 2003; Stump and Batker 1996). Since Aleuts define themselves as commercial fishermen and their social life and culture cannot be separated from the practice of fishing, I have sought to understand the ways in which this connection can be threatened and how people respond to these threats. This chapter traces Aleut identity through two major ongoing struggles: the salmon wars surrounding the Aleut and conflicts between environmental groups and fishermen over endangered species in the North Pacific and Bering Sea. These events have brought about a heightened self-awareness for the Aleut and have shaped Aleut identity in both common and heterogeneous ways. They have also solidified public opinion and media bias, both in Alaska and in the culture of environmentalism, against commercial fishing and against this particular albeit misrepresented fleet of fishermen. The burden on the Aleut to demonstrate indigenousness and possession of "traditions," both within and beyond Alaska, is constant. This chapter considers Aleut identity within a relentless atmosphere of others' denials of that identity.

Incorporating the Aleut into the larger American, Alaskan, and industrial configurations, Aleut identity is influenced by many factors, including conflicts within the fishing industry, competition from Chilean and Norwegian salmon farms, political movements against the industry, and an increasing awareness of a long heritage of marine dependency. Socially, economically, and culturally prescribed outlets to status are continually limited, eliminated, created, and shaped by local and global processes. The Aleut express idealized "free will" as self-employed fishermen, but only within external constraints and conditions. A wide range of contradictory agendas is constantly being asserted from multiple sources. Popular environmentalist discourse advocates conservation of wild resources for our "national interest," and yet most Americans love eating seafood, and wild Alaskan seafood in particular. Alaska is bound by federal constitutional mandates to preserve wild salmon for subsistence use by Alaska Natives, but the state also depends upon revenue from commercial exploits. An urban environmentalism seeks to remove humans from the landscape, or to relegate them to Stone Age economics, and upholds certain species to advance their agendas. Other Native Alaskans want access to the same resources and employ a variety of tactics to achieve this. These interests are not exhaustive, but they affect how the Eastern Aleut express local identity. Many of these interests are out of the realm of control or even influence of the Aleut, yet they have direct and indirect ramifications on Aleut daily lives. In addition, the *perception* of global processes in relation to the fisheries affects a whole host of relationships within the community. Their position as Native arctic peoples has been called into question through politically driven assessments by nongovernmental organizations (NGOs) and other entities. Dependence on global markets has made the fishermen vulnerable yet also links them to larger processes. Aleutian villages are still dominated by family-based economies, but this relatively small population influences access to valuable natural resources, which have national and global economic consequences. The reverse is also true. Aleuts have a long history of global interaction and enduring economic pressures under different political systems, and it is this cosmopolitan outlook that affects their present political position and their own perceptions of political processes.

State and federal agencies, environmental organizations, and fellow indigenous Alaskans have unsystematically colluded to dehumanize the Eastern Aleutians. Policymakers have referred to the region, its inhabitants, and its fisheries solely as "Area M" or "False Pass," without any mention of people, especially indigenous people, in debates over access to salmon. As will be shown, by creating categories such as these, a social reality is created that makes the Aleut disappear from the map.[1]

The terms "culture," "tradition," "subsistence," and "commercial" are part of the language of Alaska and are used to argue for certain rights; however, they do not mean the same things across the state (Morrow and Hensel 1992). This seemingly universal language, through which very different local realities are translated, often results in people talking past one another. This chapter also considers how this language is used and abused for particular ends. Concurrent with the salmon wars, environmental organizations have lobbied heavily against North Pacific fishermen, most recently with regard to the Steller sea lion and other species given protection under the Endangered Species Act of 1973. A significant antecedent to these movements is anthropology's misrepresentation of the Aleut on many fronts, for example, as cousins of the Eskimo and/or as downtrodden beyond hope and/or reduced to nothing after World War II. These combined events profoundly affect the social and economic activities of Aleuts, creating intense uncertainty, and may negatively determine the survivability of Eastern Aleut villages. Their small population, lack of political representation, turbulent history, lack of (conventional) material cultural display or ritual, small number of speakers of the Aleut language, geographic remoteness and expense of travel, and full participation in an industry that has traditionally been associated with white men have made it easy to overlook the living indigenous population. These factors have direct consequences concerning fishing rights. The battle between the Yupiit and the Aleut over salmon is also a debate over who is "more traditional," though, as will be shown, the Aleut were late to realize this.

SALMON WARS AND "CHUM CHUCKING"

A long-standing legal, regional, and cultural battle over the stock of origin for chum salmon between Area M (western Alaska Peninsula and Unimak Island) and Area AYK (Arctic-Yukon-Kuskokwim)

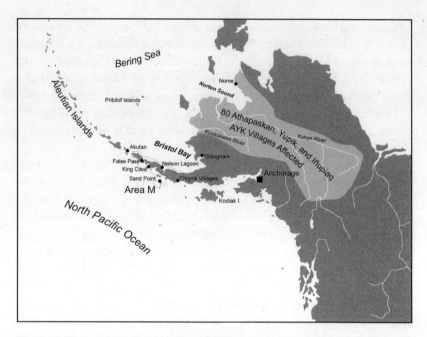

Figure 5.1
Map of Areas M and AYK, with AYK's 2000 designated disaster area

(figure 5.1) has caused stress in both regions of southwest Alaska. Chums are incidentally harvested during the sockeye fishery along the south side of the Alaska Peninsula and Unimak Island. Fishermen in this "False Pass" June fishery[2] have long been accused of taking obscene quantities of fish that do not belong to them. This is a "mixed stock" fishery, in which chum, king, and sockeye salmon swim together on their return migration to western Alaska and Asia before sorting themselves out into their rivers of origin to spawn.[3] The people of Area M fish mostly for sockeye salmon for which the canneries pay better prices than for chum salmon (in 2000 Peter Pan paid 85 cents for sockeye versus 7 cents for chum, and even less in the following years). Area AYK fishermen use chum and king salmon as subsistence staples and say that chum are also used to feed their dogs (although use of sled dogs is largely a thing of the past).[4] In addition to this chum war, Bristol Bay fishermen complain that Area M fishermen do not let enough sockeye through the passes to return to their streams. Area M fishermen had previously been allocated only 8.3 percent of Bristol Bay's forecasted sockeye harvest for June,[5] although in a 25-year average they caught only 5.9

percent of the actual Bristol Bay harvest (Aleutians East Borough, personal comm.).[6] In these salmon wars, studies can be found that support both Area M (Rogers, Boatright, and Hilborn 2000; Seeb and Crane 1999; Seeb, Crane, and Debevec 1998) and Area AYK, Norton Sound, and Bristol Bay (Eggers, Rowell, and Barrett 1991; Rogers 1990). As stated, the sockeye salmon fishery each June is when the Aleut earn most of their income for the year and harvest much of their subsistence food for use throughout the winter, and at the same time a body of social relations are constructed through harvesting, processing, and sharing activities.

There are vast differences in scale between these regions: Area AYK fishermen hold more than 1,500 commercial salmon permits with approximately 30,000 people relying on the rivers for subsistence; Area M supports approximately 200 salmon permits and slightly fewer than 2,000 people (Malecha, Tingley, and Iverson 2000a, 2000b; www.census.gov). In 2000 there were 85 purse seine, 36 drift gillnet, and 82 set gillnet permit holders who listed King Cove, False Pass, Sand Point, or Nelson Lagoon as their primary residence (www.cfec.state.ak.us). These numbers do not take into account that some individuals hold multiple permits. Though these numbers appear small when compared to the combined locally owned Kuskokwim, Lower Yukon, and Arctic salmon permits of Area AYK, it is greater when compared to the percentage of village residents in the region. In 1999 and 2000, 5.2 percent of the 29,585 AYK residents held salmon permits, whereas 10.7 percent of the 1,891 residents of Area M communities held salmon permits, or 7.5 percent of the total 2,697 Aleutians East Borough residents.[7] The Eastern Aleutian region is perhaps the best location to harvest salmon commercially, and a greater percentage of these fishermen received permits during Limited Entry.

In an effort to ensure that enough chum salmon from this mixed stock are returning to AYK to support the Yupiit's subsistence needs, the Area M chum harvest was limited, or "capped," in 1986 by the Board of Fisheries, and Area M fishermen consistently stayed well below the caps. In 2001 the Board of Fisheries abandoned the chum cap but restricted the June salmon fishery to just three days a week and threatened closure in the future. Figure 5.2 lists the restrictions to Area M's Aleut fishermen in relation to chum salmon. This list is presented less to understand the specifics and more to illustrate the set boundaries in which the fishermen must operate, combined with

AREA M REGULATIONS FOR CONSERVING CHUM SALMON

- June Fishery must begin after 10 June.
- June fishery is restricted to Shumagin Islands and S. Unimak sections.
- Sanak Island section is closed due to its historic chum catches.
- Purse seine test ratios must be 2 to 1 for sockeye to chum for two consecutive days to open the fishery before 13 June. The test fishery may continue past 13 June.
- If the fishery opens before 13 June, seine and drift can last only 6 hours in the first opening. The length of the second opening depends on ratios and chum catch size.
- First setnet fishery opens with seine fishery but for only 16 hours. It can stay open if ratio in setnet fishery is better than the 10-year average.
- There is a chum cap for June, determined by forecast harvests of chum in the AYK. Cap is adjusted based on escapements in certain AYK rivers.
- ADF&G has a priority to stay below the chum cap, not to ensure the sockeye allocation. It will close if chum cap seems likely to be exceeded.
- If the ratio is less than 2 to 1 for three consecutive days after 24 June, ADF&G may close the fishery, restrict its time, or limit fishing areas.
- Fishing closes on 30 June; no exceptions or extensions.
- All salmon must be retained on board and reported.
- Aircraft cannot be used to spot salmon.
- Seine gear is limited to 375 meshes in depth and leads of 150 fathoms.
- Gillnet gear is limited to 90 meshes in depth
- Setnet gear cannot be more than half a mile from shore in the South Unimak District.

Figure 5.2
Steps to conserve chums in the Area M salmon fishery (Aleutians East Borough, 2001)

the seasonally imposed limits. No other salmon fishery in Alaska is under such strict regulations.

In the same context, Area M fishermen have been accused of "chum chucking" – or illegally dumping chum salmon overboard that were caught as a by-product of the sockeye fishery. Years of suspicion that these fishermen were dumping chums so that they would not reach the cap prompted law enforcement officers to dive below tenders and spy on the fleet. In 2000, state law enforcement filmed chum chucking in the Shumagin Island section of the fishery and charged three seine boats with illegal dumping; this was the first arrest on the South Alaska Peninsula despite years of complaints from both the South Peninsula fishermen and those from areas with declining chum runs on the Yukon and Kuskokwim rivers (Paulin 2000). Area M's fishermen are required by state law to keep and record all bycatch chums. The fishermen charged claimed that most of what they were pitching overboard was bycatch pollock. Hostilities abound over chum chucking, and local fishermen watch one another. Of the three fishermen arrested in 2000, two were from Sand Point and one was from Washington State. Some King Cove residents were angry that this reflects negatively on all Aleutian fishermen.

Disasters

In July 2000 then-governor Tony Knowles signed a salmon disaster declaration for the Yukon, Kuskokwim, and Norton Sound areas after their salmon returns were measured at less than 50 percent of the twenty-year historical average.[8] The disaster area comprised 620,000 square kilometres and some 80 villages along the Yukon, Kuskokwim, Koyukuk, Porcupine, and Tanana Rivers (see figure 5.1, shaded in lighter grey). Almost 30,000 people, of whom 80 percent are Alaska Natives, reside in the disaster area, where the vast majority depend on salmon for subsistence and commercial use. Knowles argued that activities in the Area M fisheries were threatening the spawning needs of western Alaska salmon and the subsistence demands of its residents. He stated, "Specifically, I am writing a letter to the State Board of Fisheries that says we must take measures before the next fishing season to stop the interceptions that threaten subsistence and spawning needs of these western Alaska stocks in the Area M fishery" (press release, Knowles, 19 July 2000). The following month he reiterated: "As governor, I have a constitutional responsibility to manage for the sustained yield of Alaska's resources and state statutes clearly make subsistence the highest priority among consumptive uses of our salmon. To provide for the conservation and subsistence needs, I am calling today for action by the State Board of Fisheries and the North Pacific Fishery Management Council to halt incidental harvest of these stocks in state and federally-managed waters" (press release, Knowles, 9 August 2000). Nowhere in the governor's numerous press releases, letters to federal and state officials, speeches, and declarations is any concern shown for Eastern Aleutian residents. They were dehumanized as "Area M," and their economic lifeblood was described as "bycatch," "interception," or "incidental harvest," without any mention of Aleut people. Most of this conflict has been mediated through state agencies with minimal Aleut-Yupiit direct interactions regarding a solution. The state, therefore, made pronouncements through "constitutional responsibility" that legitimized sentiments in Area AYK and created a negative image of Area M that was adopted across the state. In this way, it dictated truth and morality through its control of communication (Foucault 1977). Stating that Area M was responsible for the situation made Area M responsible, without consideration of its people.

Complete with fish skeleton logo, Knowles named the disaster relief effort in the AYK region "Operation Renew Hope" and appointed a disaster response chief. The operation organized relief efforts by creating government jobs in the area and sending chums caught in other parts of Alaska to some of the villages. A disaster declaration from the federal Department of Commerce prompted Knowles and state senators to try to secure additional federal funds for community assistance and for scientific research on the causes of the run failures and how to rebuild the salmon stocks. Based on previous stock identification studies, mentioned above, Knowles concluded that approximately half the king and chum salmon in Area M originate in southwest Alaska (and the rest are bound for Russia and Japan). The state's map (figure 5.1) indicating a broad swath of destruction affecting 80 villages and almost 30,000 people, is a powerful image, and is certainly no match for 2,000 Aleuts in four villages within a thin corridor on the fringes of the state.[9]

The needs in Area AYK are great; the residents are not getting the subsistence food they require. The needs of the Aleut are just as critical to their survival. It is the cause for the lack of salmon that is in dispute. Causes of crashes in salmon runs are largely unknown, but they have occurred periodically for thousands of years independent of human activity (Finney 1998).[10]

In Governor Knowles's press releases and letters, he made clear that it is "imperative that all segments of the industry share in the responsibility for conservation." Although he never acknowledged that Area M is made up of indigenous people, there is a sense that he was advocating a type of "levelling out" of the standard of living for all Alaska Natives, even if that meant lowering the standard for Aleuts to a level they had never experienced. No Aleut I spoke with

Unfair fishing restrictions destroy communities.

SAVE A WAY OF LIFE. SAVE THE AREA M FISHERY.

ALEUT COMMUNITIES FOR FAIR FISHING • KING COVE • SAND POINT • AKUTAN • COLD BAY • FALSE PASS • NELSON LAGOON

Figure 5.3
Bumper sticker distributed by the Aleutians East Borough, 2000

ever disputed the hardships faced in the greater AYK region, but they simply do not think themselves responsible.

Of particular note is the fact that Aleut fishermen often refer to themselves as Area M (see figure 5.3), just as politicians and regulators use the term broadly to designate the Aleut salmon fishery and the people. "Area M – that's what our culture is; that's all we know," said one Aleut woman.

This appeal for help would perhaps have been more effective if it had highlighted the fact that unfair fishing restrictions are destroying Aleut communities. By saying "Area M," the Aleut make use of a term which they feel is reasonably synonymous with their fishery and way of life without fully recognizing that it is loaded with negative connotations.

Closing Area M: "Genocide for Votes"

The state government's solution to the fisheries problems along the western Alaska rivers was presented as a solution to the people's social as well as economic problems. Substance abuse, family violence, sexual assault, suicide, and mental health concerns are well documented in western Alaska (Fienup-Riordan 1994; Lee 1995, 2000; Palinkas 1987; Shinkwin and Pete 1982, 1983). These "solutions" are more than an economic threat to Aleuts. The state demands that all salmon user groups share the burden of subsistence conservation; but by increasing the restrictions, it may be creating in Aleut villages the same problems (or intensifying existing ones) that have plagued western Alaska villages for decades (a subject I consider more fully in chapter 6).

The term "genocide" appeared intermittently in my conversations with Aleut fishermen:

"King Cove is dying, it's going to die. Uh – In a way it's a form of genocide, I imagine. They've taken all our resources, not allowing us to fish them, giving 'em to other people. The halibut is given to the Seattle fleet. We sit down and watch them fish all spring, bringing in load after load of halibut while we can't go and get 'em. The taking of our June fishery will be genocide, and I will call it that. (Aleut seine fisherman, October 2000)

Genocide implies deliberate attempts to annihilate the Aleut population, which I do not believe is anyone's intention. But many Aleut recognize their own vulnerability, as revealed in the following comment:

Commercial fishing has become our subsistence. It's the only thing we have. And it's slowly being taken away from us, all of it is. Not slowly, it's being taken away from us fast. They're taking that away, it's genocide. There's no other hope for us down here, there's no – there's no tourists. (Aleut seine fishermen, October 2000) (continuation of quotation introduced in chapter 3)

Aleut survival depends on a successful industry. Tourism has become critical to the economic future across the Arctic as "cultural preservation through cultural presentation" (Nuttall 1998:125, on Greenland). Nadel (1984) explores how an east coast Scottish "fishing village" which no longer fishes can maintain social identity through tourism after the basis for its existence is lost. Although ecotourism has been developing in the Pribilof Islands, where fur seals are a main attraction (Merculieff 1997), a few guided hunts in the Eastern Aleutians do not make a tourism industry. There is no main attraction. Only a few King Cove fishermen have charter licences for their boats, and even fewer are licensed to guide.

Among the Aleut seine fishermen, who have far greater expenses than gillnetters, there was a profound sense of hopelessness about the future. After a seine fisherman said he could not make his payments one year, I asked what his chances would be of recovering that payment the following year. "There's no chance whatsoever," he replied. "Probably won't even have a June season according to the governor. Without the June season there is no chance of recovering. They might as well come and take the boats right now probably.

Take our houses. Put us on the streets in Anchorage, I guess" (Aleut fisherman, October 2000).

Many King Cove fishermen expressed the feeling that their livelihood is an easy platform for politicians to campaign on without having any understanding of the needs of the Aleut people or how to manage the fisheries. For example, in discussing his feelings of uncertainty, a fisherman upgraded his emotion to anger at the thought of the politicians: "Lot of anger. There's a lot of anger in this town. Simple fact is it's all political. We're gonna lose our, our whole livelihood because somebody wants some votes. That's what really, it's not for any good reason that we're gonna be losing the – just for votes. Our whole lifestyle is gonna change because of it" (Aleut fisherman, October 2000).

Many Aleut fishermen blame the salmon conflict on the state's politicians and less on the Yupiit and Iñupiat. One fisherman indicated that the state perpetuates the animosity for its own ends:

Well, there's a lot of bad feelings about it. There's bad feelings up there [in the AYK delta]. People – It's a political deal, it's always been political. The politicians will promise to get rid of Area M fishermen to get elected, and, uh, they don't worry about our votes. There's not enough to make any difference. But they, they promise, make promises like that, they, they – The state's kept this fight alive. Politicians have. Because it is always a good vote getter. (Aleut fisherman October 2000)

It is my sense that this is fairly accurate. This particular fisheries issue has been a platform for many political campaigns in the past decade. If the last major state election is a model, Area M will continue to be used in elections.

A major factor contributing to the Aleuts' negative feelings towards the state stem from inconsistencies in harvest regulations between the two regions, which many Aleut see as unfair. Subsistence regulations, like commercial regulations, vary by region of Alaska, and although different regions may require different rules to maintain the health of marine resources and balance them with the subsisting populations, the difference in regulations between Areas AYK and M appear to be largely politically driven (illustrated in table 5.1). For Area AYK, there are fewer permit requirements, no take limits, and

Table 5.1
Subsistence regulations from Areas AYK and M

Area AYK	Area M
No subsistence permit required for any species, except in a few small sections of inland rivers	Subsistence permit required for salmon, rainbow, steelhead, halibut. No permit for other fish species.
No harvest limits set on any species	Salmon limit of 250 fish
Few time limits (only in specific districts and for one day before a commercial fishing opener)	No salmon taken within 24 hours before or 12 hours following (and within a 50-mile/80 kilometre radius) of a commercial fishing opener
Gear limits: for salmon only gillnet, beach seine, fishwheel, and rod & reel are allowed; by spear in a few areas. No gear restrictions on other fish species	Gear limits: for salmon and other fish species, only seine, gillnet, and rod & reel, or gear specified on permit allowed
No record keeping required	Record keeping required on the reverse side of the permit, to be returned 31 October to the Federal Subsistence Board

Source: Reedy-Maschner 2001:67

few time limits. For Area M, they must always have permits, they have set harvest limits and time limits, and they are required to keep records of their subsistence fish on the reverse side of their permits and to turn them back in to the state.

Most Aleuts see these regulatory differences as one more piece of evidence that they have few rights. Regulations always lead to more regulations. What is most striking is that there is no record of what fishermen in Area AYK are pulling out of the rivers, whereas most fish in the Aleut take are accounted for (except for commercial removal). A sense of unfairness is felt among both the Aleut and the Yupiit; the Aleut have been regulated to the point that they spend more time "on the beach" than on the water, and the Yupiit still are not getting the fish they need. The claims both groups have made for their own rights have selectively used state and federal language.

Aleut-Yupiit-Iñupiat Relations: "Every fishery is an intercept fishery"

"The Kuskokwim Eskimo [Yupiit] say their fish is from here," one woman told me. "How can they say that? They say 'all our fish.' I don't know how *we're* going to survive" (elder Aleut woman, October 2000).

My assessment of relations regarding the salmon wars comes mostly from fieldwork in the Aleutians, from the anthropological literature on western Alaska, and from brief trips to Bethel and Nome; thus it is not a balanced picture. Nevertheless, it is the Aleut perception of the Yupiit and Iñupiat receiving favourable treatment that fuels much of their antagonism, and this sense of unfairness has grown out of the reality that the two regions are subject to vastly different rules and regulations.

The Yupiit have long claimed the resources on a different basis than the Aleut. They have used a language of indigenous rights, that they have done the same things "since time immemorial" and hence are unassimilated, unconquered, and have the unique right to use a variety of resources in quantities and customs to which no one else is entitled (Fienup-Riordan 1990a:167–91, 2000:19). They have also used the state "Subsistence Law," which gives priority to that usage of salmon. Thus, they combine indigeneity as defined by federal Indian law with state preference for subsistence to lay their claims. The Aleut, on the other hand, do not claim indigenous rights to the fish (yet) and may have a long history of commercial production, but do not consider themselves to be transformed into assimilated producers. Rather, their traditional practices have changed and modernized, and they are one of several groups who use the resources in ways that combine customary subsistence with commercial practices. This self-evaluation has not been politically effective for the Aleut.

One King Cove woman stated, "There is more political power up north in AYK. Their voices are twice as loud, heard twice as much, and they are yelling subsistence." The Aleut could simply change their rhetoric and argue on equal grounds. A borough representative counselled a group of fishermen in the Harbor House saying, "In order to fight the Yup'iks [sic], you have to say it's affecting my culture, my whole life, like they are." Recognizing that they may have to adopt the same strategies that the Yupiit and Iñupiat employ, they are, however, arguing using the same terms even though they have different meanings. When an Aleut argues for subsistence, he or she is doing so in relation to commercial activities.

"Every fishery is an interception fishery," one Aleut elder reasoned, and salmon are always bound for somewhere else. Even on the Yukon River, villagers complain that those downstream from them are taking too many fish before they get upriver. In the 1970s,

Athapaskans in Canada's Yukon Territory protested on the basis that Alaska's Yupiit and Athapaskans were taking too many Yukon River king salmon before they reached the headwaters. Trawling and other international fishing activities out in the ocean are affecting the runs before they even begin to head back to the rivers to spawn. But maybe the activities at the other end of the migration share the burden. Aleuts perceive greater political power north in the AYK area; however, they are more economically depressed. "It's like the Third World up there," a woman said. "I saw a lot of waste in those villages," said a fisherman's wife whose husband fished out of Unalakleet, an Iñupiat village on Norton Sound. Some fishermen had the opinion that the Yupiit and Iñupiat are upset because instead of being able to catch their dog food, now they have to buy it. King Cove fishermen grumble about how careless northern fishermen are, that they are overfishing rivers, ruining spawning beds, or stripping roe, and that their villages are dirty.

These depictions, I believe, are a way for the Aleut to say, "We are not to blame for their problems." Many Aleut say that the Yupiit must take care of their own rivers and villages if they want healthy salmon stocks to return to them. The Yupiit also blame their fishing problems on the "wasteful practices of both Native and non-Native fishermen" – that salmon choose which nets to entangle themselves in based on the practices of the fishermen (Fienup-Riordan 2000:52). Chum chucking is a wasteful practice, they say, adding an accusation that Aleut fishermen are recklessly turning the fish away. "If we are being wasteful, why are salmon choosing to entangle themselves in our nets?" the Aleut ask. However, logic does not necessarily enter the discussion, since these are ideological arguments for ideological reasons. The Yupiit base their greater claim to the resources than non-Natives on their long social relationship with fish and wildlife (2000:19). The Aleut do not share these beliefs and do not often challenge non-Native fishermen's roles in fishing.

Little of what the Aleut state about Yup'ik wasteful practices is based on first-hand knowledge of their villages. The following discussion, however, is with an Aleut fisherman who visited the Yukon-Kuskokwim delta several decades ago. His comments only partially reflect past practices, not those of today.

FISHERMAN: In 1920, and before that, all the Indians in the Alask – in the Kuskokwim and the Yukon, all the Indians were starving up there because of one cannery. In 1920, I think it was '20 or '21, Congress shut down all commercial fisheries on the Yukon because of this. They didn't shut down Area M. Their fishery came back even though we weren't shut down. Historically, those rivers cannot support a commercial fishery. The State of Alaska gave them two thou, upwards of two thousand commercial fishery licences, and they wiped out their own fishery. You can't fish right on the spawning grounds of any salmon stream and hope for something to come back. This is how we all feel.

KRM: Right.

FISHERMAN: The State of Alaska still actively supports roe stripping in the Yukon. Not many people know this, but they told them, the fishermen up there, to – it's okay to take the roe if they hang the fish on the banks of the stream. Fish are hanging on the banks of the stream, they're rotting, they're not doing anything with them. Years pass, this has been going on forever.

KRM: What's the logic behind hanging the fish on the banks?

FISHERMAN: They dry 'em for using for dog food or use 'em for subsistence, for food, they can be put up for food. But, ah, all they're interested in, all the fishermen are interested in, is they can't sell the fish, the fish ain't worth nothing. The rule is so they take the roe and hang the – if Fish & Game is watching, they hang them up on the bank – let it rot, and just keep fishing, nobody taking care of it.

KRM: If Fish & Game is watching?

FISHERMAN: If the State of Alaska is watching 'em they hang it up, otherwise they'll just throw it back into the stream, and take the roe.

KRM: Uh huh.

FISHERMAN: But hanging the fish in the stream bank it – and letting 'em rot is – uh, it's – All these practices got to be stopped. Historically, those streams cannot support a commercial fishery. Not 2,000 permits anyway. How many – 200 permits in whole of the Yukon could starve the whole Yukon River, the whole length of it probably if they did it right.

KRM: So why is Area M being blamed so heavily for this, for their problems?

FISHERMAN: They see us catching fish down here and (chuckles) –

KRM: You're too prosperous?

FISHERMAN: We used to be too prosperous, not no more, we have too many restrictions. We can't make any more money. I never even been paid for my, uh, insurance on the boat this year. I never worked so hard for nothing.

This fisherman claims to understand riverine ecology and sustainability better than those who live on these rivers. He builds a conscious model of Yup'ik practices and traditions, and emphasizes the state's role.

KRM: Has Area M ever considered commercially selling roe from salmon?

FISHERMAN: We can't. There's a law against that.

KRM: Is there? Why here and not there [in AYK]?

FISHERMAN: I really don't know why we're treated different. They can sell their subsistence codfish too and we can't. It's against the law for us to sell any subsistence codfish. They say we can't even smoke it and sell it. Any part of a subsistence codfish is off limits for us selling. They sell all theirs, one hundred percent of it. The eggs, they smoke it and sell it. I really don't know what the difference is between us. They are allowed unlimited amount of chums, we're allowed 250 subsistence fish. I really don't know how unlimited it is, but one guy up there told me he has a big family and he needs 7,500 chums for every member of his family.

KRM: For each?

FISHERMAN: Each member of his family needs 7,500 chums.

KRM: My god.

FISHERMAN: Compare that to our 250 fish that we're allowed to keep and not sell ... I'm glad it's there [subsistence]. And then for somebody else says he needs 7,500 subsistence per person in his family. (*Shakes head*)

Again, this fisherman claims a direct understanding and plays up Yup'ik excesses. This is not an accurate picture of activities for AYK fishermen. However, at least a decade ago, roe from commercially caught chum salmon was sold separately and the carcasses retained for home use, but never for subsistence-taken fish (Fall, personal comm.). State regulations do not allow for the sale of subsistence fish (with a few exceptions). If the fish were caught in federally managed waters under the jurisdiction of the Federal Subsistence Board, then the regulations allow for "customary trade" that includes exchanges for cash, but they cannot be sold to a commercial enterprise.

Robert Wolfe, a former research director in Fish & Game's Subsistence Division, wrote that the state considers subsistence regulations unnecessary along the Yukon River because of low levels of demand which limits production, allowing "subsistence harvests to seek their own levels by internal mechanisms" (1984:174). Hensel demonstrates, however, that *quantity* is an important cultural marker for the Yupiit. He writes that one's Yup'ik ethnicity depends in large measure on "how ethnically marked various activities are," and that processing fish in certain ways is "more Yup'ik" than others (Hensel 2001:225). Making king salmon "blankets," for example, where they are filleted with the belly sides attached, dried and smoked, is "more Yup'ik" than making salmon strips (2001:225). Quantity is important: "Drying thousands of pounds of salmon implies its constant dietary occurrence, freezing a few is dietary dabbling in comparison" (2001:225). Thus, Yup'ik identity depends in large measure on harvest abundance and method of processing. Among the Aleut, as we have seen, this same model applies, but with the addition of commercial fisheries success. Abundant harvests are desired, and methods of harvesting are important markers of being Aleut, but they tend not to measure one another's Aleut-ness based upon their daily harvesting activities.

At a 1991 meeting on this fishery with the commissioner of the Department of Fish & Game held in Bethel, a Yup'ik elder testified:

The other thing, you know, I didn't have a chance to talk to that commissioner. You know what, you know – I've been into meetings into Anchorage, hearings [on the] False Pass [fishery]. You know, we're just little people over here, what they call us, little people. We don't have much money to flash around over there in Anchorage. The guys from down there, you know, they come in with a gold watch, gold ring, you know, and they've got vests and they walk around with a cigar in their mouths, and they – when somebody talks, people listen [to them] [BRIEF PAUSE WHILE TAPE TURNED] – hurts all of us, you know. It doesn't add up, you're not with us, you just said. You know I don't talk much, you know, when they're at a meeting, but I listen.

You – you said you're – you're not going to take some actions. But I think you know, you're talking about kids, because we don't make over five thousand dollars fishing. And those guys down there make over two to three hundred thousand dollars, you know, fishing. You know, we've got kids just like anybody else, we try to feed them. And what statements you have made, it has lots of weight to the guys that's listening here.

I know, because I work with my people for a long time. I don't – like I say, I don't say much, but I *listen*. I know what's going on. I know what kind of person, you know, when they talk, what kind of person they are. That's all I have to say. Thank you. (in Hensel 1996:169)

I have quoted him at length to give a clear sense of what the Aleut are contending with. Both the Aleut and the Yupiit use similar imagery, both claiming that the other has a stronger voice in regard to Alaskan politicians. A Nome Iñupiat, Charles Johnson, wrote a piece for Smith and McCarter's *Contested Arctic* (1997), claiming that there had been no subsistence chum harvests for the previous six years because their chum salmon are "being caught in huge nets by commercial fishermen at False Pass, and the State of Alaska Fisheries Board keeps increasing their allowable catch of chum salmon. These commercial fishermen, who are mostly from Seattle and other non-Alaskan cities, are making huge amounts of money, averaging $250,000 to $400,000 per share over the same six years that we are being denied subsistence for the sake of saving the same salmon run for the benefit of these out-of-state commercial fishermen" (Johnson 1997:6). He provides no references, and his claims are patently untrue. The Board of Fisheries has decreased the allowable chum catch over time, and the Aleut, as well as the non-Native fishermen who fish alongside them, would love to make the kind of money he claims they do. Of course, he never mentions the Aleut.

The imagery of the rich, greedy white fishermen linked to Area M is constantly being thrown up, and the Aleut have been unable to contest it in an organized, effective way. At the Board of Fisheries meetings, the Aleut witness a mobilization of symbolic resources. As one man described, Yupiit and Iñupiat often attend these meetings in traditional dress, accompanied by a language translator, while a few Aleut stand at the back of the room in their jeans and boots. The Aleut do not feel they can compete with this representation. However, their boots and raingear arguably are their "dress" as fishermen (and I suspect the Yupiit and Iñupiat dress in similar ways to go out fishing). Thus, the symbolic resources that speak volumes at the local level – boats, permits, crew organization, et cetera –

weigh against them on the global stage. All the material wealth and behaviour associated with high status in the village count against them as not being "Native enough." As one Aleut fisherman told the *Anchorage Daily News* in 1999 after Native rights attorneys sued to end their June salmon fishery, "I'm a historical person too" (in Kizzia 1999).

Anthropologists working in the Yukon-Kuskokwim Delta have been reluctant to admit that Area M consists of Native fishermen, referring to it as the "False Pass intercept fishery" (Hensel and Morrow 1998:71) or "Seattle boats" (Alaska Anthropological Association meeting, Fairbanks, 2001). Hensel recognizes the above testimony as a strategic move on the part of the elder, but adds, "It is interesting to note that the Commissioner was wearing a gold-nugget-studded watch and ring. There is at least an implication that the Commissioner's visible markers link him with the *high-volume non-Native fishermen of the False Pass area* rather than the low-volume mostly Native fishermen of the lower Kuskokwim River" (1996:172, emphasis added). Though his discourse analysis is fascinating, he misses the goal of the strategic dialogue: to "de-Native-ize" and vilify False Pass Aleut fishermen, and plea for protection of the "little people" from those allegedly immoral outsiders who dabble in being Alaskan, a type of strategic essentialism (see also Herzfeld 1996). Morrow and Hensel's article "Hidden Dissentions" (1992) is about policy negotiations between Alaska Natives and non-Natives and the construction of realities. However, they fail to mention that some of the "non-Natives" the Yupiit are engaging with are, in fact, Native Aleuts, therefore affirming the Yup'ik "reality" and taking it on as their own. Nowhere in their writings do Hensel and/or Morrow acknowledge that the majority of the fishermen of the False Pass area are Aleut. In fact the words "Aleut" or "Unangan" do not appear anywhere in their discussions. Aleut fishermen do not come to Anchorage flashing money and gold jewellery with cigars hanging out of their mouths. They do not have the ear of fisheries board members. They do not make two to three hundred thousand dollars salmon fishing.

In 2004, following testimony from those across the state, the Board of Fisheries gave Area M some relief by tripling its fishing time in June and easing some boundaries on the water. Little in the way of new information was presented on the problem of Area M and salmon runs in western Alaska, leaving me to wonder what data the board bases its decisions on. While Aleut fishermen rejoiced, thousands across the state were outraged and appealed for federal intervention into the state board's decision, but to no avail. In 2007, regulations remained largely unchanged. This buys the Aleut fishermen some time, since it is more than likely that the pendulum will swing away from them in future Board of Fisheries meetings.

Discussion

Resource rights must be understood with regard to levels of political organization in play. Federal jurisdiction allows for Alaska Native status to count with regard to subsistence claims. The state does not allow for indigenous claims on paper but seems to consider it a factor in practice. "Alaska Native" is a generic classification, and there is tremendous variation. Tradition plays different roles in different contexts. Morrow and Hensel are quite right to point out that "negotiating parties often assume contested terms represent congruent realities, and that this assumption may mask deeper cultural disagreements" (1992:38), but they left a Native party off the negotiating table.

How long must a society participate in an activity before that activity becomes traditional? Hobsbawm and Ranger (1983) might classify Aleut commercial fishing as "invented tradition," where a traceable instituted set of practices implies continuity with the past. I believe, however, that it does not matter how long traditions have been in practice; it simply matters that they are considered to be traditions, that they have significance for people's actions in the present. Maschner has archaeological evidence that the prehistoric inhabitants of the western Alaska Peninsula have been netting salmon for nearly 5,000 years (Jordan and Maschner 2000; Maschner 1998, 1999a, 1999b, 2000), which is 2,500 years earlier than any evidence for people living, let alone salmon harvesting, in the Yukon-Kuskokwim delta. Based upon current data, it is probable that the ancestors of the modern Aleut were intercepting fish long before there were Yupiit living in the delta.

Efforts to open up a dialogue have been made on both sides. In 2001 the president of the Aleutian/Pribilof Islands Association (APIA) visited the president of the Association of Village Council Presidents (AVCP, based in Bethel) in the hope of "normalizing" relations between the regions and cooperating on projects and concerns that affect both regions, "although fisheries were not a specific topic of our discussions" (Philemonof 2001).

Many different Native peoples use the same terms, but they often refer to remarkably different practices and ideas, and are often at odds with the state's definitions. "Tradition" uniquely combines subsistence and commercial economies and practice for the Aleut. "Area M" was co-opted by the Aleut as a legitimate term for their fisheries and their villages without fully realizing that it was being used as synonymous with non-Natives "stealing" the fish. The languages of identity, and the processes of how practices and beliefs take on meaning, are framed within the notion of social inequity as well as cultural essentialism on both sides of the debate. The Aleut are finding their lives construed in a market economy and a political economy in ways they did not anticipate. After calling her father in False Pass to wish him a "happy Father's Day," a young Aleut woman got a dreary fishing report from him from the first opening. Her reaction was to start drinking and call me on the phone, angry: "Those stupid people down there [Lower 48]. They don't know the difference between a dog or a red or a king. They think salmon is salmon. They're so stupid! Don't they know that we only like the dogs [chum salmon] for their heads and that we eat them raw?! Don't they know that?! Down there they pay what? Seven dollars a pound? And we only get 50 cents? That's fucked up! Who's making all this money off of us?" (young Aleut woman, King Cove, July 2002).

Economic prosperity is crucial to the Eastern Aleut, but the prestige and the rights attached to the fisheries are valued even more. To buffer against the social and economic losses resulting from the shrinking salmon fisheries, groundfish harvesting is becoming crucial to Aleut fishermen. But as we shall see in the following section, turning to these fisheries has its own difficulties.

Rarely is the nature of competition and conflict among and between Alaska Natives explored. I have looked at ethnicity and identity with reference to various perceptions from others. The ways in which the Aleut are positioned is logically contradictory, but no one is clear about what categories they are using. The Aleut have been eclipsed; they are very much a part of the fishery and the landscape, but they have been made invisible by processes larger than themselves.

THE OCEAN'S *POSSE COMITATUS* AND FISHERMEN UNDER "HOUSE ARREST"

The clash of an Aleut grassroots cultural movement claiming rights to "their culture" with a powerful, wealthy international environmental movement expressing grievances in the courts was set in motion in 1998. That year, Greenpeace, the Sierra Club, and the American Oceans Campaign sued the National Marine Fisheries Service (NMFS) to limit groundfish trawling in the Bering Sea and Gulf of Alaska in order to protect the habitat of the endangered Steller sea lion that live along the North Pacific Rim. The sea lion population fell 80 percent in the 1970s, 1980s, and early 1990s, and the western stock was listed as endangered in 1997 (National Research Council 2003). This decline was blamed on trawlers over-harvesting cod and pollock, their primary food. NMFS's Office of Protected Species was found to have a legally inadequate "biological opinion" defining the effects of groundfish fisheries on the sea lion and its habitat. The environmentalists' targets were factory trawlers, massive vessels that drag the ocean's floor with mile-long nets taking everything in their path. Environmental groups cast these trawlers as high-seas pirates, raping and pillaging the sea, hiding their identities, sneaking from port to port, and flagging their vessels in countries that do not follow international regulations (Stump and Baker 1996).

Ironically, factory trawlers have scarcely been affected by the  bans; it is the local Alaskan communities that have become the "first casualties" of their campaign (Waller 1996:124). These small-boat fishermen also agree that the "global sea monsters" are overfishing, harming the oceans, and contributing to the sea lion's decline in great numbers. As described in chapter 3, the Alaska Peninsula's fishermen have become increasingly dependent on groundfish fisheries because of the volatility of the salmon industry and the shrinking crab fisheries. Large areas of the Aleut traditional fishing grounds were made off-limits in hopes that sea lion would recover.

The decline of the Steller sea lion is considered to be a commercial fishery issue, not one of community or cultural survival, and

Figure 5.4
Sticker attached to a seiner's wheelhouse, King Cove harbour

continues to ignore the fact that indigenous peoples *are* commercial fishermen. To NMFS, one Aleut girl wrote, "Yes, the Stellar [sic] sea lions are endangered, but if you take away our fisheries, we will be endangered too." The parties of the lawsuit, the environmentalists and NMFS, neglected to involve the thousands of people who spend extraordinary amounts of time in their boats on the water in either the formulation of policies or the solutions to the perceived Steller sea lion crisis. Aleut fishermen have a wealth of knowledge on predator-prey relationships, population changes, and environmental factors. Given a species that is difficult to monitor, folk knowledge is perhaps most valuable in assessing its population and behaviour, and local input in the original drafting of the "biological opinion" might have made it a more robust document. One fisherman asked, "How can they count all the sea lions in one day on a coastline of 1,500 miles or more? Sea lions migrate to follow their food just like a fisherman has to." Greenpeace's report on factory trawlers and the Steller sea lion points the finger at "intensive" commercial fishing but makes no mention of local people (Stump and Baker 1996).

Historically, the Aleut hunted sea lions for their meat, blubber, and oil, their bones and teeth for tools, sinew for cordage, flippers for boot soles, whiskers for adorning hunting visors, internal organs for waterproof clothing, and skins for covering their baidarkas. Today, sea lions have no immediate sociocultural or economic value in Eastern Aleut villages, and most fishermen agree that they are pests. They follow boats and get tangled in the nets. "They can pick fish faster than I can. Now they are protected," said one man with sarcasm. Some even joked about writing a sea lion cookbook.[11] Since 1986, the Endangered Species Act has prevented the harvest of the Steller sea lion. However, as Native Alaskans, the Aleut can legally subsistence harvest sea lions, and a few were taken in 2002, but most Aleut do not hunt them and voluntarily take measures to avoid them. As one fishermen determined:

FISHERMAN: No, eliminating us ain't gonna help the sea lion. If they want to help the sea lion they're gonna have to thin that killer whale but the killer whale is out.

KRM: Are they starving too, the killer whales?

FISHERMAN: I don't think so. They're eating whales, sea lions, seals and otters. The otter on the Aleutian Islands I figure will go on the, on the list next ... Because of the killer whales. That's documented ... And, uh, sea lions is documented too but you can't bring it up. Nobody will listen to you at a meeting about it. National Marine Fisheries won't listen to it. They're afraid of the environmentalists. Environmentalists will walk out if you show pictures of killer whales killing sea lions. We got movie pictures of it happening, and they will not watch it. Their, their answer to everything is to eliminate the fisherman.

KRM: Have environmentalists ever come out here to talk to you at all?

FISHERMAN: Yeah, we've had 'em and uh ... they said that they weren't interested in hurting small boat fisheries and all that there, but the very next year they push them all twenty miles offshore. No small boat fishery in the months of January, February and March has any business being twenty miles offshore.

KRM: Because it's too dangerous?

FISHERMAN: Dangerous. Icy. Weather? You could have flat calm weather in one minute and five minutes later it could be blowing a hundred north, northerly, and you're taking ice and if you're twenty miles offshore you are not making it back to shore.

Starting in 2002, all vessels in Area M are required to participate in the Vessel Monitoring System (VMS) to ensure that fishermen do not go near the Steller sea lion grounds. As another "emergency rule" issued by NMFS, any vessel that fishes the federal halibut, sablefish, or groundfish fisheries must carry VMS equipment. Even if fishermen are not fishing the pollock, cod, or Atka mackerel openings, they must have the VMS equipment on board and running. The system costs $2,000, and people are required to pay up front and get reimbursed. Once installed, it costs $5 per day to run, which the fishermen are responsible for. "It's like one of those ankle bracelets," several fishermen argued. "Like we're all under house arrest."

A similar case for protection is now being made for the threatened Steller's eider. Again, in the onslaught of environmentalists waving the Endangered Species Act, Aleut-Yupiit relations have come into conflict. The Yupiit, who live near the eider's nesting grounds, are accused of overharvesting the eggs:

KRM: What do you think about the eider issue coming up?
FISHERMAN: Steller eiders are doing great down here. They don't need to consider critical habitat down here, they're doing great. I guess the ones that were doing great are Russian nesting eider, but the only ones not doing great is the Alaska nesting eider. As far as I'm concerned, they can look up there where they're nesting.
KRM: Up north.
FISHERMAN: (Nods) Find out what's happening to those eggs. It all comes down to eggs. The Steller eider eggs, chum eggs ...

The next species due for listing as endangered are the sea otter, spearheaded by the US Fish & Wildlife Service (USFWS 2001), and gorgonian coral (Calcigorgia spiculifera) (Oceana and The Ocean Conservancy 2003),[12] identified throughout the Aleutian region as threatened by fishing and for which the fishermen have no defence. A federal employee recently confessed to an Aleut leader that the long-term goal of Fish & Wildlife is to depopulate the Aleutians through regulation and designate the islands and western peninsula as wilderness. The creation of the Aleut Marine Mammal Commission (AMMC) in 1998 was an indigenous effort to challenge many of the claims made on these species and to open up a dialogue between the Aleut, environmentalists, biologists, and agency representatives.

The Aleut Marine Mammal Commission

Many arctic anthropologists focus on the symbolism and meaning of subsistence hunting and fishing to arctic peoples and relationships with the environment, animals, and one another. These approaches emphasize the complex connections between human and environment, culture, social life, kinship, ritual and symbolism, sharing and reciprocity, among others (e.g., Bodenhorn 1989, 1997; Fienup-Riordan 1983b; Nuttall 1992; Riches 1982). Some anthropologists and their informants feel that quantifying these data underestimates the meanings and connections inherent in these processes and ignores people's conceptions of their own environment. A large number of harvesting studies and surveys – for example, those of Fish & Game, US Fish & Wildlife Service, and Minerals Management Service – do not include symbolism and include only quantifiable data. But while the symbolic and cultural importance of hunting and fishing must not be downplayed, indigenous peoples, particularly the Aleut, are beginning to recognize that this is not enough to combat threats to cultural survival. They need to quantify in the particular political environment in order for their voices to carry. They have to fight numbers with numbers in order to be part of the discussion at all.

This is a double-edged sword of sorts. Quantified data are often taken as facts and are used to define the limits of need and over-harvesting; the effect may be to restrict the choices people can make. Modelling the moment, on the other hand, is certainly more accurate, but it is probably less useful in political or policy discussions. Documenting frequency and sharing between communities and households is quantification of a sort, but it more accurately captures the relationships in sharing and is not about balancing quantifiable amounts of wild food (Bodenhorn 2000). The process of conceptualizing their position in terms of numbers has been a political one. Village leaders have told me that in other smaller villages they made it community policy to inflate their subsistence numbers in surveys to indicate that they harvested the limit in all species, whether they did so or not, for fear that they might lose access.

The Aleut have struggled for how to include their voices in decision-making processes with regard to their natural environment. They launched a grassroots campaign with letters from both adults and children in the villages going to the Alaska Congressional Delegation and NMFS, pleading for NMFS to get into compliance with the Endangered Species Act while still allowing them to fish. Children were called upon in schools to participate in this campaign. Girls wrote statements such as, "By closing pollock they are putting the City of King Cove on the endangered list" and "I don't know much about fishing but I know if you close fishing, I will be forsed [sic] to leve [sic] my home and my friends." Teenage boys began almost every letter with, "I am a fisherman and ... " They attended meeting after meeting and gave testimonials. They even checked for whether they themselves met the threatened or endangered criteria for listing under the Endangered Species Act![13]

The Aleut Marine Mammal Commission (AMMC) was formed in 1998 at the instigation of local tribal councils as a regional entity that gives a voice to Aleut communities in the management of marine mammals and the authority to work with NMFS and other agencies on the policies of these resources.[14] This commission is patterned after the Alaska Eskimo Whaling Commission (AEWC) and the Alaska Beluga Whale Committee (ABWC) that represent whaling communities and work with management agencies to ensure the continuation of subsistence whale hunting and the survival of arctic communities that depend upon these resources (Huntington 1989, 1992). These organizations have taken an active role in the scientific process for protecting habitats, and they exercise authority in political matters as part of the regional federally recognized tribal council. The AMMC differs from these organizations in that it has equal interest in protecting their commercial activities as it does their subsistence ones.

The commission obtained grant money to gather and disseminate information on subsistence harvests of the sea lion and supplement ongoing research efforts. Non-Native scientists need the subsistence harvesters for their biological research because they do not have the permit authority to take sea lions. The commission facilitates this collaboration and aids in the training of hunters to collect biological samples.

NMFS had in effect told the Aleut that their local observations of species abundance and behaviour, their indigenous knowledge of ocean cycles, and their local perspective on the causes and consequences of the decline of certain species were anecdotal and hence useless to them. Recognizing the need to speak in the language of science in order to be heard at all, the Aleut have hired those with the skills to train local people to collect local knowledge of sea mammals and translate those data into scientific form. As one fisherman assessed:

> They're starving to death. The killer whales are taking 'em. Too
> many Free Willys left in the world to do anything about the killer
> whale. So the sea lion will continue to decline. Sea lions used to
> travel, or be out, wherever we fished. They used to come out,
> and especially gillnet, you know, they'd take and rip big holes.
> There was a big conflict with them with gillnetters. But now the
> sea lion is scared to come off the beach. You never see them more
> than twenty feet from the shoreline because of killer whales.
> We'd never see sea lions, when there were hundreds of thousands
> of sea lions, we'd never seen them in, uh, in the bays eating, or
> in the harbours eating from fishermen on a boat. Never have
> we seen it. They're coming in now trying to keep away from
> the sea lions, er killer whales. They're hauling themselves up on
> the floats. Every time a sea lion tries to leave the shoreline, he
> gets ate. So they're starving to death from that. Until National
> Marine Fisheries and environmentalists want to go do something
> about the killer whales, they are not being serious about doing
> anything for the sea lions.

In a five-part series published in the *Sacremento Bee* in 2002, reporter Tom Knudson argued that environmental organizations are "money machines," depending on steady recruitment of new members and maintaining a "constant sense of crisis" (Knudson 2002). He found that environmental groups spend half of their raised funds on overhead and more fundraising. They rely on "poster species," like the Steller sea lion, to spark emotion in new recruits and hold on to their membership. In their multitude of lawsuits, they "force judges to act as biologists," as summarized by the editor of *National Fishermen* (Fraser 2002:4). Of course, journalists themselves fuel this kind of narrative (discussed in Cronon 1996; Milton 1993, 1996); however, Milton Freeman has shown that urban-based organizations' attacks on northern peoples are marked by "widespread ignorance" of their lifestyles and realities (1997:8-9).

In 2001 Herbert Maschner presented data on spatial and temporal variations in Steller sea lion distribution in the Eastern Aleutians to the Ocean Studies and Polar Research Boards of the National Academy of Sciences in Seattle. He argued, in effect, that there has never been a time on the North Pacific when humans were not impacting the landscape and natural resources. That is, as soon as the glacial ice retreated, the Aleut and the animals colonized the North Pacific and southern Bering Sea at the same time, and therefore the Aleut should be considered part of the ecosystem. A representative from NMFS stated, "Fortunately for us the Endangered Species Act does not require that we take into account indigenous peoples." Indigenous peoples are not accorded any rights, regardless of their history or position on the landscape.

In January 2003 the Ocean Studies and Polar Research Boards released their report on the findings of nearly $87 million in research funds allocated to determine the effects of the pollock and cod fisheries on the Steller sea lion (National Research Council 2003). The report found that these fisheries were having little effect on sea lions but that Orca predation, illegal hunting, and predator-prey relations were credible causes of the decline, something the Aleut had tried to tell them before they spent millions. One finding of the report was the need to make use of local indigenous observers (2003:154).

There is a sense that organizations such as the AMMC meet federal obligations to "hear" local people, and that the Aleut can no longer complain because they have been given a forum in which to communicate with NMFS. Wildlife co-management regimes theoretically include indigenous people in environmental management and conservation. Indigenous peoples provide TEK, traditional ecological knowledge, defined as "a cumulative body of knowledge, practice and belief, evolving by adaptive processes and handed down through generations by cultural transmission, about the relationship of living beings (including humans) with one another and with the environment" (Berkes 1999:8). TEK was originally regarded as "savage science," or based upon primitive irrational thought, and it was never actually included in scientific environmental management. Many anthropological studies in the past few decades (e.g., Agrawal and Gibson 2001; Berkes 1999; Bielawski 1992; Collings 1997a, 1997b; Fischer 2000; Freeman 1993, 1998; Stevens 1997) have shown that TEK provides important insights into natural phenomena but also that such insights regard humans as a part of nature. Rather than scolding the sciences for not including their data, the Aleut are asking how they could translate their knowledge into a form that is recognizable to modern science so that resource managers, scientists, and the Aleut can use it.[15]

"Management" of the environment and its resources is an absurd concept to many Aleutian fishermen. "The weather changes, one species will go and another will come back," said a village elder. "It has little to do with humans." Lydia Black indicated that the Aleut word for codfish translates as "the fish that stops," meaning it periodically disappears (1981:332). Many contend that state and federal regulations imposed on fishing and subsistence activities seem to follow no logic or awareness of what really affect different species. "Environmentalist" is a bad word, and most Aleut spit it out as if they have an awful taste in their mouths. "They won't listen to old timers, only to people with alphabets at the ends of their names." Regime shifts and ocean cycles are generally known by "old timers" but have yet to be incorporated into scientific decision-making processes.

The Aleut have to fight to be recognized: first as indigenous people, second as legitimate commercial fishermen, and third as a part of their own environment, possessing knowledge within it. Environmental organizations use Native peoples when their activities further the environmental agenda and deny their rights or existence when they do not (e.g., Stump and Baker 1996; Waller 1996). The Aleut recognize that commercial fishing is the only way they can continue to live successfully in their homeland, and therefore what might be considered Aleut conservation has merged with commercial fishermen's conservation and is thus in conflict with environmental agendas that tend either to uphold imagined Native principles of care (sustainability) or to eclipse humans from the landscape. Consequently, a history of fishing restrictions has edged out the next generation of Aleut fishermen, and they now must moonlight as politicians to argue for their existence.

RELUCTANT POLITICIANS

In these two ongoing struggles, political demands on the Aleut are growing. The majority of Aleut rely on the articulations of a few to speak for all. Alaska is overrun with acronyms (see appendix B). The Eastern Aleut have a plethora of political, social, and economic organizations to contend with, so many that it is daunting for most people. "We have trouble getting men to talk," said a woman who manages her family's fisheries corporation. Women stand at the political foreground because they do not fish and have the freedom to travel to Anchorage for meetings when the men must fish. For some of these women, there is a fearless way in which they attack political disputes. "It's 'cause I don't know any better so I don't get intimidated," said one woman. Meetings often coincide with fishing seasons. "Send your wives if you can't go [to testify at the Board of Fisheries meeting]," pleaded a borough representative. "At these meetings there is usually a lot of Yup'iks [sic] in their traditional clothes with a language translator and then maybe five Aleuts standing in the back." Women still choose their battles based on what their husbands, fathers, uncles, and grandfathers want and need.

The Aleut have an historical claim to fish as much as any other Alaska Native group, and perhaps they have a greater claim to fish commercially given their historical role in global economics, but that may mean little in today's political climate. Fishermen in King Cove are used to having to defend their right to fish but have yet to exercise "tribal rights" or to try to block non-Natives from fishing alongside them (in Kizzia 1999). Fishermen are reluctant to encourage their children to stay on and try to make the same living, but they also realize that their homes and villages will disappear if they do not.

Indigenous peoples worldwide have survived attempts to make them disappear through policy, assimilation, and genocide (Perry 1996). Bureaucracies are able to reflect what they want and not the reality. One way to increase global awareness is through the creation of indigenous political organizations. Aleuts are only marginal members of Native American and arctic NGOs designed to advance the goals of arctic peoples, whatever those might be. Their position in the Alaska Federation of Natives, which is meant to represent concerns of Alaska Natives before Congress and the state legislature, has been limited, partly because of the small Aleut population (Damas 1984). The Arctic Council, meant to provide a "northern voice," was criticized by Aleuts as "hardly representative," since they "don't have a voice" in the council (Lekanof in Tennberg 1996). With the formation of the Aleut International Association (AIA) in 1998, a pan-Aleut organization meant to protect the natural resources and the environment of the Aleut homeland, they became members of the Arctic Council, though the benefits of that are unclear. They are not considered to be "subarctic" peoples because that has become synonymous with Athapaskans, but their position as "arctic" peoples has also been disputed because they are geographically on the fringes. In short, their status is ambivalent, and they have not conjoined with larger organizations to affect national and international processes.

Within the state, political power is skewed away from the region at the outset. The senator for the Aleutian region is from Bethel, the hub village of the Yup'ik region. Area M fishermen have virtually no voting power in the state and make up a small percentage of the voters in their own House and Senate districts (CFEC Election District Reports). It is difficult to exercise block power because of their small population, and when mixed with Unalaska and Bethel, the Eastern Aleut disappear.

Local *perceptions* of many national and international events as bearing directly on the activities of the Aleut is often overstated, but they are very real nonetheless. For example, between 2000 and 2003, Aleut fishermen stated, "If Bush hadn't been elected, I *know* we wouldn't be fishing now" ... "The U.S. Government has never run a fishery that they didn't completely destroy. Big U.S. catcher-processors, they tell Congress what they want, Congress gives them the fish and they kill it off. They killed off this area with traps. It took twenty years to rebuild" ... "One little island nation [Japan] sets the price for every fish in every ocean of the world."

The recession in Japan, which is Alaska's major foreign market, has affected them overseas, while the salmon farms in Norway, Chile, and Canada have pushed them to the outer reaches of the domestic market. The Magnusen-Stevens Fishery Conservation and Management Act (1996) bans the authorization of foreign-based processors in state waters even though many Alaska fishermen have lost their market. Shore-based foreign processors seem to be exempt from this act, since Peter Pan Seafoods is Japanese-owned. Several fishermen thought that the sinking of the Japanese trawler *Ehime Maru* near Hawaii in 2001, in which a U.S. attack submarine surfaced and collided with the vessel and killed several of the crew, could affect the price of fish.

One way the state has attempted to pacify the Aleut voice is through what many local people are calling hush money: "The state is encouraging us to build roads, to pave, new bridge. They are trying to kill this town and trying to fix it up at the same time. The left hand doesn't know what the right hand's doing" (fisherman, King Cove, June 2002). Despite the erosion of the fisheries, King Cove's infrastructure has seen improvements. The city, tribal council, and corporation actively attracted grants for a variety of projects, but there is also a sense that the state has been so generous in order to ease the pain of rescinding fishing opportunities. In 2002 the new health clinic was completed, a new bridge to the harbour was put in, the road to the airport was under construction, a second harbour for large boats had been recently completed, plans for paving several roads were underway, and windows and siding were replaced on most homes. The projects also allowed crewmen to gain temporary land jobs in the hope of better fishing opportunities in the future.

LOOKING FORWARD

The Aleut have met opposition to their way of life on every front, from the governor's failure to consider the impact of his recommendations on Area M's people to the Native American Rights Fund's apparent neglect of Aleut Native-ness when defending Yup'ik or Iñupiat villages' attempts to block the June fishery in the 1990s (www.narf.org).[16] Economists have tried to predict the future impact of fisheries closures on Eastern Aleutian communities, forecasting bankruptcies and the loss of boats and permits (Braund et al. 1986; Northern Economics 2000), not to mention the social ramifications of closures. The state would also lose fisheries revenues and have another disaster area to contend with. There is no evidence that closing Area M's fisheries would have any positive benefit for the AYK subsistence fishery, since the restrictions already in place on Area M fishermen have done nothing to improve these stocks.

Under all this political weight, we might expect the Eastern Aleut to start innovating and broaden their economic options. This has not happened, but it is not because of lack of creativity on their part. Some have obtained licences to lead guided hunts and to charter their boats. Some specialize in boat building and repair, while others manage stores and bars. Several have diversified their fishing support to haul and store crab pots, nets, and other equipment. Others lend logistical support to archaeologists. However, all of these activities depend on the ability of residents to fish, and thus economic diversification is realistically limited to some relationship to the fisheries.

Dependence on foreign-owned canneries made the nearby Aleut village of False Pass nervous enough to build its own cooperative cannery. As part of the Aleutian Pribilof Islands Community Development Association (APICDA), Bering Pacific Seafoods opened in 2000. Sadly, it struggled from the start. In 2001 it honoured the strike during the salmon season (see chapter 3), and in consequence it did not make enough money to keep operating and was forced to close down and lay everyone off. This facility reopened in 2008 and 2009.

For saving the salmon fisheries, fleet reduction seems to be the favoured strategy of the state, masked as reducing harvest costs. The state advocates a series of steps, which include harvest cooperatives that would use less capital and less labour, permit-stacking alternatives (a voluntary consolidation program where more than one permit can be attached to a vessel with all or part of the limits of each permit), and permit buyback programs. All such proposed solutions result in fewer people fishing and fewer boats on the water. Recent talks have surfaced in King Cove for the potential of a harvest cooperative, where salmon fishermen save expenses and share profits by designating some members to fish on behalf of the entire group. The intent would be to safeguard individual fishermen against the vulnerability of the business. Some have grumbled that this is "communism," but others consider it a viable option in the future though perhaps a last resort, since it would mean "sitting on the beach" for so many. In 2002, seventy-seven Chignik seine fishermen developed a cooperative approved by the Board of Fisheries. An open, competitive fishery also occurred among twenty-two fishermen who did not want to participate. The cooperative fishery had mixed results and mixed emotions about its success, with many who "missed fishing" (CFEC Report 02-6N; Knapp et al. 2002). My own prediction, based on conversations with Aleut fishermen both for and against a cooperative, is that it would be a disastrous alternative. Negotiating the "open fishery" is part of their identity and status, and social problems within King Cove are blamed on fishermen not being able to "keep our nets in the water." Fishermen forced to watch others make their living for them, since the Board of Fisheries prohibits them from fishing other salmon fisheries (though they may be free to participate in other fisheries), might feed animosity, jealousy, boredom, and low self-esteem. The cooperative could, however, operate on a rotation basis from season to season.

The future of Alaska's wild salmon market is uncertain (Knapp 2000). Alaska's former lieutenant governor, Fran Ulmer, stated at a 24 August 2001 press teleconference that the cause of crashing salmon markets is "well known": farmed salmon from Chile, Canada, and Norway have displaced traditional markets in Alaska's wild salmon, flooding the market and driving down prices. She declared an economic disaster again for 2001, extending coverage to Bristol Bay and the Aleutians East Borough. Still considered Operation Renew Hope, the declaration itself did not trigger the release of any funds to the region covered. Instead, the governor wrote to President Bush requesting federal funds. The state intended to pursue needed research linking local people's knowledge with science and is seeking ways to improve market conditions. Operation Renew Hope continued with job training, Low Income Home Energy Assistance programs, and strategizing for the future.

The "catch-process-market-consume!" cycle that seems to characterize commercial fisheries is no longer sustainable, and many Aleut fishermen are discussing further changes within the industry. For example:

We'll have to fish differently, not getting mass volumes of fish. We'll be getting fewer fish and taking better care of them. We'll still need volume for pinks and chums, can't do nothing with them except put them in a can, but not the rest. (June 2003)

The Japs are broke, they're buying cheap fish. We can't sell to a Jap outfit no more. The Borough needs to do like Prince William Sound and get a market. The market can't be a broke country. I'd rather see them [Peter Pan] give up. I'd rather start World War III with the Japs than give them free fish. (June 2003)

Salmon prices will come up, I think. They have to. (June 2003)

Despite an uncertain future, King Cove expanded its harbour to provide protected moorage for 48 large fishing vessels of between 25 and 50 metres. The hope is for King Cove to become a central port for the Gulf of Alaska and Bering Sea. One man predicted that fishing will not disappear entirely, but it could easily be limited to sport fishing and ecotourism.

Foreign-farmed salmon is indeed forcing change in the Alaskan industry. A visit to a Chilean operation by Aleutians East Borough representatives found it to be such an advanced system of raising and processing fish that Alaska's canneries would have to completely retool in order to compete. Much of the processing plants are automated, so they do not have to hire a large labour force, and they are highly sanitary where labourers wear lab coats, gloves, and

masks. The highest grade of fish is sent overnight to high-end restaurants around the world.[17] Major drawbacks of salmon farms are
both environmental and economic, including the growing recognition that the farms are producing fatty fish using vitamin injections
and dyes, releasing diseases to wild stocks, and polluting the waters
around the farms (Barcott 2001; Montaigne 2003).

North Pacific fishermen must contend with the growing world
market of fishing. Fish can be purchased from all over the world
today, not just from local regions. Consumers and restaurants also
focus on fish that are trendy to eat (for example, orange roughy was
popular in the 1980s but not today, and grouper is now a popular
fish in restaurants but was virtually unheard of fifteen years ago).

The Aleutians East Borough developed its own marketing scheme
emphasizing a regional brand of fish called Aleutia in 2002. In partnership with the Alaska Fisheries Development Foundation (AFDF),
Trident Seafoods Corporation, and Orca Bay Foods, Inc., the foundation buys the highest-quality[18] sockeye salmon at about 95 cents
per pound from participating fishermen, more than double what the
canneries offered in 2002. Customers specify the type of fish and
amount that they want before the fish is caught. Trident, located
in Sand Point, receives about $1.60 per finished pound of fish and
keeps the roe as trade for part of the custom processing. Orca Bay
Seafoods is also buying bycatch coho from the red salmon fishery.
However, moving fish on ice from the Alaska Peninsula to market in
the Lower 48 is very expensive, most of the cost being between Sand
Point and Anchorage (ADN 2003).

Regional product differentiation is "more than slapping a cute
sticker on it and sending it away" (Jones in ADN 2003). Aleutia pro-
moters hired third-party inspectors to certify the quality of fish at all
stages: from catch to processing to transport to market, using new
language like "Give the customer what they want." It is only recently
that Eastern Aleut fishermen have concerned themselves with what
happens to the fish once they sell it, since it is the fishing more than
the fish that drives social and cultural dynamics. This new marketing plan will profoundly alter the ways in which Aleut fishermen
actually fish.[19]

CONCLUSION

The majority of Aleut see levels of government, policymakers, and
environmentalists as competing interest groups. Salmon are valuable

resources, not only for the state's revenues but also for the satisfaction and health of Native peoples. A precedent of dehumanization and ignorance set by anthropologists and bureaucrats facilitated the Steller sea lion campaign against North Pacific fishermen, giving them an easy forum to tug at the heartstrings of urban environmentalists on behalf of an understudied species. Governments and NGOs are easily swayed by the notion of the "traditional." In the case of Federal Indian Law, indigeneity does not depend upon traditional behaviour, and the Aleut have not asserted rights based upon indigeneity. The reality, however, seems to be that the more "indigenous" people seem, the more comfortable governments and agencies feel in giving them certain rights. The Aleut have been made to "disappear" in these political processes but have nevertheless attempted to gain a political voice, with mixed outcomes.

It could be argued that much of the Native Arctic is in a debate over whose culture is the most ruined just as much as in the debate about whose culture is the most intact. The development of the commercial fisheries was uneven across Alaska, and the Aleut homeland has a geographic advantage because it is within both the oceanic and riverine environments used by salmon. Though "ethnic revival" is too strong a concept here, Smith's definition of its significance – that "it is at one and the same time an attempt to preserve the past, and to transform it into something new, to create a new type upon ancient foundations, to create a new man and society through the revival of old identities and preservation of the 'links in the chain' of generations" (1981:25) – does apply. Richard Daly gave comprehensive expert testimony in the landmark Delgamuukw case in British Columbia, in which he worked with the Gitksan and Wit'suwit'en to document and validate two cultures for the court, and legally prove they were still indigenous people in the modern world and deserved self-governance and land ownership. This testimony failed to persuade the judge, in part because Daly's descriptions of the cultural matrices were complex and fluid. Since that time, First Nations peoples have simplified and reified sociocultural practices so that they can be understood by the courts. The Aleut may have to essentialize themselves, that is, to pluck some aspects out of their cultural matrix to uphold as icons.

But as Shore (1996:9) argues, "Ironically, at the very moment that many ethnic groups have turned to identity politics and highly essentialized notions of culture as ideological supports for their own autonomy and authenticity, many anthropologists have abandoned the culture concept altogether as too essentialist, preferring the more politically and historically charged concepts of discourse, interest and strategy" (see also Baumann 1996; Cowan, Dembour and Wilson 2001). This is an approach that contributes directly to a loss of indigenous community identity and political power. Wachowich's (2001) study of identity construction among the Inuit of Nunavut via representational media and outside attempts to document their "traditional culture" found that Inuit engagement with outsiders is itself a form of subsistence that supports traditional hunting through well-funded projects. Inuit, she argues, use idealized iconic categories of their own identity to "produce" traditions and reap social, political, and economic benefits, what Myers calls "culture making" (Myers 1994:680, discussed in Wachowich 2001:12). To maintain their roles as fishermen, the Aleut are at a similar juncture where they must develop cultural icons and "market cultural representations on a global stage" (2001:ii) to be part of the dialogue on their own future.

The Aleut have lived through millennia with a distinct ethnicity and culture in relative geographic isolation. They have integrated ethnic multiplicity and have shaped the modernization of their communities. Aleut survival has been challenged throughout history, but current circumstances and conflict have triggered a heightened awareness of identity, ethnicity, and culture, and an awareness that their continued existence may depend upon how these elements are perceived by the world. This is just as much a "hunt for identity" (Rasing 1994) as it is fishing for food, for social cohesion, and ethnic survival. Environmental organizations like Greenpeace also used the rhetoric of the national interest, arguing that saving the ecosystem is for the wealth of the nation. Their preservationist mindset removes humans from the environment while stating that humanity (a nebulous group rarely defined, but seemingly excluding indigenous or rural people) needs wilderness and animals. The Aleut have been making meaning for one another through action and interaction, but now they have to make meaning for a heterogeneous other that seeks to overwhelm them and discursively erase them from the landscape. Throughout the salmon wars and the environmental campaigns, the Aleut have continually engaged themselves in the debates, though in small numbers. In this process, they have become painfully aware that not only do the opposing representatives have little understanding of who they are, but they seem not to know why Aleuts are even at the table.

Social science has the potential to play a significant role in commercial fisheries management, but thus far in this context it has been an afterthought without provision for its meaningful inclusion in decision-making processes. Although all federal agencies signed a document that compels them to contact local communities before a project is considered, let alone carried out, and to discuss all potential impacts with them, this rarely happens.[20] This neglect is deliberate, I believe, in the concern that local people might introduce information that would destabilize a growing trend or perception. The Aleut are by no means "natural conservationists," but they do have a strong attachment to landscape and the ecosystem. Debates in the Aleutians are beginning to resemble Freeman and Kreuter's (1995) discussion of whales in the High Arctic, where resources take on an iconic mode and represent something more than food.

Throughout these processes, sets of rules have been created that the Eastern Aleut must live by but have little control over. The following chapter considers Aleut behaviour within the local as well as larger structures of power. If fishermen do not own or influence decision-making processes that have direct bearing on their daily activities, they may be reluctant to comply with the rules.

6

Disenfranchised Aleuts

ALEUT IDENTITY IN THE FACE OF SOCIOECONOMIC
VULNERABILITY

"There was a hole in my heart watching the fleet go out without me," said a seiner over coffee on the day of the first June opening. He had fished every year of his life, ending in that summer of 2002 when his stepson ran his boat with his own permit. In uttering these words, he appeared at once frustrated, angry, nostalgic, worried, and sad. Life as he knew it was changing. He was losing his foothold in fishing and his identity as a first-rate seiner as a result of low fish prices and short openers. Fishing is the only thing he had learned to do.

Crises of resource depletion and resource access have daily consequences for the Aleut. The fishing franchise, upon which the foundations of much of their understanding are built, and through which they interact, communicate, share, and make meaning, is in many respects in danger of disappearing. This chapter attempts to answer the big questions that have been asked all along: What are the consequences to individuals and villages if the commercial fisheries are no longer accessible? What are the prospects for sociocultural or economic retention and recovery? What happens when the socioeconomic lifeblood of one Native group is removed in order to preserve the subsistence lifeblood of another though both are crucial to both societies? As I have shown in the previous chapter, the conflict is not defined as one between groups; it is one in which there are many players with multiple agendas, and taking from one group will not necessarily solve the problems of the other.

As we have seen, fishing is a communal activity that binds the village together while allowing for individual striving and self-expression. Men have tremendous responsibilities and expectations placed upon them while more often than not being structurally denied opportunities to fulfill those expectations. Interpersonal stresses, openly blamed on fishing crises, seem to manifest themselves as alcohol use and abuse, family violence, petty crime, and mischief. A woman in False Pass once told me, "When fishing is good they [the fishermen] have pride and spend their money on themselves and toys for their kids. If the fishing is bad, they spend it on alcohol and waste away." In the absence of fishing, many Aleut face a loss of community and culture and must confront a world outside fishing, outside the village, which they do not fully understand and sometimes fear. Here, I evaluate their own hypothesis: the fewer people allowed to fish commercially (due to a whole host of reasons), the greater the problems within the community. I consider whether losing this crucial source of status has a measurable social effect on the community.

The argument has been put forth time and again that the roles and ideals of the dominant society (mainstream America) are being imposed upon Native Americans (who always have unequal access to those ideals) and is responsible for high rates of crime, violence, and social ills (e.g., on the Aleut see Berreman 1964, 1978:228–30; Jones 1969a, 1976; Merculieff 1997). When Dorothy Jones wrote about Aleut health, education, child welfare, and aggression, she was writing against the prevailing assumption that in rural Alaska, Native people were weak-willed, childlike, and easily addicted people who could not solve their own problems, and she called for reforms to take specific social factors into account in order for government agencies to provide effective services. However, one consequence of her reframing "the problem" was the tendency to define everything as a response to white American impositions. Instead, measurements of social conflict must come from those embroiled in it within an empirically mapped social and political framework. The Aleut do not see themselves as responding to "American" ideals or institutions; they see themselves as Americans. Instead of assuming roles of victimhood, they voluntarily grasped commercialization in order to raise their own standards of living and create an economic base that ideally would provide for many generations to come.

Social conflict in the North today is common, with high rates of alcoholism, child neglect, sexual assault, suicide, homicide, and mental health problems plaguing arctic rural communities at diverse levels (Berman and Leask 1994; Bloom 1975; Briggs 1994; Fienup-Riordan 1994; Hisnanick 1994; Lee 1995, 2000; Palinkas 1987; Shinkwin and Pete 1983; Wood 1997, 1999a, 1999b). Attempts to investigate the reasons for high crime rates in the Far North have concluded that there is little or no relationship to Western variables such as joblessness or market forces, and hence no economic explanation (e.g., Wood 1997). This may be because economic success is a common Western measurement for social success, and success in these communities is not reducible to financial well-being. The nature of status and prestige among northern peoples is sometimes measured economically but often is tied to other aspects of society, such as hunting prowess, sociopolitical skills, leadership skills, artistic skills, and, sometimes, deviant behaviours. Success, then, can be a combination of multiple factors that involve social, cultural, political, and financial capital (Bourdieu 1977). For the Eastern Aleut, cultural success equals success in fishing and is evaluated in terms of the captain's ability, the boat's catch, crew capacity, time spent on the water, and sharing networks, as well as income. Income increases the ability to pour their earned resources back into their symbols of identity and empowerment, and to increase their social position. When these means are inaccessible, sources for gaining status and recognition must be sought in new areas.

Disenfranchised men who have no alternatives to social and political status often find themselves in conflicts. This is clear from data on village-based societies (e.g., Chagnon 1992; Robarchek and Robarchek 1998), on nation-states (Daly and Wilson 1988, 1989, 1994; Wilson and Daly 1985), and on inner-city gangs (Jankowski 1991), and it is present in the Arctic as well (e.g., Palinkas 1987). Young men are the most likely participants in all forms of violence (Daly and Wilson 1988) as well as the most risky behaviours (Wilson and Daly 1985). However, risk is also culturally defined (Douglas and Wildavsky 1982) and has possibilities that can often be calculated; uncertainty, on the other hand, cannot be calculated and can generate different reactions (Giddens 2002).

My research was instigated in part by several local Aleut and the Aleutians East Borough making a speculative connection between social problems in the community, especially among youth, and problems in fishing. There are assumptions implied in the use of crime data to measure social unrest. Statistical data reveal provocative correlations, which can then be grounded, analyzed, and challenged qualitatively. For the Aleut, crime or social deviance is defined as the violation of codified laws, as well as the violation of social or cultural rules beyond the state's definitions.

There are caveats to examining crime data, since most of the published data are quantitative and their collection and interpretation are fraught with biases (e.g., Moyer 1992; Wood and Trostle 1997). In Alaska, as in many other parts of the world, problems in law enforcement processes result in higher arrest, conviction, and longer sentencing of some portions of given populations than of others (Schafer, Curtis, and Atwell 1997). Studies recognizing cultural differences in administering criminal justice are rare (see exceptions: Banks 1997; Blurton and Copus 1993; Morrow 1993, 1994). There are subtle discrepancies between inside and outside definitions and understandings of law that present difficulties in knowing what these crime data represent (e.g., Morrow 1992; Walker 1997). Patterns identified through the quantitative analysis of events and actions are held in this light.

Natives have been recruited as law enforcement officers, putting themselves and their families in difficult positions, and the officers are often called upon to perform duties beyond their job descriptions (Wood 1999b; Wood and Trostle 1997). These individuals are often judged strongly by the community, though they are welcomed over a state trooper. Aleut adjudication methods (outside the law) are also examined for whether there are village councils or local leaders who have authority within and between families. In nearly all village-based societies, the severity of the crime (although it is unclear if the concept of crime actually applies) is determined to some extent by the relationships between the participants, especially the degree of consanguinity (Daly and Wilson 1988). Resolution tactics chosen by many lineage societies are determined by relatedness, with disputes between lineage members adjudicated within the lineage, and disputes between individuals in different lineages requiring more formalized adjudication methods. Handling disputes at the family or village level without involving the police could be viewed as a means of self-preservation against the overarching state or as something that is none of the police's business. In King Cove there is a strong police presence, but there are also less formal familial and community influences. An analysis of the justice system would require a volume all its own; here, I consider how some Aleuts get into the system and why.

In the following sections, I focus on young adults and household relationships and consider the role of alcohol, which some Aleuts have stated "drives the community," fuelling both positive and negative aspects of community life. Within this, I consider how the Aleut model their own problems. I then describe aspects of community structure, from bars to law enforcement, and how they are perceived in the community. I turn to civil and criminal data at the end, since the village data are meant to inform the interpretation of the crime data, advocating a more culturally and socially specific approach to social problems.

A GENERATION ADRIFT

Change is difficult to establish in a few years of fieldwork, but baseline data comes from the Aleut themselves and from a history of regulatory intensification. For them, there has been a rapid erosion of the customary lifeway since 1995. This is not generally regarded as a cycle. One man observed, "Younger people don't really understand the significance of these short openings. When I was young, they started fishing in May and didn't have any closings throughout the season." Another man declared, "We used to fish year round. Salmon all summer, then we'd jump on a crab boat for the winter. We never had to wait very long." Limited Entry cut off future generations from full membership in fishing. Fishermen before them have been mentors, with young men in apprenticeships. All the incentives (financial, social, and cultural) have been there for them to stay in the fisheries, yet few can now hope to own their own boats and permits. Many a young man in this generation still lives with his parents and crews for whomever will hire him. In many instances, the young man is a father, and his children are being raised by his girlfriend in her parents' home. To extend the nautical metaphor, most of the current generation is drifting between transitory roles in fishing and a kind of social "Sargasso Sea" of idleness.

Despite the difficulties, there is significant pressure on boys to fish, the pressure coming from both adults and peers. Wage employment starts early for children where, as crew, a boy can make upwards of $10,000 in one summer. (As a consequence, it is not uncommon for teens to owe thousands of dollars in income tax.) An elder warned, "They see dollar signs. They think it's gonna last."

In a discussion of youth behaviour with King Cove's tribal council members, there were disagreements on the severity of their situation. "They have a different mindset [than we did growing up]" stated one man. "Every one of these kids will get in trouble with the police department before they graduate from high school. It was different when I was a kid." A woman retorted, "You just didn't get caught. There were no police back then, just — and that's it [referring to the Aleut man who was the only community police officer after King Cove became a second-class city]. Now there are all these damned police running around." The man continued, "We used to fight, hit and get hit. Knock each other down. I've seen kids fight now and knock each other down. They'll get someone down and they'll *stomp them*. I've seen it." They cited media exposure as an influence, but with regard to what was ultimately responsible, they did not know. In the vein that Bourdieu critiques the effects of media and television as reproducing dominant cultures in others, media exposure has certainly influenced social interactions among the Aleut, but it must not be implicated as "causing" young men and women to be aggressive or create mischief.

The liminality between the rites of passage that Turner described, in which there is freedom in behaviour and relationships with few expectations or roles in society (1967:101), partly applies to the liminality of Aleut youth. Young men have more freedom to engage in recreation, drinking binges, and parties, to have sexual partners with no expectations, and for whom the penalties for breaking laws are less strict because they are considered to be "acting their age" – "age" being flexible, depending on the responsibilities and expectations taken on or placed upon the person. For some, however, enormous expectations have already begun in terms of providing subsistence and care for members of their families, as described in chapters 3 and 4. For these young men, there is a frantic element to their lives where they just want to get on with the next stage of life but have nothing to get on with.

On several occasions, young men's limited role in fishing seemed to affect their interactions with me, in that they were fairly confident until it became apparent that I was well aware of the fishing situation and their plight within it. Simply asking if they fished or whom they

fished with was loaded with meaning. This was first made apparent
at an interview in an elder's house when I was still learning the ins
and outs of fishing. The elder was extremely hungover and did not
remember our phone conversation at 3 o'clock in the afternoon the
day before, during which I had set up the interview, and he offered to
cook me a salmon patty dinner. "That was just about when the lights
started to go out," he said. A young sometimes-crewman in the neighbourhood (though it had been two years since his last hire) came into
the house and settled on the couch with a beer. After a long chat about
mundane topics, the conversation suddenly turned antagonistic:

NEIGHBOUR: You white people should stay the hell out! This is our
state!
ELDER: Ah! Don't pay any attention to him. He's a drunk.
NEIGHBOUR: The United *State* of Alaska, that's what I'm talking
about! We support you guys down there. You'd be nothing without
us!
KRM: Could be. (*Long pause*) Are you a fisherman?
NEIGHBOUR: Okay.
KRM: You don't fish?
NEIGHBOUR: Okay. (*Long pause*)
KRM: What do you do?
NEIGHBOUR: I used to fish with — and —!
KRM: What do you do now?
NEIGHBOUR: I build HUD houses sometimes. (*Drained the beer and
left*)

This excerpt does not adequately convey the hostility of this
conversation. My asking about whether the neighbour was a
fisherman was taken as a direct threat to him. Where he had been
belligerent and haughty before, he withered almost immediately and
left the house. Though he is married with a family to support, he is
intermittently employed and is less known for his performance in
fishing than for his drunken foibles. During the next visit, only after
I accepted a beer from the elder, did this man decide that I was okay
to talk to again.[1]
    Similar problems face young women. For example, after their
18-year-old daughter spent another night in jail for drinking and
almost running an officer off the road in her car, the advice this
couple got from an elder was, "Get her outta here!" The elder had

Table 6.1
Survey results regarding community concerns for youth

1 Alcohol abuse
2 Lack of alternative activities
3 Lack of after-school activities
4 Teen pregnancy
5 Lack of motivation
6 Too much idle time

Source: EATS, 1999

already sent his own daughters out ("out" means "to Anchorage"), the last one rather recently. "There's nothing here for them to do except drink and get into trouble." Some have gone to Anchorage to begin college, but many of them returned just as confused about their lives as when they left. A young woman who received a full scholarship to a technical college decided that she would miss her friends too much and would not leave. Yet "I've got to get outta here" was a mantra for so many young women.

The issues that plague young Aleut men affect women in different ways. "Women can make themselves feel useful having babies," a health worker observed, and they do. Teen pregnancy was listed as the fourth greatest concern for youth in a survey of health workers, law enforcement, schools, and community residents conducted by EATS in 1999 (table 6.1).

Young Aleut women prefer to partner with successful Aleut fishermen, but mate preferences have been strained in recent decades because these basic criteria are harder to find in young men. When one young woman told me, "I don't normally like white guys, unless they're really, really tan," I asked if she preferred Native men. "Yeah," she said, "but the ones around here suck." The lack of potential Aleut mates outside King Cove was a real concern for many women. One young woman was disgusted with the high school in Palmer, Alaska (north of Anchorage), where she spent a year because "there weren't any Native guys up there." A significant trend in many rural Alaska Native villages is for young women to marry non-Native men and leave the village (Hamilton and Seyfrit 1994a, 1994b), which may have to do with access rather than preference. This trend does not affect Aleut villages in a measurable way, and though women do find Aleut mates, it seems that they prefer those who are not just fishermen but who stand to inherit a permit and boat.

The future aspirations of many young people are conflicted. So many of them simply stay home, torn between wanting to live and fish in the village and discovering a life outside it. The following was said by the relative of a young woman who had been thinking of going to college but began to get into trouble with drugs and alcohol a few months before the time she was to start: "It's a communication thing with your parents, you know. You don't say nothing. We all grew up with that. She was trying to fill out her scholarship paperwork and her parents wouldn't help her. She's lost like so many kids. So many are in the same boat. They're just out of high school. It's frightening out there. She's in a rut, like so many kids in this town" (July 2001)

This scenario is not uncommon. Young people who are presented with opportunities outside the village begin to sabotage their prospects before they even leave. This young woman was sent to an alcohol treatment facility in Anchorage for six weeks, where she was in counselling and was medicated. By and large, the young tend not to speak out to parents and other adults, especially to assert goals which their parents may not support. This passage also presents the conflict that many parents feel: they do not want to teach their children how to leave the village but do not want to see them struggling if they remain.[2]

Many adults recognize that young people need experiences outside the village in order to successfully protect fishing rights and ensure their future. One mother was able to take her children to Anchorage and outside the state on a regular basis, but was deeply concerned about the rest. "Few kids are interested in college," she said. "Money is good fishing, they're here, they're comfortable. It's scary out there. They're intimidated, don't want to confront the newness because it is such a contrast. If the school would send kids out on trips it might alleviate it."

Another mother was conflicted: "Out there, you know (*shakes head*). They're so protected right here. When kids leave, I hope they come back and I hope they don't." Adults have cited out-migration as a concern for young people, yet the reality is that so many continue to stay in the community, if not at their parents' homes, in difficult times. A police officer speculated that they grew up with such closeness, both living together on the boat and at home, that they will not leave that comfort. "When I give a 24-hour sight and sound order," said the officer, "it's not difficult [to comply with] because they live together." One young man who owns his own house in King Cove continued to live in his parents' home. The next generations are also presented with notions of fear of the outside. One woman from False Pass said, "I told my kids, 'this is a little place and look at all the bad things that happen. Can you imagine what happens out their [in cities]?'" She despairingly added, "I hope you find some good things here."

So what are the alternatives? After a few weeks of little return in fishing, one fisherman said, "Fall back on the stuff I learned in high school, I guess." Another said, "Guess I'd better look for a welding job." (Welding is one of the few alternative skills taught in the high school.) In most Native American societies, joining the US military is a viable alternative for many young men (and sometimes women), giving them renewed respect (e.g., Hackenberg 1972; O'Neill 1999). For as militarized as the Aleutians are, it is remarkable that Eastern Aleut youth tend not to consider this an option. In previous generations, a large number of King Cove men were drafted into the army during the Vietnam War, and one man joined the air force.[3] World War II's generation of King Cove men ran army transports, supply ships, and cargo ships for the military. This was before a draft but also before Native Americans were fully considered viable for military duty and still had second-class status (except, perhaps, the Navajo code talkers). But today, few look to this kind of alternative.

Among the Innu of Labrador, Hugh Brody found that increased political activity is related to a decrease in violence (personal comm., March 2000). Disadvantaged or deprived individuals sometimes try to redress their situation through political action, but this can depend on the type of deprivation, such as economic, health and welfare, social, or political (A. Smith 1981:28). Eastern Aleut young men are politically inoperative right now. As more young men find themselves disenfranchised, they may channel their frustration into politics, since "existing data suggest that political and status deprivations are more closely related to political action than economic or service wants" (A. Smith 1981:28).

Reinterpreting Harrison's *The Mask of War* (1993), Bowman found that in the villages of the Manambu lineages in Papua New Guinea, men's cults were interrupting peaceful trade and gift exchange between communities by performing rituals that compel members of their villages to perceive cooperative exchange as aggressive, creating an "us" (often kin relations) and a "them" (distantly related kin or neighbours). These "warriors in waiting" created new identities for themselves, as well as for members of their communities. The male organizations "produced" war in order to give themselves a particular identity, plucked out of a larger, peaceful network of social interaction (Bowman 2001:33–4). Like the men Bowman described as "warriors in waiting," (2001:34) these young men are "fishermen-in-waiting," seeking ways to affirm an alternative identity with new distinctions and new prestige. An "imitate-the-high-in-status" mechanism was proposed by Barkow where the status-conscious adolescent follows behavioural strategies that result in social prestige by imitating popular peers (1994:130). Abbink adds that this mechanism fails when young men stall their own initiations and changes in social status (2001:132). Rather like a graduate student's completion anxiety in an unfavourable job market, many young Aleut men deliberately hold themselves back and delay any possibility of upward social mobility. While young Aleut men have tried to create alternative identities for themselves, they have been less creative in finding new routes to status and even less successful at compelling the rest of the village to recognize these as legitimate. The new routes to status that Eastern Aleut youth have created border on illegality and often include defiance of laws, drinking, vandalism, and seemingly trivial altercations. The young are torn between what they perceive outside the community and fishing, yet they cannot fully participate in one or the other. I attempt to quantify their plight later in this chapter.

FAMILY

There is a collective sigh of relief among women as soon as the men leave for fishing. In the salmon season, they normally do not see the fleet for the whole month of June. This is a time for women to do things they might not do when their husbands or fathers are in the house, such as starting craft projects, going to the bar, and visiting friends more often. Women are also bracing themselves for the potential consequences of a bad fishing season or even a good fishing season. Bad seasons can lead to tension, abuse, or anger. Good seasons have been implicated in hedonistic behaviour, causing men to feel invincible, chasing women other than their wives or leaving to party in Anchorage.

Women have said they have counted on that time apart, on that respite from their spouses. With the June fishery severely curtailed, fishermen continually return to the harbour between short-term openings, reducing these breaks to only a few days at a time. Constant homecomings have required women to remain alert to their husbands' needs and can produce rising tension after each poor fishing opener.

At the start of this chapter, I began with a man in the process of being edged out of fishing because of financial, political, and personal circumstances. Whether edged out entirely or just for a season, several fishermen were forced to stay home in the course of my fieldwork. One fisherman who was stuck at home in 2002 said, "Look at me! I'm sitting ashore! Even if I were out there [fishing] I'd be fighting for a crew. It's impossible and I'd go backwards [further in debt]." They were angry, and they explained their situation as beyond their control.

Uncertainties abound, from opening to opening, season to season, year to year. People are always looking for alternatives to disappointing seasons, whether it is to insert themselves into different fisheries or to compensate for the current setbacks with explanations. These compensations can take liquid form, which produces other concerns.

GOOD FISHERMEN ARE NOT DRUNK FISHERMEN

"I made my beer money anyway," one fisherman told me. "I brought in seven reds this trip. Better to have the fish in my house than selling it this year" (crewman July 2002). The only places to buy alcohol in King Cove are the Native-owned liquor store, the Native-owned bar, and the Native Corporation-owned bar. The liquor store goes from being fully stocked to virtually empty in the first week of June as fishermen supply their boats for the salmon season. Most captains have a "no drinking" policy on board, except between openings and when not on duty.

An elder in King Cove recalled major changes in the village after the first bar was built in the 1970s. People used to go from house to house celebrating with home brews such as salmonberry wine. Now that there are public drinking venues, he said, household parties have become less frequent, and they seem to occur mostly when money is tight because the bars are more expensive than buying from the liquor store. One King Cove couple averaged their yearly bill for alcohol, cigarettes, and paying babysitters to watch their children while they go to the bar at $23,000. "It costs a lot to drink out here," many people have noted, but the high cost seems not to be a deterrent.

As in many towns and neighbourhoods, the bars tend to act as community centres. For men, they are a kind of secondary social centre after the Harbor House. For women, the bars are second to one another's homes. Between openings, fishermen and crews crowd the bars, sometimes before they have even showered. It was rumoured that the Corporation Bar would not cut people off if they were too drunk anymore because they were losing money. However, I have seen many people get thrown out over the years. At the Native-owned bar, the owner watches out for her relatives drinking there. One night, when a non-Native visitor tried to buy a round of shots for several of the owner's uncles sitting at the bar, she told the man that one had a bad liver, another had already had too much, and the other needed to go home to his wife.

Among many adults and teens in King Cove, including the non-resident fishermen and their crews, the state of drunkenness is an almost daily experience. One elder, pointing at a sheepish young man hovering in his doorway, complained, "This guy here was banging on my door at 4:30 this morning looking for beer. Somebody's always looking for beer." While some whites will mention alcoholism as a problem and one that should arouse guilt, reference is seldom made to alcoholism among Aleuts.

The overwhelming majority of reported crimes and domestic violence involve the consumption of alcohol by one or both parties. Almost all calls at the King Cove Police Department are alcohol-related; in the sixteen months one police officer has worked for the force, he had only one call that did not involve alcohol. "If it wasn't for alcohol, we wouldn't see minors in here [the police station]," said the chief. He was relieved, however, that minors were mostly drinking instead of using drugs, though a growing concern of his was that locals were going to Anchorage to buy drugs and bring them back to sell.

Several teenagers have DWIs (driving while intoxicated) on their records and their drivers' licences revoked. One 17-year-old had a DWI and drove all the time anyway. His mother asked me not to let him borrow any vehicles from the residence where I was staying. He later got drunk one night and wrecked the family car by driving it into the pilings of a house. Several grown men have numerous DWIS and cannot drive. In one family, a 40-year-old man had to ask his young niece for rides around town on his four-wheeler, since he was not allowed to drive even that.

There are a few cases of people in King Cove who drink in the morning and then clean up and try to hide it for work or for a fishing opener. Excessive drinking is implicated in reduced participation in fishing because it slows efficiency. Captains are frequently "beached" because their crew was drunk or severely hungover. The state of drunkenness can be quite dangerous on boats and is the reason for a number of accidents, "man overboard" emergencies, and deaths.

A discussion about alcohol in False Pass found one man linking problems of drinking to the harsh environment: "Look around you. There are active volcanoes all around. People are responding to the wind and the weather." Others argued that people drink because of a lack of activities. A woman in False Pass said that men do not like to drink at home but will go off with other men. "People here don't just get drunk for a day, but for a week." She continued, "I ask drunks, 'why do you hate yourself so much?'" Nancy Lurie (1971) proposed pan-Native American drinking as the "world's oldest on-going protest demonstration."

One man was concerned that in poor fishing years, gambling would be seen as a potential money-making activity. I observed two women spend approximately $500 each one night on pull-tabs, the legal cardboard slot machine introduced by the tribal councils.[4] These women set a garbage can between them and pulled the tabs as fast as they could. One woman let her cigarette burn all the way down to her fingers and scorched her hand because she was so engrossed in pull-tabs.

There is variation in the extent to which people within King Cove identify drinking as a problem, but it is clear that drinking, gambling, and problems in fishing are intimately related. As one elder said during the poor salmon season of 2002, "No way will I be going to the bar tonight. Too many fishermen. There'll be lots of fights because it's a bad season." As seasons open and close, fishermen race to the bars to celebrate or commiserate, their performance at sea easily discernable by their behaviour.

CULTURE AND CRIME

Among villagers, "crime" is a term mostly reserved for the behaviour of transient cannery workers. Deviance and crime are locally defined based upon what constitutes acceptable behaviour. For example, the truck I had rented had a smashed windshield, no signal lights, one headlight, and windshield wipers that turned on and off at whim; the passenger door and windows would not open; the engine died at every turn or if going downhill, and the key was stuck in the ignition. An Aleut woman riding with me joked, "I don't think this thing is even King Cove legal!" "King Cove legal" was used to describe anything from driving drunk to battered vehicles with expired licence plates to hunting caribou out of season.

There can be a clash between state and Aleut definitions of crime which for some depends on the situation. In many instances, those about to be arrested for petty crimes have told the police that since they were "local," their behaviour was acceptable. A police officer described how sometimes people he has just arrested will sit in jail in total disbelief, saying "Man, I can't believe I'm in trouble." Even though they have been arrested, they do not believe they have done anything wrong.

A disproportionate number of Alaskan Natives, both adults and youths, are found in the justice system; Alaska Natives make up 36 percent of the prison population but only 15.6 percent of the state's population (Alaska Dept. of Corrections, 2000 Offender Profile; Census 2000; Schafer, Curtis, and Atwell 1997). The reasons for this are contested. Alaska is under Public Law 83–280, known as federal statute PL 280, which in 1953 extended civil and criminal jurisdiction of the state to include Natives on Native lands (Case 1984:14). Alaska Native self-government is now limited by or concurrently shared with the state. The law has been interpreted to give more extensive jurisdiction in criminal matters rather than civil (Case 1984:27). While the Aleut certainly have local definitions of crime, they are also citizens of the State of Alaska and the United States, which have codified descriptions of what constitutes crime. The Aleut are intimately aware of these external conditions and participate directly in the American judicial system. It is critical that quantitative data collected as a by-product of Aleut interaction with the more global judicial system be used in comparison with the local constructions of criminal behaviour identified during fieldwork.

Social service agencies merge the Aleut with larger entities; for example, the Indian Health Services (IHS) and the Division of Family and Youth Services (DFYS) combine the Aleutians with the Anchorage regional service centre, skewing the data to the urban population or mixing them with Alaska Natives in general and making the Aleut disappear in the statistics. Studies involving violence and crime in Anchorage lump Eskimo, Athapaskan, and Aleut ethnicities in their survey findings (e.g., Huelsman 1983). To the statistical researcher it seems that Native is Native and the separation of ethnicities would be less impressive. Though these studies indicate that there is a great deal of unreported crime among Alaskan Natives on Anchorage's "skid row," they are not particularly useful to someone asking whether people from Aleut villages commit crimes in Anchorage and, if so, what the circumstances are at home and "in town."[5] Where law enforcement places strict rules on the availability of data, the legal system treats most of its records as public information (excluding some juvenile records). Much of the crime data in Anchorage and in King Cove come from public records made available by the Alaska Court System in Anchorage. In addition, the King Cove Police Department has provided statistical summary information for a five-year period (1997–2001), including monthly breakdowns of incidents, activities, and calls.

Law Enforcement in King Cove

The composition of the King Cove police force has changed several times since 2000; the force generally consists of a chief and three officers. Throughout most of my fieldwork the police chief was a local Aleut and a member of one of the largest lineages. The officers were usually from outside the community or outside Alaska and had been in King Cove a relatively short time. "All the good ole boys are gone," one woman lamented, stating that they would have given a drunk driver "a good talking to" instead of arresting him/her. There is also a Village Public Safety Officer (VPSO) who doubles as the fire chief. The purpose of the VPSO program is to provide a police presence in remote villages of Alaska that cannot afford conventional police, ideally hiring local people to fill the roles; it is funded in part by the state.[6] The village's budget crisis, due to lost revenue from the fishing predicament, resulted in the police department losing an officer and the position in 2002. "A three-man department is tough because of the burnout factor," said the police chief. "We can't afford to lose any more. They are very expensive to replace."

Community members described a love-hate relationship between the community and the police force. According to one woman, "Cops are harassing their kids when they are in trouble, but if something happens to them they ask, 'Where are the damn cops?'" Several teenagers noted that people behave in different ways depending on which officer is on duty, because they know they can get away with certain things. "There's some of the 'white man' stuff," one woman said; some consider the white police to be targeting Aleuts. She stated that when she was younger (just ten years ago), the cops would "make fun of Aleuts." My interviews with non-Native officers indicated an "us versus them" attitude, with them referring to Aleuts as "these people," for example, out of earshot of the locals. None of the officers I interviewed are still employed with the department, since clashes with the community resulted in their being fired. The Aleut chief of police experienced difficulties of his own, saying he had to arrest family members in the past, which put him in a difficult but sympathetic position.

King Cove's jail is more of a "holding facility" with two cells. Some jail guards make prisoners sit alone in the cells, but mostly they watch television outside the cells in the holding pen. Microwavable meals are provided by the state and the inmates have access to Bibles, comic books, magazines, and a shower. For the local inmates, family members "baby them" and bring them food. They can bring in their own blankets and even their own television set if it makes them comfortable. Prisoners from the cannery are watched more closely and not let out of the cells. Those arrested watch a video that advises them of their rights, and all arraignments are done by telephone with Anchorage. The magistrate is in Cordova. Security is somewhat lax: young women and men still on probation from their own offences were hired to guard prisoners.

Law enforcement is mixed, experiencing constant employee turnover and operating on a strained budget, but by and large the King Cove Police Department is an effective, respected group, whose place in the community is understood as necessary, if at times difficult. The mayor has hiring and firing entitlement, and officers are sometimes in a difficult position with respect to community leaders' families; enforcing laws against them or even mishandling a situation as defined by a leader can cost them their jobs.

COURT AND CRIMINAL DATA

As stated, "crime" is used most often with reference to cannery workers. Many of the recorded crimes in King Cove occur at Peter Pan Seafoods. "A fresh crop of cannery people might make me want to lock my door," said one local man. Prior to 2000, there was a poor to non-existent security screening system for workers at the cannery. Peter Pan hired convicted murderers, escaped convicts, and people with long "rap sheets." In the spring of 2000 it hired an escaped convict from Kansas and the state had to extradite him. That same year, the cannery hired a permanent security guard for the first time. He tries to handle the problems before they become criminal, but the police deal with them after that point. The police chief was relieved that "the whole picture has changed now." They have a screening system that includes background checks on potential cannery workers. "It's costly to bring a person in here. They were losing manpower and money having to ship them out. And it was a strain on city services, both the PD [Police Department] and clinic ... They have a different management. They don't fool with troublemakers now."

Peter Pan is fairly isolated from the rest of the community such that there is not much conflict between its workers and local residents. They work around the clock and rarely have time off, but when they do it frequently happens that cannery workers will take over the bar and the local people will leave. Cannery workers and community members occasionally tussle over women or other matters, but these almost always occur at the bar and involve alcohol.

The call ratio between the city and the cannery for the last few years indicates that a small percentage of the total calls to the Police Department are made by the cannery, but a large percentage of the total arrests are related to Peter Pan Seafoods (see figure 6.1).

Figure 6.2 illustrates the calls and incident reports by month for the King Cove Police Department. Note that during the last half of 1997 and the first half of 1998 there is an increase in the number of calls, a point I will return to later. If we revisit the monthly schedule of activity and economics illustrated in chapter 3, January to February are spent crabbing and groundfish fishing, March is busy with another groundfish opener such as black cod, April is for herring fishing, May is salmon preparation, June to September is spent salmon fishing, October is for King crab, Permanent Fund Dividends

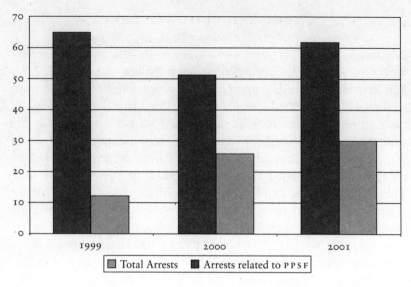

Figure 6.1
Three-year activity report, King Cove Police Department, 1999–2001 (King Cove Police
Department)

are distributed in November, and they may fish groundfish IFQs
again in December.

The monthly breakdown in the number of calls coincides in large
part with the schedule of workers arriving for the cannery. Based on
these data, the King Cove Police Department indicated that there
was almost a schedule in which criminal activity could be predicted.
The department ranked the top three problems as alcohol, assault-
ive behaviour, and domestic violence assaults. "What accounts for
this?" I asked. "The textbook answer," said a police officer, "is that
work here is seasonal. People go out, they make a pile of money, then
they don't have work. And there's nothing to do here. So then they
start drinking. They get new rigs, spend it all fast. The money runs
out. That's when the problems start. They start fighting. It's a cycle
that repeats itself and they can't get out of it."

Violations during fishing seasons do occur. During crabbing seasons, one man complained that the crab fishermen were "like a
bunch of pirates" and told of a crabbing crew that stole a quarter of
a million dollars from Peter Pan in 2000.[7] "The state troopers came
in and caught up with them in Dutch," he added. "They bragged to

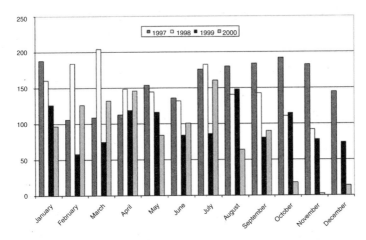

Figure 6.2
Monthly breakdown of calls/incidents to the King Cove Police Department,
1997–2000

the wrong friends, I guess, with a $10,000 reward out." In October 2001 the *Anchorage Daily News* reported a crab boat stranded in Cold Bay that had been burgled of crab pots and crab. Within the King Cove fishing fleet, small fishing violations are generally overlooked by other fishermen *if the violator does not get caught* and *if the violation does not impinge on others*. If he or she does get caught, then the ramifications can be socially more devastating because the behaviour reflects on the status of the entire fleet, particularly in the chum war, and the fishermen share the same fate. In the span of fieldwork, the only admission of dumping chum salmon was by one crewman's mother, who felt that her son did not have a choice. Small transgressions are usually ignored; otherwise the Aleut tend to police one another on the water for incidents such as robbing another's subsistence nets.

Enforcement of fishing violations can be both cooperative and antagonistic with Fish & Game authorities. As I have argued, if people do not own or at least influence the decision-making process with regard to rights and regulations, they are more likely to ignore the rules. In McCay's "Pirates of Piscary" article (1984), she found that piracy in New Jersey, defined as fish and shellfish poaching, is a cultural response to a long history of restrictive fisheries legislation and the intensified enforcement of restrictions, sustained by a myth that the government discriminates against commercial fisher-men and that they are justified in illegal fishing. Piracy is considered a "natural law" and "unalienable right" of the commoners to access the commons (1984:34). Compliance is at issue, and people who do not agree with the laws may not follow them.

Local Transgressions, Public and Private

Most recorded crimes are petty larceny and are often connected with the cannery. Even these are few and far between, and almost all involve alcohol. A mental health provider predicted that I would not detect the crimes that he sees in the crime statistics and that there are more interpersonal crimes than any other type. He knew of no reported rapes, though they do occur, particularly date rapes, he said, adding, "Men out here don't want to get you drunk because they like to see you happy." One woman personally knew of assaults, underage drinking, vehicle accidents, and sexual abuse that were not reported: "I don't know if it's just because it's a small town or what." King Cove is not an anonymous place, and this plays a role in the type of crimes that are most prevalent and most reported.

"Nothing ever gets reported," stated one young woman, who spoke of her friends being raped by local young men when they were all drunk at parties. A health worker believed that there is a perva-sive feeling that nothing will be done about these crimes and that their justification for this view is a history of police isolation: "The police live in an isolated social enclave; they are in the community but not a part of it." The police, the health worker argued, did not pursue many of the more serious crimes. He saw every kind of drug entering King Cove on fishing boats from all over the North Pacific but believed that the law enforcement officers made little effort to curb this. Drugs come in "helter-skelter," he said, mostly marijuana, some cocaine, and hybrid drugs, but alcohol is preferred. He added, "Adults buy booze and give it to the kids. They're not prosecuted. You won't see this in the crime stats."

Non-Native non-locals have informed on child welfare problems to police and welfare agencies in the past (Jones 1969b:299), and there is some evidence that this continues today. A False Pass woman complained to me about "non-Native Christian women" informing the Division of Family and Youth Services of problems in her family.

At the time of our conversation, she was waiting for a DFYS investi-
gator to arrive as a result and was extremely resentful: "They won't
take my kids away or they'll have a fight!"

Most crimes are "private," meaning they are not openly discussed
or reported. There are, however, also many "public" crimes, those
that occur out in the open and are on everyone's lips. The crime of
the decade seems to have occurred just before I arrived to begin fieldwork in the spring of 2000: a man stole a taxicab. He was drunk at
the bar, called a cab, and was waiting in the car while the driver went
back inside to look for more rides. He got bored waiting, jumped
into the front seat, found the keys in the ignition, and drove around
and eventually home. His sister called him to tell him that the cops
were looking for him, so he locked himself in his house. The police
had to "kick the door down." He had only been out of jail for a day
or two when I met him. "From 8 to 10, I'm in the pen," he joked.
His family brought him food while he was in jail. "Hard time," he
laughed. Thus, crimes discussed out in the open are often less serious, with no victims.

The Angry Young Men and Women

The crime data for young men and women are difficult to quantify because most crimes of those younger than 18 years of age are
either not reported or are unavailable because the records are closed.
Looking at age-sex specific data, significant patterns emerged. In the
database of crimes compiled from court records, looking just at
criminal offences such as DWIs, assault, theft, disorderly conduct,
attempted sexual abuse, malicious destruction of property, and vio-
lating domestic violence restraining order, I considered the age of
the defendant at the time of the incident and separated them out for
males and females. Figure 6.3 illustrates a type of "young male syndrome" as described by Wilson and Daly (1985) but also a "young
female syndrome." However, for the men, two patterns of criminal
activity are in evidence, the first occurring for those between the
ages of 17 and 23, and the second occurring for those between the
ages of approximately 27 and 40. This could reflect an extended
"young male syndrome" where men who have tried to enter the
fishing industry as more than crewmen have not been successful and
engage in behaviours which they might not otherwise attempt.

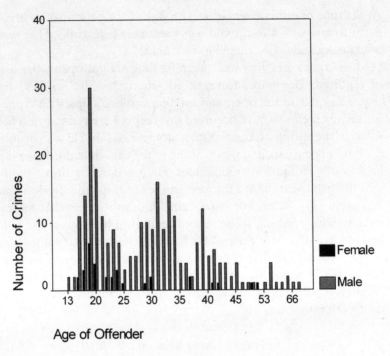

Figure 6.3
Offender sex and age data for number of crimes between 1990 and 2002, King Cove

Men and Women

There cannot be a "'gender-free' interpretation" of crime (Archer 1994:6). This is not to suggest that crime and violence are male problems rather than human problems, as some feminist writers propose (Archer and Lloyd 1985), but rather that there are significant sex differences in homicide, crime, domestic violence, sexual assault, and same-sex violence. Statistically, there are vast gender differences in overt acts of violence, which overwhelmingly find male perpetrators (Archer 1994; Daly and Wilson 1988; Dobash and Dobash 1992); but, of course, acts committed by women often go unreported more than acts committed by men. If the prevalence of certain types of crime is related to negative constraints on cultural and social identity or individual success, then central to sex differences are questions of male/female roles and interactions. The relationship between aggressors and victims is also crucial.

In examining court cases of domestic violence, only 14.9 percent of plaintiffs/petitioners in domestic violence cases were male.

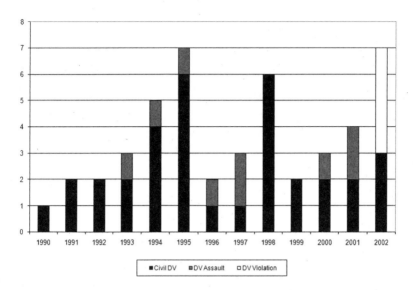

Figure 6.4
Civil and criminal cases of domestic violence filed by King Cove residents, 1990–2002

Table 6.2
Number of male and female plaintiffs/petitioners in domestic violence cases filed,
1990–2002

	Civil DV	Assault DV	DV violation	Percent
Female plaintiff/petitioner	27	9	4	85.1
Male plaintiff/petitioner	7	0	0	14.9

Instead, men were defendants/respondents in 85.1 percent of the cases (see table 6.2). The cases where men filed as plaintiffs often involved children and endangerment to them. A health provider stated that "violence is prevalent" and often related to alcohol. "Violence is not seasonal *per se*, but it changes with fishing," she argued. She knew of court-mandated alcohol counselling cases as a result of domestic violence.

The location in which the crime appears in the court system is significant when considering domestic violence. Few cases reported in King Cove actually made it as far as the magistrate in Cordova. Cases of domestic violence committed in Anchorage were more likely to involve the courts. This could indicate that domestic violence among the people of King Cove was more prevalent when they were staying in Anchorage. My sense, however, is that victims of domestic violence were more willing to involve the police in Anchorage than the police in King Cove. One elder told me how her husband used to beat her to unconsciousness on several occasions, and when she called the police they would take him away just long enough for him to sober up, and then they would bring him right back to the house. Another woman stated that when she called the police on her abusive husband, they took him to his mother's house instead of arresting him. There is little alternative for the police either. Both of these women were speaking of incidents that were ten or more years old but still very fresh in their minds. In one case, a woman described the situation in her family saying, "My kids seen him beat me, but this last time they saw me fight back." She and her children had moved out of the house two weeks earlier but were still spending a lot of time in it with her husband. "I moved out for one year before, but — started sleeping over and eating there [at her new house]." The *bidarki* reference made in chapter 4, in which men are stuck to their spouses and hard to pry off, seems accurate for these relationships. These stories also illustrate the absence of alternative social service organizations such as shelters or safe houses.

Conflict Resolution and Punishment

There are counselling services to turn to but no women's shelter or youth halfway house. There is a great deal of movement of children and adults between homes, and some of it is in avoidance of conflict, though that is rarely stated. Children sometimes slept on my couch because their parents were fighting. I was told of one woman with two children who has waited outside her home in any kind of weather, holding her children against her for warmth, until her abusive husband turns off the lights so she knows it is safe to go back inside.

In Nelson Lagoon (pop. 80), there is a community-wide "zero tolerance" policy for spousal and child abuse, according to the VPSO. Anyone who violates this policy will be expelled from the village. This type of policy works in a place of so few people and limited social services. In King Cove, with ten times the population of Nelson Lagoon, this does not exist as a policy, and it might not work because of village size, the influence of certain families, and structures in place to legally and socially deal with family violence. However, some individuals have been banished, which is probably

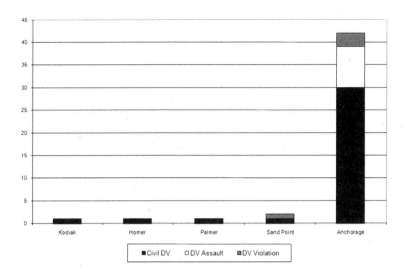

Figure 6.5
Number of domestic violence cases involving King Cove residents filed by court
location, 1990–2002

the strongest form of punishment imposed community-wide. In
some hunter-gatherer societies, banishment was believed to be tantamount to spiritual or physical death (e.g., for Inuit, see Briggs
1970). In King Cove it is tantamount to losing one's identity, even
though such people are not formally stripped of tribal membership.
Banishment means no longer being able to visit or fish, and having
limited contact with family. Two cases of banishment were reported
to me, one of the alleged perpetrator of sexual abuse of a minor
and the other involving vehicular manslaughter of a young man.
My sense in these two cases was that banishment from the village
has more devastating consequences than any sentence the legal system could impose. King Cove is evaluating prospects for creating
a tribal youth court within the provisions of PL 280 in the hope of
effectively adjudicating youth matters locally and keeping offenders
in the community.

SOCIAL CONFLICT AND FISHING?

Are problems in fishing responsible for social conflict? Running
numerous paired correlations using variables associated with fishing
and crime, a number of relationships emerged. I expected rates of

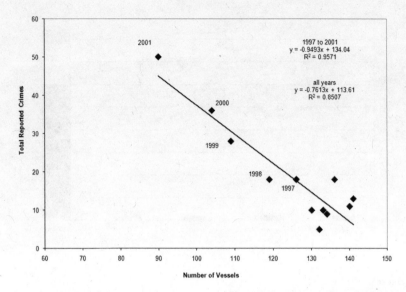

Figure 6.6
Total reported crimes versus number of fishing vessels. As the number of fishing vessels
in King Cove decreased between 1997 and 2001, crimes filed in the Alaska court system
increased.

crime and deviance to increase as opportunities to fish decreased. In
Greenland, the number of criminal court cases increased in villages
where fisheries landings had decreased, and in villages where landings had increased the crime rates were below average (Hamilton,
Lyster, and Otterstad 2000:207). However, I found no relationship
between any of the crime statistics and red, chum, king, or pink salmon harvesting. As access to salmon decreased, then, the need to fish
alternative species increased. Thus, fluctuations in access to these
alternatives should coincide with changing crime rates.

Figure 6.6 shows that as the number of vessels fishing decreases
and as wealth is in fewer hands, the number of reported and prosecuted crimes, violent and non-violent, increases. Between 1997
and 2001 (more recent data were incomplete), there is a linear
increase in reported crimes. The number of decreasing vessels and
increasing crime may be spurious and simply a by-product of the
reduction in the fleet through time and increasing crime through
time. However, it may also mean that the fewer people fishing, the
greater the amount of crime. It could also reflect the greater dispar-
ity between the haves and have-nots as being relative rather than

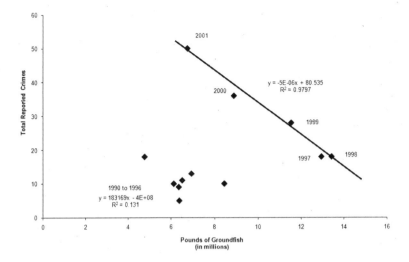

Figure 6.7
Relationship between amount of groundfish harvested by the King Cove fleet and crimes found in the Alaska court system

absolute, and the fact that there are decreasing opportunities for recognized status.

Figure 6.7 illustrates the intensification of groundfish fishing, this being their reserve strategy, which occurs more intensively when the salmon season was poor. Groundfish fishing requires IFQ (individual fishing quota) shares; in other words, one has to have been assigned shares for the right to fish based on historical catches for the vessel owner. These quotas fluctuate with the total allowable catch set by the North Pacific Fisheries Management Council. When expansion is restricted, crime rates seem to follow the number of fish landed in reverse. As seen in figure 6.2, showing the monthly breakdown of calls/incident reports to the King Cove Police Department, in the last half of 1997 and the first half of 1998 there was a strong increase in these calls and incidents. This time period coincides with that given above, during which the numbers of crimes break away from the cluster of the previous years and increase linearly. Though these are two different datasets, and the *calls* appear to decrease in the years to follow, read together they might indicate a significant event contributing to the rise in crimes.

As we saw in chapter 5, restrictions on groundfish fisheries began in earnest in 1997 in relation to endangered species. Again, between

1997 and 2001, there is a linear increase in numbers of crimes with
the decline in pounds of groundfish harvested. Thus, groundfish
appear to be related to crime rates from 1997 to 2001, but not in the
six years before, in which crime floats independent of the amount
of fish harvested. Communities with smaller populations along the
North Pacific have shown an out-migration in quota shares since the
program was implemented in 1995, possibly indicating their frustration with restrictions or the sale of shares to satisfy immediate
financial needs.

"ANCHORAGE'S NEXT STREET PEOPLE"?

"We'll all have to move to Anchorage, it's cheaper to live. We'll be
Anchorage's next street people" (seiner, October 2000). This Aleut
seine fisherman and elder could see no opportunity for financial
recovery in the absence of a full salmon fishery, and he feared that
he and his relatives would be forced to find a life in Anchorage in
the near future. Anchorage's Fourth Avenue has become a kind of
skid row for the city's homeless. Many are Native people who did
not succeed in their home villages and have come to Anchorage,
where they panhandle and live in shelters (Huelsman 1983). Though
Huelsman's data are lumped for all Native peoples on the streets of
Anchorage, in my own experiences there are noticeably few Aleuts
(so far).

A white, male health provider stated, "I feel a personal sense
of burden to kids to look beyond the fishing industry. There are
physical limitations too. There's a kid here with knee problems. His
brothers both fish and he feels left out, angry. I tell him he can do
lots of other things. You don't have to live here to be an Aleut"
(King Cove, June 2000). But maybe you do. Aleuts pride themselves
on their continued survival in their traditional homeland. Fienup-
Riordan sees the mobility and urban migration of the Yupiit to be
an expansion of the Native community and a sharper affirmation
of Yup'ik identity across boundaries (2000:ch.5). In contrast, the
Aleut do not have the population or village numbers that the Yupiit
have, and out-migration is seen more in terms of a trickling away of
their relatives and their society. While some maintain second homes
in Anchorage, the physical connection to the village and the annual
return to fishing are essential to their lives.

Once you leave the fisheries, there is little chance of re-entry: "There's no chance for us, none whatsoever down here," I was told. "And they've taken from people that were doing really well too, all on their own. They've stripped down, right down to the – This community will be a welfare community if anybody stays here the way it's going. I'm not sure Peter Pan will even open without the June fishery" (seiner, October 2000). Other Alaska Natives have asked plaintively if they have stopped being Native because they moved away from the village. I have never heard urban Aleuts mention this. There are an estimated six hundred Aleut Corporation shareholders residing in the Lower 48, primarily in Washington and Oregon.[8] It would be interesting to discover how many of them maintain connections with Aleutian villages.

A health provider interviewed in 2000 (now no longer employed by Eastern Aleutian Tribes) described a "weird blend of traditions" in the village, where "a lot gets swept under the cultural rug." He saw culture, however it is defined, being used as a "convenience thing, especially with younger ones," used only when it is to their advantage to be *cultural*. It costs a lot of money to live out in the bush, and housing subsidies, full medical coverage, and other such benefits are granted to locals solely because they are Native. This man said that when they have the option to leave the community to work, they state that they do not want to abandon their family or their culture. "But," he argued, "are they concerned about culture or is it simple economics?" "What's the difference?" I asked. True, they get benefits in the community which they would not receive elsewhere, but this man believed that these benefits were largely financial. He believed that culture is portable without acknowledging that it is tough to be Aleut away from an Aleut village – that being Aleut is to fish, to relate to the community, to share food, and to live off the land and sea.

Suicide

As a final point, I want to include a discussion of suicide. The suicide rate among young men in their late teens and early twenties is high for all of Alaska,[9] but it is extraordinarily high in Aleutian communities. Between 2000 and 2007 there were three suicides and three failed attempts in the Eastern Aleutians, and two other suicides within the three years prior to my starting the research – figures that are strikingly high in a small population. Whereas in some arctic societies elders choose their own moment for dying (Balikci 1970; Mary-Rousselière 1984:439–40), suicide here is an offence against the community and is usually committed by young men in complicated circumstances.

In the first month of fieldwork in 2000, a teenage boy whom I had known for a few years committed suicide in Cold Bay. He was living with his grandparents and, rumour has it, had warned his mother in Sand Point that if she married her fiancé, he would kill himself. He did just that the day before the wedding. There was a funeral service for him at the small chapel (a converted Quonset hut) with pictures and candles, almost like a "shrine," as one man described it.

One elderly couple told me about their 40-year-old son's suicide during the winter of 2000. He had been a marine, stationed all over the Pacific. His parents said military service "messed him up" and he shot himself shortly after a friend of his, who had also been a marine, killed himself in the same way. In False Pass, one woman who has lived there fifteen years counted six suicides in that time. She said one 16-year-old boy who used to work for her killed himself when "some guys got him drinking all night and he shot himself the next day."

Most suicides in the Eastern Aleutians involve alcohol. According to a village health provider, the classic theory for the occurrence of suicides is that people get alienated and isolated from the community. However, she stated that it is practically impossible for that to occur in these communities because they are very "close knit" and "nobody's really alone." Another woman, an Aleut elder, expressed concern that I was staying alone in a hotel room and made sure that I had her phone number and knew that I could drop in anytime. "Don't let yourself get closed in, especially in bad weather."

By contrast, another health provider believes that young men feel "stuck." They go to Anchorage and find that they do not fit in and cannot make the same money that they made fishing. It is not unusual for there to be 13- and 14-year-olds who have yet to leave King Cove and 50-year-olds who have never been beyond Anchorage. This health worker knew of no suicides committed by women at that time (however, after our conversations, in 2001, a woman in Nelson Lagoon took her own life). She said, "Women can make themselves feel useful by having babies and raising families." She found a high correlation between alcohol and depression, "but the question is, what comes first?" Alcohol is a depressant, but people also self-medicate with alcohol. She gave a lot of credit to the theory of lack of light causing depression. Light stimulates the pineal gland that produces seretonin. The Eastern Aleutians see an average of 60 sunny days each year. False Pass's health aide estimated that one in three adults in the Aleutian chain are on some type of antidepressant, and she linked this to the grey weather, given her own experience.

Several authors have claimed that suicide and violence are common in arctic societies because these hunting cultures are "experienced in killing" (Pentikäinen 1983:135) or because "children are conditioned to a predatory life from the time they can toddle" (Lantis 1960:24). I find these notions preposterous; knowledge and skills in hunting do not make people violent or more prone to take their own lives; they simply make them good hunters. However, using the framework of life history in which to examine behaviour, it is significant that morbidity and mortality are constant threats. Life expectancy for whites in Alaska is 75.2 years versus the 68.5 years for Alaska Natives (Alaska Bureau of Vital Statistics 1995). It is my sense that low life expectancy has a profound effect on people's behaviour, with individuals engaged in more risky behaviours if there is a chance that their lives will be cut short anyway. Sex differences in risk-taking behaviour are evident, where young men take greater risks in behaviour such as driving too fast, fighting, showing off, and are more likely to die in the process (Barrett, Dunbar, and Lycett 2002:114). There are lots of behaviours for women that could be defined as risky, but they are less likely to be life threatening. Rites of passage for young men achieving manhood often involve risky behaviour; this is a kind of "social puberty" (Van Gennep 1960:65) as well as "competitive advertising" of their maturity and prowess (Barrett, Dunbar, and Lycett 2002:115). I should add that there were unconfirmed suggestions of homicide in two old suicide cases and in one accidental death case. These statements were made by family members in disbelief over the circumstances of the deaths.

There are old stories of young Aleut women jumping from Russian ships into the freezing sea or young men cutting their throats to avoid enslavement or because of grief over being forcefully removed from their families and villages (Sauer 1802/1972; Hrdlicka 1945:208). Veniaminov wrote in 1840 that mourners of family members who died an accidental death might commit suicide or give away most of their possessions (family members who were killed by another person were avenged instead). Veniaminov attributed suicide to oppression by the Russians, that one would rather take one's own life than suffer persecution – what one scholar called "ethnocide" (Pentikäinen 1983:127). Wife exchange gone awry was also a reason for suicide: a husband might kill himself if he did not get his wife back (1983:127). Jones wrote that suicide was preferred over "receiving a physical blow" (1976:14); in other words, instead of enduring humiliation, young men would rather die.

Aleutian villagers are actively seeking the causes of suicide and ways to prevent it. King Cove's school received a Suicide Prevention grant, which funded a "Teen Center," built in the 1990s, and provided training to faculty and staff to help them identify the warning signs of suicide. Most villages have a suicide prevention coordinator. I hesitate to speculate on the reason for the frequent incidents of suicide, but in the cases that I am aware of, family members of the victims variously cited their sense of hopelessness, uncertainty about their future, lost love, and past regrets, but ultimately could not fathom a reason for the suicides' decisions.

CONCLUSION

Returning to the hypothesis that restricted access to fishing and fewer fish caught amounts to an increase in social problems, it appears that fishing is a double-edged sword for many individuals. In good fishing years, there is an increase in alcohol problems, drug use, adultery, and divorce. In bad years, there is an increase in depression and anxiety, alcohol use, family violence, and relational problems. When there is a surplus of money, there is hedonistic behaviour. When there is a deficit, there is a lot of anxiety, tension, irritability, and people looking for someone to blame. But it is not sufficient to link these problems solely with economic highs and lows. A good fishing year means more than just catching a lot of fish and making a lot of money.

Salmon fishing is the primary identity for King Cove's fishermen and families. When it is restricted, the first step is to intensify salmon fishing further. The second step is to expand into fishing for other species, notably groundfish. The third step is to intensify fishing for other species. When these options fail, an increase in community-wide problems is revealed.

Conditions where there are no alternative outlets to status in the Eastern Aleutians are developing in the context of changing social systems that, by default, create limited entry systems and place the possibility of achieving status in the hands of a few individuals. Thus, we can predict that in cases where we remove social, political, economic, or other culturally prescribed means of gaining status, men will seek alternative routes, which may include criminal activity and aggression. But contrary to the prehistoric and ethnohistoric periods in the Far North, violent behaviour today does not lead to success in arctic communities, although there may be some individual perception that it does. Today, when an individual has a choice or opportunity for alternative forms of competition – such as Native arts, hunting, or, in Alaska, village basketball games – many of the same accolades formally given to successful warriors are now given to the most celebrated artists or sports stars (Blanchard 1983; Collings and Condon 1996; Condon 1987, 1995; McDiarmid 1983). Sled-dog racing is encouraged as an alternative to drinking and substance abuse in Yup'ik villages, because it requires a good deal of time and energy and there is no time to get into trouble (Hensel 1996:198–9n8). Eastern Aleutian village-based juvenile delinquency and suicide prevention programs include funding to increase culturally appropriate creative outlets and sports participation (EATS, personal comm.). But even among these alternative roles and identities, some individuals are left behind. In a broader sense, King Cove residents are nervous about their future, and there is an element of lost control over their livelihood.

I argue that all societies have some individuals who strive for status along culturally prescribed avenues of social success. These routes to social success in King Cove are tied directly to the fisheries. In many cases, a loss of access to these outlets of status and prestige, especially for young men, has resulted in a sense of disenfranchisement that often leads to social deviance. Suicide, spouse abuse, assaults, and non-violent crimes are seen as symptoms of a growing sense of hopelessness among Aleut youth. A sense that no matter how much effort one puts into the socially prescribed behaviours that signify what it means to be a "good" man or women, they will never be able to acquire the rewards that should come from such a social investment. They are torn between a desire to participate in their heritage and the recognition that it may be fruitless. The result has been increased levels of teenage pregnancy, alcoholism, spouse abuse, and petty crime. Why these behaviours? Because they are seen, at least among their peers, as possible outlets to status. Access to alcohol, sex, and violence are the only means that some individuals have to stand out among their contemporaries. If it can be shown that the root of decisions to participate in socially deviant activities is proportionate to alternative outlets to status and prestige, then new social mechanisms oriented towards these outlets can be implemented.

Local Aleuts share to some extent a conceptualization of criminal or anti-social behaviour with that of the larger Western society. But the Aleut also perceive these behaviours through what they believe are the explanations, linking them continually to fishing. People model problems within the village, their households, and their personal lives in relation to fishing, and there is powerful language in the healing powers of subsistence and commercial harvesting. Healthy fisheries and full involvement in fishing, sharing, and relating is crucial to the social health of the community.

Identity in Context

Many men go fishing all of their lives without knowing that it is not fish they are after.

Henry David Thoreau (1817–62)

THE LAND FROM THE SEA

Eastern Aleut villages at the turn of the twenty-first century are intimately intertwined with a volatile way of life on a volatile landscape. The Eastern Aleut not only maintain access to the resources upon which they have traditionally depended, but they have translated this access into a contemporary commercial economy through both active and passive conditions, creating an unusual cultural continuity and a social system dependent on participation in the industry.

A great deal of arctic anthropology privileges subsistence over commercial aspects of life. At the same time, there can be an assumption that "progress" moves from subsistence to commercial economies. Here, commercialization is neither a threat to traditional ways nor is it a natural progressive stage, but instead it is part of the sociocultural processes that are the foundation of the community. Aleut fishing activities are sometimes similar to those of non-Natives or other Alaska fishing communities, but there are aspects that give worth to the Aleut that make this fishery their own. For a boy to be a man, he must fish and must strive to one day have a boat, crew, stable marriage, and large family. Thoreau's observation in the nineteenth century suggests that the lifestyle is the draw, not the actual fish (which may explain why catch-and-release fishing is popular). For the Aleut, however, it is both a way of life and the fish. Fish are both sold and eaten. Fishing represents what Bourdieu outlined as identity through practice, in which fishing is a franchise that allows the Aleut to maintain individual identity, social relationships, and collective identity.

The fishing industry did not happen to the Aleut; rather, they have taken control of what they can. They voluntarily migrated away from smaller villages to the more profitable amalgamation villages. Fishing was by no means a new activity, and local knowledge was expanded through participation in the industry to include a broader fishing range and more species. It is this industrialization that has provided an occasion for the Eastern Aleut to live in their homeland and emphasize cultural distinctiveness. Commercial fishing is by no means the "wage gathering" of the foraging Naiken of South India, where jobs were exploited for their wages and incorporated into customary foraging strategies (Bird 1982); nor is it practised in order to maintain the subsistence base as found throughout much of the Arctic (e.g., Rasing 1994; Wolfe 1984). Instead, commercial fishing is the practise of culture itself and is interrelated with individual identity. The activity is never referred to as a job or a career in the way that "land jobs" are, and land jobs are always considered temporary until the opportunity for crewing on a boat improves. The Aleut do not perform rituals surrounding fishing; the fishing itself is the ritual.

The first chapter outlined the major arguments in which status is brought to the forefront of identity development and maintenance. Changes in fishing have major ramifications for Aleut identity. The way to understand the problem is to "define the terms" using culturally salient categories. Anthropologists have argued that identity is a stable phenomenon in modernity, but in a postmodern world it is believed that we can avoid fixation and keep our options open. Assuming every individual has equal opportunities available to him or her, the postmodern ideal would allow everyone to freely choose identity classification tailored with individual style. We are, however, unevenly bound by the unconscious and by the social world. Culture is shaped simultaneously by psychological processes that influence thought, motivation, and emotion, and by social processes that influence social interactions, motivation, and choice.

The Aleut define themselves in an unconventional way. Their way is unrecognized by government and bureaucracy as a "way of life" for indigenous people. They are most often acknowledged as having a "mixed" economy but are lumped with other groups as being subsistence-based when acknowledged. Otherwise, the Aleut are whitewashed. Thus, there is variability in Alaska Native economic exchange and thus in their self-definitions. These are understudied and misunderstood people. I hope to have challenged the ways in which many anthropologists examine hunter-gatherers and Alaska Natives, and describe the development of commercial industries within a Native population, looking at how we measure success and failure specific to a society.

In chapter 2 I produced a vibrant history of the Eastern Aleutians out of a historiographically difficult record, one that is particularly sketchy for the Alaska Peninsula. My reading of Aleut history suggests cultural complexity and a marine identity through several major units of time. The living generations of Aleuts are in some ways disjointed from history because of their ancestors' estrangement from painful twentieth-century events. Recognizing the potential of the fishing industry, Aleuts migrated from smaller villages to build profitable towns. This was a progressive move without a rejection of the past. Participation in the fishing industry raised the standard of living among Aleuts. This was the intention of the Aleut; they recognized the potential of commercial enterprise.

My reading of history is important for today's events. The development of commercial industries was mutual among Aleuts and newcomers. History has important implications for current political battles, but is as yet untapped. This history is likewise critical in matters of status and pride in being Aleut. To be a "kayak hunter" in the Russian era was to be sought after, conscripted, and transported because of the specialized skill one possessed. The desired skills of power and accuracy in sea otter hunting transformed into skills of running a boat, organizing a crew, and bringing in fish. These skill requirements were later accompanied by a system that limited participation and put automatic capital in the hands of some, and actively stripped others of their identity and often their ability to live in their village.

In chapters 3 and 4, I showed how closely connected subsistence and commercial fisheries are, and continued to build my argument that being Aleut is the practice of combining these systems. The fishing franchise is a system of interaction, complementarity of men and women, proscription, and obligation. Limited Entry added a layer of proscription that set the stage for future relations and opportunities, such that there are multiple limited entry systems, and access to fishing assets allows for access to many social and cultural resources.

Women are within men's public sphere, and through sharing and fulfilling obligations are critical for the men to be successful.

Fish distribution forms the fabric of a range of social relationships and etiquette. As Gluckman wrote, "It's not the beer that counts: the invitation to drink is a symbol of recognition of kinship" (1965:45). Some feel more justified in receiving fish, while some feel burdened by the obligation to provide fish to certain people but not others. I illustrated the burdens placed upon crewmen and captains, and how they must negotiate status. Most crewmen cannot work their way up to being a captain, which goes against the grain of social organization. This phenomenon is crucial to an understanding of variability in men's status. I presented the distribution before the production because it is important to know the demands placed on people engaged in various aspects of fishing before we examine how recognized fishing assets are obtained.

The Aleut captains are commercial fishermen and are out for profit, but they hire kinsmen (not necessarily the best fishermen). Thus, they are average capitalists but better family men. I showed how, in making crew selection, Aleut boat captains maximize productive effort sometimes, but more often they consolidate productive effort. In this way I hope to have shown how the evolutionary propositions of Maynard-Smith (1964) can be used to explain some aspects of indigenous societies in a modern economic context. The state blames resource exhaustion on the perceived capitalistic drive and competitiveness of Area M's fishermen, but the data show that their decisions are not based on maximizing profit. Nadel-Klein examined "how capitalism can create and then dismiss a way of life" in Scottish fishing communities (2003:1), and in many ways the Aleut have been encouraged by capitalism, only to have their access to the fisheries eroded. The US economy is based upon growth, not sustainability. The Aleut simply want their present relative affluence to be a permanent condition.

The current fisheries system is set up to exclude many people from fishing and gives unequal access to indigenous commercial fishermen. With the Limited Entry system, the rights of the person and the rights of property became set apart. Prior to this system, the fisherman had rights in the open fishery based on his own initiative and his known negotiable position within the society. His status depended on his participation in fishing (or sea otter hunting or fur seal hunting) as a routine group event visible to the rest of the society.

Limited Entry added the state, creating a sharp divide between those with fishing capital and those without. As described in chapter 1, the quest for status is itself a "limited entry system," in which the defined prestige-allocation criteria can be filled only by some, not by all. The imposed system put the majority of the resources in the hands of a few, further limiting options for upward social mobility. Those with the resources have rapidly intensified fishing effort through the technology of extraction. The fish buyers, necessary entities for the Eastern Aleut to do business, represent another conflicting group interest and are controlled by (disguised) foreign corporate interests.

In chapter 5 I moved from intercommunity to international relations and considered differential government and bureaucratic perspectives on indigenousness through two major ongoing struggles: the salmon wars and environmental dehumanization. The idea of indigenous peoples in commercial economies is not fully recognized in Alaska. Contrary to the Aleut, the Yupiit and Iñupiat promote themselves as authentically indigenous. This notion of "the traditional" has held sway with government regulators and anthropologists. The Aleut have taken a different track, arguing that they have rights as commercial fishermen. Indeed, the Aleut took on the term "Area M" as it became synonymous with their fisheries, with every player in the salmon wars speaking the same terms but with vastly different meanings. I also considered the effects of listing the Steller sea lion as endangered and the ramifications on the Aleut depending on how the problem is defined. Millions of dollars have been appropriated to study the sea lion decline, but these studies often start with assumptions about commercial fishing. The Aleut are desperately seeking to avoid governmental dependency. The state, whose social services are already stretched, should share in their fears.

Chapter 6 considered those who are being left out of the fishing system and asked what is happening to them. Young Aleut men are not turning to crafts or sports but to alcohol and petty crime. Here, I attempted to explain why criminologists cannot find Western correlates of crime in indigenous communities, and argued that correlates must be locally defined. Aleut well-being, measured through fishing access, sharing, and family relationships, seems to have an inverse relationship to fishing.

On the occasions when I found myself on boats, the crews of fishermen were often acting tough, showing off, and berating one another for the benefit of their audience. But when it came time to tie up to a dock or to load gear, all the individualistic behaviour disappeared, and they began moving in concert, understanding both the tasks and one another with nods and mumbles over the loud engine. There was solidarity and mutual understanding in their actions. However, both before the task and afterwards, the individualized and competitive aspects came to the forefront of behaviour again. The culture of fishing provides cohesion, often between kin members on the boat and on land, as well as community vitality and cultural continuity, while allowing for individual expression, success, and identity.

FISHING FOR IDENTITY

Following Rasing's discussion of "hunting for identity" among the Iglulingmiut (1994:170–2), the Aleut are fishing for identity. However, fishing does not have dual meaning in this headline: they are not in search of their identity, but they are desperately seeking to be accurately understood as legitimate commercial fishermen and as indigenous people. Area M is not a fishery of "outsiders," as the majority of the State of Alaska believes; they are local Aleut men and women with long-term vested interests in continuing their livelihood and securing rights for future generations.

Change is seldom witnessed in the course of fieldwork. This is not the case here. The social health of the Eastern Aleut is directly related to commercial fishing, especially to status roles within the system. Fishermen who are currently active in fishing are reluctant to admit that certain fisheries need a moratorium or reduction in order to recover or grow to a healthy population. It is mostly the retired fishermen who will discuss options for restoring fish stocks. One retired fisherman was frustrated that Fish & Game was opening a Tanner crab season "and not letting them come back before opening the fishery full force." Younger fishermen believe that populations have to rebound too, but there is too much at stake socially and economically to admit it.

Celebrations surrounding fishing are changing. For example, during the Fourth of July, which is perhaps the biggest community-wide celebration of the year, fishermen used to do a "boat parade" and run their boats out in the bay in a queue. "Not no more," said one woman. "They don't want to waste the fuel, I guess."

The theme of Aleut culture is expressed in ritual by means of the symbols connected to the social and cultural context of the daily life of Aleut fishermen. Cultural transmission is the process of passing on culturally relevant knowledge, skills, attitudes, and values from person to person or from culture to culture. The Aleut maintain a profound relationship with the sea, so strong that, especially for the younger generations, it partially excludes a broad knowledge and experience of the interior land, except for good places to hunt caribou and waterfowl. Even the first community clinic was a ship that made annual visits that patients skiffed out to meet in the bay.

Fishing is an ensemble of beliefs, sentiments, and practices that is visible and tangible. The small, close community of King Cove shares, to some extent, emotional characteristics. Problems within fishing are challenging at the emotional level; for example, when a boat sinks or someone is lost at sea, the whole community claims the loss. In the early 1990s, when a boy was killed by a bear, for months after the incident others in the community shot and killed every bear they saw as a kind of retribution. When the price of fish is low, when the fishermen are not catching enough fish to satisfy their needs, the entire community shares in the stress and frustration that this brings, but the extent to which individuals feel this difficulty is uneven and depends on factors of prior assets, household need, family networks, and expectations.

Part of identity is to have a future. Fishermen are always weighing the potential of the next opening, the next season, and the next year. The hope of this continuity is the place where identity is renewed seasonally as well as generationally.

A behavioural health clinician once told me that their individualized treatment modalities have got the cart before the horse, that they should be focusing their efforts on "community self-definition and identity development." Only after these were better established would they have some foundation upon which to build individualized interventions. He emphasized "unresolved grief" (masquerading as a multitude of things and manifesting in a significant amount of drug and alcohol abuse), both confounded with and maintained by dependence on unpredictable government funding streams. In combination, he argued, these create "marked psychological inertia." A number of other non-Aleut social or health service workers, though temporary, emphasized contact with "white civilization" as having the most significant impact on Aleut society because of the cultural discontinuity it created. At the individual level, these workers all pointed to a sense of self that is adrift in an unpredictable socioeconomic environment driven by forces outside local control, but they did not really know what "type" of sense of self was appropriate or, in their words, was "adaptive" for the Eastern Aleut. One health worker pointed to the fact that local people have "evolved to cope with unpredictability." He even proposed that alcohol abuse could be the norm and "would best be studied in context before simply being 'changed' as an expression of transient majority culture values." Statements from the Alaska Native Tribal Health Consortium support the idea that behavioural health services should be responsive to local realities.

There are elements of Eastern Aleut culture that seem to hold great tenacity, whilst other elements seem to be so fragile that the culture and society could easily vanish. The Aleut are dependent on unreliable resources and unreliable government funding sources while enduring a cumulative series of regulations meant to preserve the rights of other indigenous people. In the future, the cannery could realistically operate independent of the local fleet. The disconnect with difficult twentieth-century events, in which one woman said, "We grew up not knowing any of this. Our parents never talked about it," as well as the uncertainties of the fishing industry, indicates that the Aleut might not be able to fully grasp either the past or a future, putting them in a vulnerable position. The past, however, seems to be crucial to maintaining their lives as fishermen, establishing legitimacy. Cultural awareness/revival is becoming a survival strategy.

THE COSMOPOLITAN ALEUT

Worldwide, there are many cases in which industry has become a cultural construct, both a livelihood and a cultural foundation intertwined with every aspect of society. For example, when Margaret Thatcher closed the coal mines in Britain, the Great Miners' Strike of 1984–85 was an unsuccessful fight with the government in which the miners were struggling to maintain the only life they knew (Beynon 1985). And in the Copperbelt, after the bottom fell out of the copper market, Zambian miners experienced a rapid decline economically, socially, and culturally, having intertwined significant aspects of their lives with the copper industry (Ferguson 1999).

Modernity is assumed to be corrupting. Here, I have examined various forms of social dis-ease but do not uphold a Golden Age of Aleut past life. The Aleut are not outside modern times: they watch television, play basketball, speak American English, drive trucks, listen to Top 40 music, and argue over events in Iraq and Washington, DC. They are very much a part of American life, even if sometimes it can be an uneasy fit. A young Aleut woman about to travel outside Alaska for the first time said, "I'm gonna get a lot of igloo shit, huh?"

The Aleut have a mixed Russian and Scandinavian heritage, and it is the descendants of foreigners who are the living Eastern Aleut. The Aleut homeland does not border with other Native groups and hence Aleuts do not express Nativeness with they same intensity as is done in other parts of Alaska. They have developed a successful economy, but the fisheries change yearly, given both natural and human activities. Business diversity is not likely or feasible. Population increases have been small but significant because of economic limitations, and the village has continued to expand along the edge of the bay. Realistically, this could be the last generation of fishermen in King Cove, and perhaps the last generation of village residents, since they have been excluded from receiving federal community development funds *because* of their relative economic success in fishing.

Ultimately, our appreciation of hunting, gathering, and fishing societies must be thought about in terms of "the customary practice of change" (Bodenhorn 2000/2001:25). The irony of the Aleut case is that they are being pushed into simplifying their complex cultural matrix and essentializing themselves in order to gain recognition as indigenous people and survive in their homeland. Minnegal et al. (2003) show how in Victoria, Australia, commercial fishermen turn to "conventional props of tradition" to establish themselves generationally in a landed community with a specialized knowledge in order to combat threats to their place in the industry, even though they are sometimes only first- or second-generation fishermen who relocate frequently, thus creating a politicized identity of person, place, and practice. The Aleut stand firmly in historical, generational, and experiential tradition, but they are learning to reshape this as their identity to present to outsiders. Sahlins (1976) wrote that economic models are sometimes taken as deterministic or as common sense such that the social and cultural data are ignored. For the Eastern Aleutians, the subsistence model does not capture the range of beliefs, behaviours, and practices. "Indigenous commercial economies" captures more of that range, including changes in skill requirements, from training in harpoon throwing with power and accuracy out of baidarkas in their youth to running large, powerful boats and organizing crewmen. After all, the world's hunter-gatherers are people "who hardly seem to hunt and gather anymore" (Myers 1988:273).

Identity development in the Aleut village of King Cove is a process involving both lived experience (i.e., "I'm Aleut, I'm a fisherman") and outside forces and perceptions (i.e., "This is not a *real* village") simultaneously combined with symbols of status and prestige that relate to the past and present. Socioeconomic change will not be detrimental if it enables identity to expand around core principles that are maintained. Nothing is static; internal and external factors have an impact on identity. The Aleut show that social conflict may produce common symptoms but arises from culturally salient causes. These issues are very complex even in small places.

APPENDIX

Subsistence Tables

Table A
Local species commonly used by the people of the Eastern Aleutians, based on interviews and dinner invitations

Terrestrial mammals	*Marine mammals*
Caribou (*Rangifer tarandus*)	Harbor seal (*Phoca vitulina*)
Domestic cow, feral (*Bos taurus*)	Steller sea lion (*Eumetopias jubatus*)
Porcupine (*Erethizon dorsatum*)	California sea lion (*Zalophus californicus*)
Red fox (*Vulpes vulpes*)	Sea otter (*Enhydra lutris*)
Brown bear (*Ursus arctos*)	Northern fur seal (*Callorinus ursinus*)
	Whale (multiple species)

Fish	*Marine invertebrates*
King salmon (*Oncorhynchus tshawytscha*)	Red king crab (*Paralithoides camtschatica*)
Sockeye salmon (*Oncorhynchus nerka*)	Dungeness crab (*Cancer magister*)
Chum salmon (*Oncorhynchus keta*)	Tanner-opilio crab (*Chionoecetes opilio*)
Pink salmon (*Oncorhynchus gorbuscha*)	Tanner-bairdi crab (*Chionoecetes bairdi*)
Coho salmon (*Oncorhynchus kisutch*)	Butter clam (*Saxidomus gigantean*)
Pacific herring (*Clupea harengus*)	Pacific littleneck clams (*Protothaca*
Dolly varden (*Salvelinus malma*)	*staminea*)
Pacific cod (*Gadus macrocephalus*)	Razor clam (*Siliqua patula*)
Black cod (*Anoplopoma fimbria*)	Octopus ("cuttlefish") (*Octopus dolfleini*)
Pacific halibut (*Hippoglossus stenolepis*)	Black chitons, or *bidarkis* (*Katharina*
Red rockfish (*Sebastes alutus*)	*tunicata*)
Walleye pollock (*Theragra chalcogramma*)	Mussels (*Mytilus edulis*)
Sculpin (*Myoxocephalus sp.*)	Snails (*Fusitriton oregonensis*)
Greenling, or "pogies" (*Hexagrammos sp.*)	Sea urchin (*Strongylocentrotus*
	droebachiensis)
	Sea cucumber (*Bathyplotes sp.*)

Waterfowl and eggs	*Plants/berries*
Canada goose (*Branta canadensis*)	Salmonberries (*Rubus chamaemorus*)
Brant (*Branta bernicla*)	Cranberries (*Vaccinium uliginosum*)
Emperor goose (*Philacte canagica*)	Mossberries (*Empetrum nigrum*)
Pintail (*Anas acuta*)	Blueberries (*Vaccinium uliginosum*)

Mallard (*Anas platyrhyncos*)	Wine berries (*Cornus suecica*)
Willow ptarmigan (*Lagopus lagopus*)	Petrushki (*Ligusticum hultenii*)
Seagull eggs	Pushki (*Heracleum lanatum*)

Table B
Subsistence salmon harvests (numbers of fish) in King Cove per year, 1985–2007

1985	4,201	1993	6,865	2001	7,060
1986	2,889	1994	6,588	2002	7,543
1987	4,525	1995	8,137	2003	9,219
1988	3,721	1996	9,905	2004	8,189
1989	4,942	1997	7,277	2005	8,237
1990	4,542	1998	6,458	2006	7,154
1991	5,699	1999	6,939	2007	5,718
1992	5,856	2000	6,460		

Source: Annual Salmon Management Reports (ASMR), Fish & Game, Kodiak

Abbreviations

ABWC	Alaska Beluga Whaling Committee
ADF&G	Alaska Department of Fish and Game
ADN	*Anchorage Daily News*
AEB	Aleutians East Borough
AEBSD	Aleutians East Borough School District
AEWC	Alaska Eskimo Whaling Commission
AFDF	Alaska Fisheries Development Foundation
AHA	Aleutian Housing Authority
AIA	Aleut International Association
AMMC	Aleut Marine Mammal Commission
ANCSA	Alaska Native Claims Settlement Act
ANILCA	Alaska National Interest Land Conservation Act
APICDA	Aleutian Pribilof Islands Community Development Association
APCFA	Alaska Peninsula Coastal Fishermen's Association
APIA	Aleutian Pribilof Islands Association
AS	Alaska Statute
ASMR	Annual Salmon Management Reports
ATC	Agdaagux Tribal Council
AVCP	Association of Village Council Presidents
AYK	Arctic–Yukon–Kuskokwim
BIA	Bureau of Indian Affairs
BOF	State Board of Fisheries
BOG	State Board of Game
BP	Bering Pacific Seafoods
CAMF	Concerned Area M Fishermen
CDL	commercial driver's licence

CDQ	community development quota
CFEC	Commercial Fisheries Entry Commission
CHA	community health aide
DCED	Department of Community and Economic Development
DFYS	Division of Family and Youth Services
DPS	Alaska Department of Public Safety
DWI	driving while intoxicated
EATS	Eastern Aleutian Tribes
EEZ	Exclusive Economic Zone, 200-mile limit
EFH	essential fish habitat
ESA	Endangered Species Act
F/V	Fishing Vessel
GOAC3	Gulf of Alaska Coastal Communities Coalition
HUD	Housing and Urban Development
IFQ	individual fishing quota
IRA	Indian Reorganization Act
KCC	King Cove Corporation
LLP	Limited License Program
Lower 48	The 48 contiguous continental United States
MMPA	Marine Mammal Protection Act
M/V	Marine Vessel
NARF	Native American Rights Fund
NGO	non-governmental organization
NICWA	National Indian Child Welfare Act
NMFS	National Marine Fisheries Service
NOAA	National Oceanic and Atmospheric Administration
NPFMC	North Pacific Fisheries Management Council
NWR	National Wildlife Refuge
PAF	Pacific American Fisheries
PFD	Permanent Fund Dividend
PL	Public Law
PMA	Peninsula Marketing Association
PNAC	Pacific Northwest Aleut Council
PPSF	Peter Pan Seafoods, Inc
RAC	Regional Advisory Council to the Federal Subsistence Board
RATNET	Rural Alaska Television Network
RSW	refrigerated sea water
SFA	Sustainable Fisheries Act

TEK	traditional ecological knowledge
UCR	Uniform Crime Report
USCG	US Coast Guard
USF&WS	US Fish and Wildlife Service
VFR	visual flight rules
VHF	very high frequency
VMS	Vessel Monitoring System
VPSO	village public safety officer

Notes

CHAPTER ONE

1 In papers presented at the 2006 annual meeting of the American Anthropological Association in San Jose, CA, "identity" was the most prevalent topic, appearing in 37 papers and symposia.

2 This "tragedy" posits fish as a common property resource that is over-exploited by individual fishermen because there is no benefit for them to conserve in ways that privately owned resources might be protected (Hardin 1968). Durrenberger and King argue that fish are not common property resources in state societies but are state property that is heavily regulated and accessible only to certain constituents (2000:3–4).

3 The science and/or business of cultivating fish or shellfish under controlled conditions.

4 The fishing crisis Aleuts face is one of many (McCloskey 1998; McGoodwin 1990), the collapse of the Atlantic cod fishery perhaps receiving the most publicity (Carey 1999; Chantraine 1993; Haedrich and Hamilton 2000; Kurlansky 1997). In the PBS Frontline series *Empty Oceans, Empty Nets* (2001), it was argued that there is "serial depletion" of marine resources and fish cannot reproduce quickly enough to keep up with current demands. There is intensified fishing pressure even though the global catch has decreased. Species caught today were barely considered edible a decade ago. Bycatch (the unintended or unwanted species caught in the context of other fishing, often commercially unusable or undesirable at the time) is argued to be the greatest concern, with 20 million metric tons discarded worldwide (four times the US fleet catch, Pacific and Atlantic).

5   The Aleutians West Census Area has an Aleut population of approximately 1,500. Many Aleuts also reside in Anchorage (see also Morgan 1976) as well as in the Pacific Northwest, where approximately 600 Aleuts live in Washington and Oregon and are members of the Northwest Aleut Association.

6   "Fisher" has entered the social and political jargon as more politically correct and gender inclusive. Many women who fish reject the term (Allison, Jacobs, and Porter 1989:xix; Fields 1997), and many Alaskan fishermen understand a fisher to be a "furry animal related to the marten" (Lord 1997:xi). The Aleut use only the term "fisherman," and they understand it to include women who fish.

7   Annual cheques are issued to every Alaska resident based upon the state's earnings from oil revenues. In 2002 they were us$1,540.76 per resident; in 2003 they were us$1,107.56, and in 2004 they were us$919.84.

8   Congress passed ANCSA (PL 96–487) as a means of settling land claims with Alaska Natives. Contrived as an improvement over the failed policies of allotment and termination in the Lower 48 (Berger 1985; Case 1984; Flanders 1989), ANCSA was rendered through the formation of thirteen regional for-profit corporations, twelve regional non-profit social service corporations, and over two hundred village corporations. Legislation provided a land settlement totalling 44 million acres (17.8 million hectares) and a cash settlement of us$962 million divided between the thirteen regional corporations. Individuals became shareholders of the village, non-profit, and regional corporations.

9   The Aleut International Association (AIA) was formed in order for Aleuts to become members of the Arctic Council, and its staff overlaps with APIA.

10   Health care is managed by APIA for the Belkofski Tribe instead of EATS.

11   E.g., Bodenhorn 1988, 1989; Caulfield 1997; Condon 1996; Dombrowski 2001; Fienup-Riordan 1983b, 2000; Jolles 2002; Kruse 1991; Langdon 1991; Nuttall 1992; Wheeler 1998; Worl and Smythe 1986.

12   Jones gave fictitious names for the villages (New Harbor for King Cove and Iliaka for Unalaska) to disguise informants. However, the villages were easily identifiable through her descriptions.

13   At the time of her fieldwork, the Russian Orthodox church had not yet been built in King Cove.

14   Recent omissions in Hall 1988; Smith and McCarter 1997; and Lee and Daly's 1999 *Cambridge Encyclopedia of Hunters and Gatherers*.

15   I introduced the term "Fourth World" to a group of Aleut fishermen in the Harbor House one morning over coffee. They thought it was "ridiculous"

because it sounds worse off than "Third World" and implies an even lower standard of living.

16 "Subsistence" is a poor word for the activities and beliefs that it is used to describe in Alaska. In most definitions, "subsistence" refers to means of support or providing sustenance, often the barest means. For the Aleut, "subsistence" is a local word, with local meaning.

17 The lack of discussions on commercial activities or on commoditized exchange in many parts of the Arctic could also reflect that there are laws against such activities, not that sale and exchange do not occur. At the same time, laws do not explain why people might not sell wild foods; for example, the Iñupiat of Barrow did not sell their whale meat even when it was legal to do so (Bodenhorn 2000/2001).

18 The "skipper effect" – that a captain's personal ability to locate and harvest fish determines the amount caught – has been debated in opposition to technological and ecological variables, such as boat size, crew, and effort (Pálsson and Durrenberger 1990; Gatewood 1984; McNabb 1985). Success for Aleut captains is explained by a combination of variables, including luck, which sometimes looks like the "skipper effect" and sometimes does not.

19 The conical hat also increased the bearer's height so that he would appear taller than everyone around him.

20 Other discussion of sports arenas as social centres where relationships get "worked out" are found in Rabinowitz's work on Palestinian-Israeli relations via basketball in *Overlooking Nazareth* (1997) and in Sprott's (1997) article on basketball and sled dog racing as part of intervillage rivalry in the Iñupiaq village of Noorvik.

CHAPTER TWO

1 Famously known as Seward's Folley. The purchasing price for this allegedly barren land was US$7.2 million.

2 The first expedition under these same orders found Bering passing through the strait that bears his name and landing on St Lawrence Island, but he never sighted the American continent.

3 The major voyages were as follows. 1743–47: Basov, sergeant of Okhotsk Port Command, went in search of sea otters "like Jason in search of the Golden Fleece" (Berkh 1823/1974:2). 1745–46: a detachment wintered over on Agattu and Attu and encountered Aleuts. 1747–64: merchant Andreian Tolstykh spent time in the Andreanof Islands (named after him),

but his notes from his final voyage were lost in a shipwreck; testimonials by Tolstykh and his companions Vesiutinskii and Lazarev were recorded and eventually presented to Catherine II. 1752: merchants Bashmakov and Serebrennikov recorded wildlife and Aleut life on Adak Island. 1759–62: Glotov, Solov'ev, and tribute collector Ponomarev happened upon the Fox Islands and "established friendly relations," according to Liapinova (1996:25), but most accounts describe how they brutally killed Aleuts and burned their villages (Black 1977; Golovin 1983:107).

4   Between 1803 and 1806, Captains Kruzenshtern and Lisianskii (1814) collected Aleut artifacts, while Langsdorff (1813–14), a naturalist on this voyage, made ethnographic descriptions. Between 1817 and 1819, Golovin set sail (1979, 1983). Artists on the voyages of Litke and Staniukovich made collections and detailed drawings of Aleut life, 1826–29 (Litke 1987). Khlebnikov (1994), a Russian-American Company employee, made an attempt to reconstruct Aleut social history in 1818–32.

5   A number of primary sources have yet to be translated or published.

6   E.g., Bank 1958; Dumond 1987; Dumond and Bland 1995; Hoffman 1999; Laughlin 1963, 1980; Maschner *et al* 1997; Maschner and Reedy-Maschner 1998; McCartney 1974, 1984.

7   E.g., Berreman 1956, 1964; Black 1984; Jones 1976; Lantis 1970, 1984; Marsh 1954; Marsh and Laughlin 1956; Milan 1974; Ransom 1946; Robert-Lamblin 1982b; Rubel 1961.

8   Whaling was done by smearing aconitum poison from monkshood root on lances that had ownership marks on them (Collins, Clark, and Walker 1945:29).

9   Social and cultural differences coincided with linguistic boundaries. Linguistic differences were the bases of prejudice; folklore about survivors of raids only learning or remembering the "baby talk" of their local language are in evidence (Bergsland 1959:124–6; Black 1984:43–4; Khlebnikov 1994:173; Netsvetov 1980).

10 Louis Choris (1795–1828) was on the voyage with Otto Von Kotzebue between 1815 and 1817.

11 Versions of these "outside men" can be found in many societies as enemy bushmen (e.g., E. Basso 1978).

12 In the High Arctic whaling was and is a cooperative effort, yet it is still heroic for all participants and a route to status for the captain (Burch 1998a, 1998b).

13 A map of the ethnonyms of dialect areas as described by Aleuts living on Unalaska indicates at least ten distinct groups, though the local names of those in the far east and west are unknown since, for example, it is

unlikely that Shumagin villagers called themselves *Qawaqngin,* "those beyond the Easterners" (Black 1984:x).

14 The Tlingit had attacked and taken over these Russian headquarters for two years. Alexander Baranof, as governor of Alaska, built up a force to retake Fort Sitka. It is unclear how many of his men were Aleut rather than Alutiiq.

15 Aleuts still live on the Commanders today and face severe economic and social problems, but they have no representation in the regional legislature (Krivoshapkin 1996; Lebedeva 1993).

16 Boas (1899) examined property marks on Iñupiat hunting weapons of whale and walrus and concluded that they were most likely identity markers for the individual hunter to claim his kill. In the whale hunt, meat was divided between those whose marks were found on the weapon that killed the whale and the people of the village who discovered the beached animal. If there were multiple harpoon points in the animal, then the owner of the point closest to the head received the meat. Marks could be individual or communal, and ornamental variation between villages was greater than within them. See also Worl (1980) on current practices.

17 Clams are now sent to Anchorage for testing each year.

18 This is still common. In King Cove, for example, four brothers of one family are married to four sisters from another.

19 In the Molly Hootch case of 1975, Native students sued the Alaska state-operated school system, compelling the state to provide secondary schools in rural Native communities (Case 1984:203–4). The state legislature established Regional Educational Attendance Areas, which the Aleutians East Borough now administers.

20 One man had a record shop in King Cove several decades ago where orders were placed from Unalaska to Nelson Lagoon for Scandinavian music by Stan Bierstad and Yumpalong Yanson singing fishermen's songs with such names as "Who Threw the Halibut on the Poop Deck?"

21 Fish traps were located in the path of migrating salmon, which were corralled into a pot in the centre of the trap and then brailed out of the pot and onto a tendering vessel. The state built into Alaska's constitution requirements for maintaining adequate escapement.

22 Antitrust laws following the 1890 Sherman Antitrust Act prevent this kind of monopoly. The processors can own their own boats but cannot own quotas, so they contract with fishermen and privately owned tenders in quota or permit fisheries. Processor-owned vessels can, however, fish for species not regulated by permit or quota. The 2005 crab rationalization program, however, allocates quota shares to processors, harvesters,

and communities, effectively shrinking local participation in crab fisheries (Lowe 2008) and setting a dangerous precedent for other Bering Sea and North Pacific fisheries.

23 Bering Pacific Seafoods operated only for two years, closing because of low salmon runs and high production costs. It opened again for the 2008 and 2009 seasons.

CHAPTER THREE

1 Alaska is the only coastal state in which the coast guard requires boat registration, because the state does not have a separate boating safety program.

2 The current federal subsistence fisheries management plan, which became effective on 1 October 1999, expands federal management of subsistence fisheries to Alaskan rivers and lakes within and adjacent to federal public lands. The plan is in response to the 1990 *Katie John* legal case and was implemented to comply with the rural subsistence priority established by ANILCA on federal waters. Created by President Carter in 1980, ANILCA locked up 104 million acres (42 million hectares) as federal public lands. It also established a rural subsistence priority, regardless of ethnicity. This priority was not added to Alaska's constitution because many felt that it discriminates against urban Alaskans. The state made the decision not to appeal the *Katie John* case in the US Supreme Court in 2001. A rural priority as a Constitutional Amendment is supported, and *subsistence is a priority over all other uses.*

3 Wolfe and Walker's (1987) survey of subsistence harvests in Alaska, which considers developmental impacts to subsistence productivity, does not include a single Aleut village.

4 A celebrated meal served by friends in King Cove that my husband and I rave about, which has been recreated several times since, is a steaming pile of king crab legs and a bottle of Johnny Walker Black, and that's it.

5 This excludes a few non-Native teachers, clinicians, cannery managers, and cannery labourers.

6 I used Family Tree Maker Version 9.0. Several women and a few men pored over the genealogy with me, which I would then update on the computer, print out, and take right back to them and to others for editing.

7 Unlike that found in most Native American societies, the Aleut do not appear to have a problem with obesity, in part, I think, owing to the physical demands of fishing and processing, and to diet.

8 Fish & Game reports do not show this gap statistically, but officials know that it exists. How this influences their policymaking I cannot say.

9 This is not just "talk." Peter Pan Seafoods has explored the possibility of expanding a cannery-owned fleet. However, another cannery in a nearby Aleut village has been dubbed "the evil empire" for doing just that. Canneries are able to form as part of the License Limitation Program (LLP) and own vessels that can fish in federal waters for any species not regulated by permit or quota.

10 *Ikura* is salmon roe; *sujiko* is processed caviar still in the egg sack; *surimi* is a fish paste used in many commercial fish products.

11 For example, it will not buy fish off a boat with a dog on board, because dogs tend to relieve themselves on the deck, which pollutes the fish holds below.

12 This refers to mature salmon which have started their spawning migration from the sea to freshwater, and their skin begins to change from bright silver to the shade and colour of sexually mature fish.

13 In 2003 the old clinic was converted into a "community co-op" where a small group of women meet for a sewing circle.

14 This is a measure to ensure that enough salmon pass through the Aleutians on their way to rivers in western Alaska, described in chapter 5.

15 Descriptions of each operation are from interviews, observations, and www.adfg.state.ak.us. Some of the sketches are my adaptations from the ADF&G pamphlet *What Kind of Fishing Boat is That?* (1999), and others are mine.

16 Compiled from www.cfec.state.ak.us

17 "Greenhorn" comes from the Middle English "*greene horn*," the horn of a newly slaughtered animal, and refers to an inexperienced newcomer.

18 The Aleutian Pribilof Island Community Development Association (APICDA), which is the federal program designed to develop the economies of six Aleutian communities and manages the CDQ programs for them, specifically excludes King Cove and Sand Point because of their salmon fishery.

CHAPTER FOUR

1 Barkow 1975, 1989; Batten 1992; Blum 1998; Buss 1994; Hrdy 1999; Ridley 1993; Symons 1979.

2 Type of gillnet boat with the net reel on the bow and the wheelhouse at the stern.

3 This is a shift from a century ago: for the then Eastern Aleutian villages of Unga, Wosnessenski, Belkofski, Sanak, Morzhovoi, Old Morzhovoi, and Akutan there were 175 males to 234 females (Hooper 1897:17–23).

4 Teen pregnancy is cited as a concern for EATS, but it seems to be less of a worry in King Cove because the family support systems are firmly in place.

5 My husband becoming a father for the first time at the age of forty-two was considered most unusual, since a good number of Aleuts his age are grandparents. His nickname given by our Aleut friend was "old man," chosen for having a younger wife and starting a family later in life than most.

6 Many adult fishermen suffer from time to time too, but were slow to admit this to me, since it can be regarded as the test of a true fisherman.

7 Several women seek out white fishermen passing through because they are "related to everyone in town"!

8 This road was not completed because it would have to pass through Izembek National Wildlife Refuge; instead, King Cove built it partway and uses a hovercraft to cross the water to the town of Cold Bay.

9 Laughlin (1980:10–15) discusses life expectancy data from Veniaminov's time to the early twentieth century and found that they had considerable longevity in those years compared with other Alaska Native populations as well as with colonial settlements in the eastern United States. See also Harper (1976) and Alexander (1949).

10 Generally speaking, a longer timeframe and more data are required to consider evolutionary patterns.

11 Cold Bay, as a government town, does not follow this pattern.

12 Perfect Drift finished in tenth place.

CHAPTER FIVE

1 This is a fairly common strategy. For example, the Atomic Energy Commission defined the Northwest Arctic as "empty space" when it wanted to test its toys there. See Coates (1991) on Alaska Natives and the construction of the Trans-Alaska Pipeline.

2 The salmon pass through a corridor between the tip of the Alaska Peninsula and the first Aleutian Island of Unimak. The pass and the Aleut village located there are called False Pass, so named because it is narrow, shallow, and difficult to navigate. "False Pass" has been used as synonymous with Area M.

3 Salmon are anadromous fish; they live in the sea but reproduce in fresh water (a stream or lake). They live in fresh water as fry, mature in salt water, and then return to fresh water to spawn and die. Sockeye and king salmon travel up to 1,600 kilometres upstream to spawn. These fry rear in freshwater lakes for one or two years, then swim out to the ocean.

Sockeyes return to spawn in their fourth year, and kings return between their third and seventh years. Chum and pink salmon fry head for the ocean; chums return in three to six years and pinks return in two. Coho, or silver, salmon return to their natal streams in two to four years.

4 "The mainstays of traditional transportation, the kayak and dog team, are only incidental to modern life" (Hensel 1996:49). Dogs have been replaced by snowmachines (1996:53), and dog mushing is now the sport of dog-team racing (1996:67).

5 The Board of Fisheries adopted the "Policy for the Management of Mixed Stock Salmon Fisheries" (5AAC 39.220), limiting the maximum percentage of sockeye harvest allowed for South Unimak at 6.8 percent and the Shumagins at 1.5 percent.

6 This allocation was rescinded at the January 2001 Board of Fisheries meeting in Anchorage in an effort to satisfy Bristol Bay salmon fishermen.

7 www.census.gov; Malecha, Tingley, and Iverson 2000a, 2000b.

8 Alaska Division of Emergency Services, 2000. Fisheries disaster declarations are not new to Alaska. In 1953 the entire state was declared a federal disaster area due to a lack of fish. It should be noted that Yukon, Kuskokwin, and Norton Sound regions also were declared disaster areas in 1998. Bristol Bay and Kuskokwin River regions were declared disasters in 1997.

9 Most maps of Alaska cut off the Aleutians altogether or inset the island chain somewhere in Prince William Sound. This treatment in maps adds to a sense of marginalization, prompting the Aleut Corporation to stretch the Aleutian chain across the cover of its first annual report in 1972 and to place a shrunken mainland floating aimlessly in the North Pacific (Morgan 1980; Reedy-Maschner 2001).

10 Salmon fry mortality to predation by other fish species and birds can be extensive during their migration, estimated at between 15 percent and 85 percent on lakes and rivers in Canada and Alaska. Bruce Finney's study of marine nitrogen in the salmon-spawning lakes of the North Pacific found that the greatest measure of productivity is not based solely on how many fish spawn in that stream but on how many fish die there (Finney 1998, Finney et al. 2000). When salmon die, they deposit marine nitrogen in the freshwater streambed, which nourishes the growth of plankton, an important nutrient for young salmon. Nitrogen 15, which he translated into actual salmon, is taken up by the plankton and deposited in the sediments. Finney cored these streambeds and found huge fluctuations in productivity over the last few thousand years. Yearly fluctuations in salmon runs are of no significance given the centuries of wavelike crests and troughs.

11 A cookbook compiled in the 1980s by the King Cove Women's Club – a group of elder women who sponsor the Fourth of July celebration each year – contains a recipe for Pot Roast Sea Lion Meat, a mixture of sea lion ribs, lard, and spices.

12 Oceana has launched an aggressive campaign to preserve deep sea corals and stop trawl fishing from the Aleutians to California. Its website, www. oceana.org, shows reports, maps, videos, and press kits for outsiders' involvement and has added a new site, www.SaveCorals.com.

13 The act specifies an "endangered species" as "any species which is in danger of extinction throughout all or a significant portion of its range other than a species of the Class Insecta determined by the Secretary to constitute a pest whose protection under the provisions of this Act would present an overwhelming and overriding risk to man." Any recovery plan must "give priority to those endangered species or threatened species, without regard to taxonomic classification, that are most likely to benefit from such plans, particularly those species that are, or may be, in conflict with construction or other development projects or other forms of economic activity" (Endangered Species Act of 1973).

14 This excludes the Pribilof Islands villages because they have their own organization.

15 Nadasdy (1999) warns that integrating traditional knowledge with scientific agendas forces indigenous people to conform their knowledge to fit management or scientific language, giving power to resource managers. I give indigenous Alaskans more credit, since the Aleut (and many other groups) have organized commissions in which science and TEK are not separated, as one feeding information to the other, but inform one another.

16 In *Native Village of Elim v. State of Alaska*, Norton Sound villages claimed that the False Pass June fishery is unlawfully intercepting chums bound for their streams. Under the Sustained Yield Clause of the Alaska Constitution, Elim argued that the Board of Fisheries must sustain a specific yield of salmon throughout the stock's migratory range to preserve Elim's subsistence. The Native American Rights Fund filed a motion in the state court siding with the Iñupiat community against Aleut fishermen to compel Fish & Game to take steps to minimize chum harvests. The NARF's siding with one Native group against another raises the question of whether the Iñupiat and Yupiit are seen as "more traditional" than Aleuts and hence more deserving of salmon rights. The court declined the motion and referred the final decision to the governor. In *PMA v. Rosier,*(1995), five Aleut tribal councils, two village corporations, PMA, AEB, and Concerned Area M Fishermen (CAMF) sued the Fish & Game commissioner, Elim,

and the Arctic Regional Fish & Game Council for actions using "emergency powers" following the Board of Fisheries decision to reject the commissioner's proposal to lower the chum cap. A 1999 Supreme Court ruling
agreed that the BOF is successfully managing the mixed stock and that the
False Pass fishery is having little effect on the chum salmon upon which
Elim depends.

17 These fish farms are still producing carnivorous fish, which feed on fishmeal produced in wild fish canneries.

18 Participating fishermen are required to attend a quality training session.

19 In December 2002 the school principal in Sand Point named his daughter
Aleutia (AEB *Fish News*, 3 January 2003).

20 The policy document *Principles of Conduct for Research in the Arctic*,
prepared by the Interagency Social Science Task Force on the recom-
mendation of the Polar Research Board, was signed by the National
Science Foundation, Environmental Protection Agency, Office of Science
and Technology, National Aeronautics and Space Agency, Smithsonian
Institution, and the US Departments of Commerce, Defense, State, Health
and Human Services, Energy, Transportation, Interior, and Agriculture.
Basic guidelines require all proposals and research to be assessed for the
potential human impact and the appropriate communities to be informed
regularly. Most studies on the Steller sea lion issue are therefore in violation of this federal policy.

CHAPTER SIX

1 Whether or not you drink alcohol can be a measure of someone's willing-
ness to associate with you, and turning down libations can be seen as a
value judgment or snub. Declining a beer can insult your host.

2 Parental ambivalence towards education has been recorded in other Aleut
communities (Kleinfeld 1971).

3 In the context of fighting over salmon rights, several people from the
AYK region publicly accused the Aleut of being "draft dodgers" during
the Vietnam War. Aleut veterans were greatly offended. That the others
would consider this a valid line of reasoning to introduce to the conflict
is interesting – almost as if they did not consider the Aleut to be "good
Americans," and another reason why they should not be allowed to fish.
Based on my own interviews, a disproportionately large number of Aleuts
have served in the military, beginning in World War II.

4 Alaska's current charitable gaming program allows virtually any organization, from labour unions to political parties, to raise money through

pull-tab permits. Pull-tab game pieces are sold for one dollar apiece at the bars. Here, this money goes to the Agdaagux and Belkofski tribal councils and is used for financial assistance to needy tribal members (see also Riches 1982 on redistribution).

5 The Division of Records and the Division of Information Services and Criminal Analysis of the Anchorage Police Department provided no answers: they do not break down their database by ethnicity, sex, or village of origin, or even distinguish victim versus suspect. I was referred instead to their annual statistics report on their website, www.anchorage. ak.us, which offers only general information. The Alaska Department of Public Safety also provided statistical information for Aleut villages, collected as part of the Uniform Crime Reporting system (UCR), created to ensure comparable data at the state and federal levels. The King Cove Police Department is a "non-contributing municipal agency" in the UCR system (only St Paul and Unalaska provide annual data), though they did participate in 1999. Ideally, these crime data include offence description, data/time, alcohol/drug involvement, age, sex, race, and victim-offender relationships; however, there were huge gaps in their database. More specific information is protected in the Alaska constitution, Alaska statutes, and the Victim Rights Act of 1991. Data older than 1987 has been purged from their files. The extracts that were provided to me represent only crimes reported, not calls for service.

6 VPSOs have a high turnover in villages across Alaska, and Aleut villages are no exception (Wood 1999b; 2000). They are ranked according to the date of original hire. King Cove's VPSO is ranked 24 of 80, having been hired in 1995. All other VPSOs in Aleut villages have been in those positions for only a few years.

7 Many crab fishermen also described themselves as pirates.

8 Members of the Pacific Northwest Aleut Council (PNAC).

9 Suicide is the fifth leading cause of death in Alaska, compared with ninth in the United States (Alaska Bureau of Vital Statistics 1995); it is the second leading cause of death for 15- to 24-year-old American Indians and Alaska Natives (American Psychological Association Congressional testimony, May 1999).

References

Abbink, Jon. 2001. Violence and Culture: Anthropological and Evolu-
tionary-Psychological Reflections on Inter-group Conflict in Southern
Ethiopia. In *Anthropology of Violence and Conflict*, ed. B.E. Schmidt
and I.W. Schröder, 123–42. London & New York: Routledge
Acheson, James. 1981. Anthropology of Fishing. *Annual Review of
Anthropology* 10:275–316
– 1989. Management of Common-Property Resources. In *Economic
Anthropology*, ed. S. Plattner, 351–78. Stanford: Stanford University
Press
ADF&G. 1999. *What Kind of Fishing Boat Is That?* Pamphlet. Juneau:
Alaska Department of Fish & Game
www.adfg.state.ak.us. Alaska Department of Fish & Game's official website
ADN. 2003. Facing New Competition, Alaska Fishermen turn to Regional
Brands. *Anchorage Daily News*, 3 March
AEB Fish News. 2003. Sand Point Newborn Named Aleutia. Aleutians
East Borough *Fish News*, 3 January. www.aleutianseast.org
Agrawal, Arun, and Clark Gibson, eds. 2001. *Communities and the
Environment: Ethnicity, Gender, and the State in Community-Based
Conservation.* New Brunswick, NJ: Rutgers University Press
www.alaska.com. 2002. *Where the Males Are.* Alaska trivia. Access date:
November 2002
Alaska Bureau of Vital Statistics. 1995–2002. Annual Reports. www.
health.hss.state.ak.us/dph/bvs. Access date: January 2003
Alaska Department of Corrections. 2000. Offender Profile. www.correct.
state.ak.us. Access date: December 2002
Alaska Division of Emergency Services. 2000. Yukon, Kuskokwim, and
Norton Sound Commercial Salmon Harvests. www.ak-prepared.com/
ykn/images/newpag1.jpg. Access date: December 2002

www.aleutcorp.com. Website of the Aleut Corporation, Anchorage, Alaska

Alexander, F. 1949. A Medical Survey of Aleutian Islands (1948). *New England Journal of Medicine* 240(26):1035–40

Alexander, Richard. 1979. *Darwinism and Human Affairs*. Seattle: University of Washington Press

Allison, Charlene. 1988. Women Fishermen in the Pacific Northwest. In *To Work and to Weep: Women in Fishing Economies*, ed. J. Nadel-Klein and D.L. Davis, 230–60. St John's, NF: ISER, Memorial University of Newfoundland

Allison, Charlene, Sue-Ellen Jacobs, and Mary Porter. 1989. *Winds of Change: Women in Northwest Commercial Fishing*. Seattle: University of Washington Press

Ames, Kenneth, and Herbert Maschner. 1999. *Peoples of the Northwest Coast: Their Archaeology and Prehistory*. London: Thames & Hudson

www.anchorage.ak.us. Municipality of Anchorage, Anchorage Police Department link

Anderson, David G. 2000. *Identity and Ecology in Arctic Siberia: The Number One Reindeer Brigade*. Oxford: Oxford University Press

Anderson, D., W. Anderson, Ray Bene, Richard Nelson, and Nita Sheldon Towarak. 1998. *Kuuvanmiut Subsistence: Traditional Eskimo Life in the Latter Twentieth Century*. Kotzebue, AK: National Park Service

Archer, John, ed. 1994. *Male Violence*. London: Routledge

Archer, John, and Barbara Lloyd. 1985. *Sex and Gender*. Cambridge: Cambridge University Press

Balikci, Asen. 1970. *The Netsilik Eskimo*. Garden City, NY: Natural History Press

Bancroft, Hubert. 1886. *History of Alaska, 1730–1885*. (*The Works of Hubert H. Bancroft* 33). San Francisco: The History Book Company. Reprinted New York: Antiquarian Press, 1959

Bank, Theodore P. 1956. *Birthplace of the Winds*. New York: T.Y. Crowell
– 1958. The Aleuts. *Scientific American* 199(5):113–20

Bank, Theodore P., and R. Williams. n.d. Urgently Needed Research on Aleut Culture. *Bulletin of the International Committee on Urgent Anthropological and Ethnological Research* (Vienna, Austria), 17:7

Barcott, Bruce. 2001. Aquaculture's Troubled Harvest. *Mother Jones*, November/December

Barkow, Jerome. 1975. Prestige and Culture: A Biosocial Interpretation. *Current Anthropology* 16(4):553–72
– 1989. *Darwin, Sex, and Status: Biological Approaches to Mind and Culture*. Toronto: University of Toronto Press

– 1994. Evolutionary Psychological Anthropology. In *Handbook of Psychological Anthropology,* ed. P.K. Bock. Westport, CT: Praeger Publishers

Barkow, J.H., L. Cosmides, and J. Tooby, eds. 1992. *The Adapted Mind: Evolutionary Psychology and the Generation of Culture.* New York: Oxford University Press

Barrett, Louise, Robin Dunbar, and John Lycett. 2002. *Human Evolutionary Psychology.* Princeton: Princeton University Press

Barth, Fredrik. 1969. Pathan Identity and Its Maintenance. In *Ethnic Groups and Boundaries: The Social Organization of Culture Difference,* ed. Fredrik Barth, 117–34. Prospect Heights, IL: Waveland Press

Basso, Ellen. 1978. The Enemy of Every Tribe: "Bushmen" Images in Northern Athapaskan Narratives. *American Anthropologist* 5(4):690–709

Basso, Keith. 1996. *Wisdom Sits in Places.* Albuquerque: University of New Mexico Press

Batten, Mary. 1992. *Sexual Strategies: How Females Choose Their Mates.* New York: Putnam

Baumann, Gerd. 1996. *Contesting Culture: Discourses of Identity in Multi-ethnic London.* Cambridge: Cambridge University Press.

Benedict, Ruth. 1934. *Patterns of Culture.* Boston: Houghton Mifflin

Berger, J. 1992. *A Long and Terrible Shadow: White Values, Native Rights in the Americas: 1492–1992.* Seattle: University of Washington Press

Berger, Thomas. 1985. *Village Journey.* New York: Hill & Wang

Bergsland, Knut. 1959. Aleut Dialects of Atka and Attu. *Transactions of the American Philosophical Society* 49(3):1–128

– 1994. *Aleut Dictionary Unangam Tunudgusii: An Unabridged Lexicon of the Aleutian, Pribilof, and Commander Islands Aleut Language.* Fairbanks: Alaska Native Language Center

– 1997. *Aleut Grammar = Unangam Tunuganaan Achixaasix.* Fairbanks: Alaska Native Language Center

– 1998. *Ancient Aleut Personal Names, Kadaangim Asangin/Asangis: Materials from the Billings Expedition, 1790–1792.* Fairbanks: Alaska Native Language Center

Bergsland, Knut, and Moses Dirks, eds. 1990. *Unangam Ungiikangin kayux Tunusangin; Unangam Uniikangis ama Tunuzangis; Aleut Tales and Narratives.* Collected 1909–1910 by Waldemar Jochelson. Fairbanks: Alaska Native Language Center

Berkes, Fikret. 1985. Fishermen and "The Tragedy of the Commons." *Environmental Conservation* 12(3):199–206

– 1999. *Sacred Ecology: Traditional Ecological Knowledge and Resource Management*. London: Taylor and Francis

Berkh, Vasilii Nikolaevich. 1974 [1823]. *A Chronological History of the Discovery of the Aleutian Islands: or, The Exploits of Russian merchants: With a Supplement of Historical Data on the Fur Trade*. Trans. D. Krenov, ed. by R.A. Pierce. Khronologicheskaia istoriia otkrytiia Aleutskikh ostrovov. Kingston, ON: Limestone Press

Berkhofer, Robert F. 1978. *The White Man's Indian*. New York: Vintage Books

Berman, Matthew, and Linda Leask. 1994. Violent Death in Alaska: Who Is Most Likely to Die? *Alaska Review of Social and Economic Conditions* 29(1):1–12

Berreman, G.D. 1953. A Contemporary Study of Nikolski: An Aleutian Village. MS thesis, University of Oregon

– 1954. Effects of a Technological Change in an Aleutian Village. *Arctic* 7(2):102–7

– 1956. Drinking Patterns of the Aleuts. *Quarterly Journal of Studies on Alcohol* 17:503–14

– 1964. Aleut Reference Group Alienation, Mobility, and Acculturation. *American Anthropologist* 66(2):231–50

– 1978. Scale and Social Relations. *Current Anthropology* 19(2):225–45

Bettinger, R. 1991. *Hunter-Gatherers*. New York: Plenum Press

Betzig, Laura, ed. 1997. *Human Nature*. Oxford: Oxford University Press

Beynon, Huw, ed. 1985. *Digging Deeper: Issues in the Miners' Strike*. London: Verso

Bielawski, E. 1992. Inuit Indigenous Knowledge and Science in the Arctic. *Northern Perspectives* 20(1):5–8

Bird, Nurit. 1982. *Conjugal Units and Single Persons: An Analysis of the Social System of the Naiken of the Nilgiris* (S. India). Unpublished PHD dissertation, University of Cambridge

Bjerkli, Bjørn. 1986. *Identitet og Etnisitet Blant Aleuter i Alaska*. Bergen, Norway: Institute of Social Anthropology, University of Bergen, Hovedfagsaavhandling

Black, Lydia. 1977. Ivan Pank'ov: An Architect of Aleut Literacy. *Arctic Anthropology* 14(1):94–107

– 1981. Volcanism as a Factor in Human Ecology: The Aleutian Case. *Ethnohistory* 28(4):313–40

– 1982. *Aleut Art: Unangam Aguqaadangin/Unangan of the Aleutian Archipelago*. Anchorage: Aleutian/Pribilof Islands Association

– 1984. *Atka: An Ethnohistory of the Western Aleutian Islands*. Alaska History, no. 24, ed. R.A. Pierce. Kingston, ON: Limestone Press

– 1987. Whaling in the Aleutians [French summary]. *Etudes/Inuit/Studies* 11:7–50

– 1998. Animal World of the Aleuts. *Arctic Anthropology* 35(2):126–35

Black, Lydia, and S.V. Ivanov. 1991. *Glory Remembered: Wooden Headgear of Alaska Sea Hunters*. Juneau: Friends of the Alaska State Museum

Black, Lydia, and Jerry Jacka. 1999. King Cove. In *The History and Ethnohistory of the Aleutians East Borough*, ed. Black et al., 97–112. Fairbanks: University of Alaska Press

Black, Lydia, and Natalia Taksami. 1999. Belkofski: 1824–1989. In *The History and Ethnohistory of the Aleutians East Borough*, ed. Black et al., 79–96. Fairbanks: University of Alaska Press

Black, Lydia, Sarah McGowan, Jerry Jacka, Natalia Taksami, and Miranda Wright. 1999. *The History and Ethnohistory of the Aleutians East Borough*. Fairbanks: University of Alaska Press

Blanchard, Kendall. 1983. Play and Adaptation: Sport and Games in Native America. *Anthropological Papers* 24:172–95

Bloom, J.D. 1975. Patterns of Eskimo Homicide. *Bulletin of the American Academy of Psychiatry and the Law* 3(3):165–74

Blum, Deborah. 1998. *Sex on the Brain: The Biological Differences between Men and Women*. London: Penguin

Blurton, David M., and Gary D. Copus. 1993. Administering Criminal Justice in Remote Alaska Native Villages: Problems and Possibilities. *Northern Review* 11:118–1<41

Boas, Franz. 1899. Property Marks of the Alaskan Eskimo. *American Anthropologist* 1(4):601–13

Bodenhorn, Barbara. 1988. *Documenting Iñupiat Family Relationships in Changing Times*. Vols. 1, 2. Report prepared for the North Slope Borough Commission on Iñupiat History, Language, and Culture Commission and Alaska Humanities Forum

– 1989. "The animals come to me; they know I share:" Iñupiaq Kinship, Changing Economic Relations, and Enduring World Views on Alaska's North Slope. Doctoral dissertation, Cambridge University

– 1997. Person, Place, and Parentage: Ecology, Identity, and Social Relations on the North Slope of Alaska. In *Arctic Ecology and Identity*, ed. S.A. Mousalimas. Los Angeles: International Society for Trans-Oceanic Research 8

– 2000. It's Good to Know Who Your Relatives Are but We Were Taught to Share with Everybody: Shares and Sharing among Inupiaq Households. In *The Social Economy of Sharing: Resource Allocation and Modern Hunter-Gatherers*, ed. G.W. Wenzel, G. Hovelsrud-Broda, and

N. Kishigami, 27–60. Senri Ethnological Studies 53. Osaka, Japan: National Museum of Ethnology

– 2000/2001. It's Traditional to Change: A Case Study of Strategic Decision-Making. *Cambridge Anthropology* 22(1):24–51

Bohannan, Paul. 1995. *How Culture Works*. New York: Free Press

Borgerhoff Mulder, Monique. 1987. On Cultural and Reproductive Success, with an Example from the Kipsigis. *American Anthropologist* 89:617–34

Bourdieu, Pierre. 1977. *Outline of a Theory of Practice*. Translated from the 1972 French original. Cambridge: Cambridge University Press

– 2000. *The Logic of Practice*. Translated from the 1980 French original. Cambridge: Polity Press

Bours, Hélène, Matthew Gianni, and Desley Mather. 2001. *Pirate Fishing Plundering the Oceans*. Greenpeace International. www.greenpeace.org. Access date: December 2002

Bowman, Glenn. 2001. The Violence in Identity. In *Anthropology of Violence and Conflict*, ed. B.E. Schmidt and I.W. Schröder, 25–46. London: Routledge

Braund, Stephen & Associates. 1986. *Effects of Renewable Resource Harvest Disruptions on Community Socioeconomic and Sociocultural Systems: King Cove*. Report for the US Department of the Interior, Minerals Management Service, Alaska OCS Region, Anchorage, Alaska. Social and Economic Studies Program Technical Report no. 123 (419 pp)

Briggs, Jean. 1970. *Never in Anger: Portrait of an Eskimo Family*. Cambridge, MA: Harvard University Press

– 1982. Living Dangerously: The Contradictory Foundations of Value in Canadian Inuit society. In *Politics and History in Band Societies*, ed. E. Leacock and R. Lee, 109–31. Cambridge: Cambridge University Press

– 1985. Socialization, Family Conflicts, and Responses to Culture Change among Canadian Inuit. *Arctic Medical Research* 40:40–52

– 1994. "Why Don't You Kill Your Baby Brother?": The Dynamics of Peace in Canadian Inuit Camps. In *The Anthropology of Peace and Nonviolence*, ed. L. Sponsel and T. Gregor, 155–81. Boulder, CO: Lynne Rienner

Brodkin, Karen, and Karen Sacks. 1983. *Sisters and Wives: The Past and Future of Sexual Equality*. Contributions in Women's Studies, no. 10. Chicago: University of Illinois Press

Brown, Donald. 1991. *Human Universals*. New York: McGraw-Hill

Brown, William, and Clive Thomas. 1996. Diversifying the Alaskan Economy: Political, Social, and Economic Constraints. *Journal of Economic
Issues* 30(2):599–608

Burch, Ernest S., Jr. 1974. Eskimo Warfare in Northwest Alaska.
Anthropological Papers of the University of Alaska 16(2):1–14

– 1984. The Land Claims Era in Alaska. In *Handbook of North American
Indians,* vol 5, *Arctic,* ed. D. Damas, 657–61. Washington, DC: Smithsonian Institution Press

– 1998a. *The Cultural and Natural Heritage of Northwest Alaska.* Vol.
7, *International Affairs.* Prepared for NANA Museum of the Arctic,
Kotzebue, Alaska, and the US National Park Service, Alaska Region,
Anchorage, Alaska

– 1998b. *The Iñupiat of North Alaska.* Fairbanks: University of Alaska
Press

Burch, Ernest S., Jr, and Thomas Correll. 1972. Alliance and Conflict:
Inter-Regional Relations in North Alaska. In *Alliance in Eskimo Society,*
ed. L. Guemple. Seattle: University of Washington Press

Burch, Ernest S., Jr., and Linda Ellanna, eds. 1994. *Key Issues in Hunter-
Gatherer Research.* Explorations in Anthropology Series. Oxford: BERG

Buss, David M. 1994. *The Evolution of Desire: Strategies of Human Mat-
ing.* New York: Basic Books

– 1997. Just Another Brick in the Wall: Building the Foundation of
Evolutionary Psychology. In *Human Nature: A Critical Reader,* ed.
L. Betzig, 191–3. Oxford: Oxford University Press

Carey, Richard Adams. 1999. *Against the Tide: The Fate of the New
England Fisherman.* Boston: Mariner Books, Houghton Mifflin

Case, David S. 1984. *Alaska Natives and American Laws.* Fairbanks:
University of Alaska Press

Cattarinussi, Bernardo. 1973. A Sociological Study of an Italian Community of Fishermen. In *Seafarer and Community,* ed. P. Fricke, 30–43.
London: Croom Helm

Caulfield, Richard. 1997. *Greenlanders, Whales, and Whaling: Sustainability and Self-Determination in the Arctic.* Dartmouth College/University
Press of New England

Census. 2000. www.census.gov. United States Federal Census

www.cfec.state.ak.us. Commercial Fisheries Entry Commission website

CFEC. 2002. *Chignik Salmon Purse Seine Fishery: Summary Data on
Issues Related to the 2002 Cooperative Fishery.* Commercial Fisheries
Entry Commission Report 02–6N. December. Juneau, AK

CFEC Election District Reports. 2000. *Counts of Registered Voters and Their Permits by Election District.* Commercial Fisheries Entry Commission. cfec.state.ak.uk/Mnu_Summary_Info.htm

Chagnon, Napoleon. 1988. Life Histories, Blood Revenge, and Warfare in a Tribal Population. *Science* 239:985–92

– 1992. *Yanomamö.* 4th edition. San Diego: Harcourt Brace Jovanovich

Chamberlain, Alexander F. 1951. Aleuts. *Encyclopedia of Religion and Ethics* 1:303–5. New York: Scribner's

Chance, Norman. 1990. *The Iñupiat and Arctic Alaska: An Ethnography of Development.* New York: Holt, Rinehart, and Winston

Chantraine, P. 1993. *The Last Cod Fish: Life and Death of the Newfoundland Way of Life.* St John's, NF: Jesperson

Coates, Peter. 1991. *The Trans-Alaskan Pipeline Controversy: Techonology, Conservation, and the Frontier.* London: Associated University Presses

Cohen, Abner. 1974. *Urban Ethnicity.* ed. A. Cohen. ASA Monograph 12. London: Tavistock

– 1981. *The Politics of Elite Culture: Explorations in the Dramaturgy of Power in a Modern African Society.* Berkeley: University of California Press

Cohen, Anthony. 1993. Culture as Identity: An Anthropologist's View. *New Literary History* 24(1):195–209

– ed. 2000. *Signifying Identities: Anthropological Perspectives on Boundaries and Contested Values.* London: Routledge.

Collier, Jane, and Michelle Rosaldo. 1981. Politics and Gender in Simple Societies. In *Sexual Meanings: The Cultural Construction of Gender and Sexuality,* ed. S. Ortner and H. Whitehead, 275–329. Cambridge: Cambridge University Press

Collings, Peter. 1997a. Subsistence Hunting and Wildlife Management in the Central Canadian Arctic. *Arctic Anthropology* 34(1):41–56

– 1997b. The Cultural Context of Wildlife Management in the Canadian North. In *Contested Arctic,* ed. E.A. Smith and J. McCarter, 13–40. Seattle: University of Washington Press

Collings, Peter, and Richard Condon. 1996. Blood on the Ice: Status, Self-Esteem, and Ritual Injury among Inuit Hockey Players. *Human Organization* 55(3):253–62

Collins, Henry, Austin Clark, and Egbert Walker. 1945. *The Aleutian Islands: Their People and Natural History.* Washington, DC: Smithsonian Institution.

Condon, Richard. 1987. *Inuit Youth: Growth and Change in the Canadian Arctic.* New Brunswick, NJ: Rutgers University Press

– 1990. The Rise of Adolescence: Social Change and Life Stage Dilemmas in the Central Canadian Arctic. *Human Organization* 49:266–79

– 1995. The Rise of the Leisure Class: Adolescence and Recreational Acculturation in the Canadian Arctic. *Ethos* 23(1):47–68

– 1996. *The Northern Copper Inuit.* With J. Ogina and the Holman Elders. Norman, OK: University of Oklahoma Press

Condon, Richard, Peter Collings, and George Wenzel. 1995. The Best Part of Life: Subsistence Hunting, Ethnicity, and Economic Adaptation among Young Adult Inuit Males. *Arctic* 48(1):31–46

Corbett, Helen, and Suzanne Swibold. 2000. The Aleuts of the Pribilof Islands, Alaska. In *Endangered Peoples of the Arctic: Struggles to Survive and Thrive.* ed. M.M.R. Freeman, 1–16. Westport, CT: Greenwood Press

Cordell, John, ed. 1989. *A Sea of Small Boats.* Cambridge, MA: Cultural Survival

Cowan, Jane, Mary-Bénédicte Dembour, and Richard Wilson, eds. 2001. *Culture and Rights: Anthropological Perspectives.* Cambridge: Cambridge University Press

Coxe, William. 1787. *Account of the Russian Discoveries between Asia and America.* 3rd edn. London: Cadell and Davies

Cronon, William. 1996. *Uncommon Ground: Rethinking the Human Place in Nature.* New York: W.W. Norton

Crowell, Aron, Amy Steffian, and Gordon Pullar, eds. 2001. *Looking Both Ways: Heritage and Identity of the Alutiiq People.* Seattle: University of Washington Press

Cruikshank, Julie. 1998. *The Social Life of Stories: Narratives and Knowledge in the Yukon Territory.* Lincoln: University of Nebraska Press

Dall, William H. 1870. *Alaska and Its Resources.* Boston: Lee and Shepard

Daly, Martin, and Margo Wilson. 1988. *Homicide.* New York: Aldine de Gruyter

– 1989. Homicide and Cultural Evolution. *Ethology and Sociobiology* 10:99–110

– 1994. Evolutionary Psychology of Male Violence. In *Male Violence*, ed. John Archer, 253–88. New York: Routledge

Daly, Richard. 2004. *Our Box Was Full: An Ethnography for the Delgamuukw Plaintiffs.* Vancouver: University of British Columbia Press

Damas, David, ed. 1984. *Handbook of North American Indians.* Vol. 5, *Arctic.* Washington: Smithsonian Institution

Davis, Dona Lee. 1988. "Shore Skippers" and "Grass Widows": Active and Passive Women's Roles in a Newfoundland fishery. In *To Work and*

to Weep: Women in Fishing Economies, ed. J. Nadel-Klein and D.L.
Davis, 211–29. St John's, NF: Institute of Social and Economic Research,
Memorial University of Newfoundland

Davydov, Gavriil Ivanovich. 1977. *Two Voyages to Russian America,*
1802–1807. Trans. C. Bearne, ed. R.A. Pierce. Kingston, ON: Limestone
Press

www.dced.state.ak.us. Alaska Department of Community and Economic
Development

DHHS. 1997. *Commercial Fishing Fatalities in Alaska: Risk Factors and*
Prevention Strategies. Publication no. 97–163 US Department of Health
and Human Services, Centers for Disease Control and Prevention,
National Institute for Occupational Safety and Health, Division of
Safety Research. Washington, DC: DHHS

Dillon, Patrick. 1998. *Lost at Sea.* New York: Touchstone

Dobash, R. Emerson, and Russell P. Dobash 1992. *Women, Violence, and*
Social Change. London: Routledge

Dombrowski, Kirk. 2001. *Against Culture: Development, Politics, and*
Religion in Indian Alaska. Lincoln: University of Nebraska Press

Douglas, Mary, and Aaron Wildavsky. 1982. *Risk and Culture: An Essay*
on the Selection of Technical and Environmental Dangers. Berkeley:
University of California Press

Downs, Michael. 1985. Sociocultural Change and Ethnic Identity: The
Effect of the Alaska Native Claims Settlement Act in Unalaska, Alaska.
PHD dissertation, University of California, San Diego

Drucker, P., and R.F. Heizer. 1967. *To Make My Name Good: A Re-*
examination of the Southern Kwakuitl Potlatch. Berkeley: University of
California Press

Dumond, Don. 1987. *The Eskimos and Aleuts.* London: Thames and
Hudson Ltd.

Dumond, Don, and Richard Bland. 1995. Holocene Prehistory of the Northernmost North Pacific. *Journal of World Prehistory* 9(4):401–51

Durrenberger, E. Paul, and Thomas King, eds. 2000. *State and Commun-*
ity in Fisheries Management: Power, Policy, and Practice. Westport, CT:
Bergin & Garvey.

Durrenberger, E. Paul, and Gísli Pálsson. 1986. Finding Fish: The Tactics
of Icelandic Fishermen. *American Ethnologist* 13:213–29

Dybbroe, S. 1996. Questions of Identity and Issues of Self-Determination.
Etudes/Inuit/Studies 20(2):39–53

Dyck, N. 1985. *Indigenous Peoples and the Nation-State: Fourth World*
Politics in Canada, Australia, and Norway. Social and Economic

Research Paper no. 14. St John's, NF: Institute of Social and Economic Research, Memorial University of Newfoundland

Earle, Timothy. 1997. *How Chiefs Come to Power: The Political Economy in Prehistory.* Stanford: Stanford University Press

The Economist. 2003. A New Way to Feed the World (p. 9) and The Promise of a Blue Revolution (pp. 19–21). *Economist* 9–15 August

Eggers, D.M., K. Rowell, and B. Barrett. 1991. Stock Composition of Sockeye and Chum Salmon Catches in the Southern Alaska Peninsula Fisheries in June. *Fisheries Research Bulletin* no. 91–01. Juneau: Alaska Department of Fish & Game

Ehrenreich, Robert, Carole Crumley, and Janet Levy, eds. 1995. *Heterarchy and the Analysis of Complex Societies.* Archaeological Papers no. 6. Washington, DC: American Anthropological Association

Elliott, H.W. 1880. *Report on the Seal Islands of Alaska.* Washington, DC: Govt. Printing Office (188 pp.)

– 1886. *Our Arctic Province, Alaska and the Seal Islands.* New York: Scribner's

Ellis, Bruce. 1992. The Evolution of Sexual Attraction: Evaluative Mechanisms in Women. In *The Adapted Mind*, ed. J.H. Barkow, L. Cosmides, and J. Tooby, 267–88. New York: Oxford University Press

Ellis, M. Estelle, ed. 1977. *Those Who Live from the Sea: A Study in Maritime Anthropology.* New York: West Publishing Company

Empty Oceans, Empty Nets. 2001. Public Broadcasting System, Frontline Series

Endangered Species Act. 1973. Complete text at www.endangered.fws.gov/esa.html

Endicott. 1988. Property, Power, and Conflict among the Batek of Malaysia. In *Hunters and Gatherers*, vol. 2, *Property, Power, and Ideology*, ed. T. Ingold, D. Riches, and J. Woodburn. Oxford: BERG

Erikson, Erik. 1968. *Identity: Youth, and Crisis.* New York: W.W. Norton

– 1980. *Identity and Life-Cycle.* New York: W.W. Norton

Fall, J.A., R. Mason, T. Haynes, V.Vanek, L. Brown, G. Jennings, C. Mishler, and C. Utermohle. 1993. *Noncommercial Harvests and Uses of Wild Resources in King Cove, Alaska, 1992.* Technical Paper no. 227. Juneau: Division of Subsistence, Alaska Department of Fish & Game

Fassett, H.C. 1960 [1890]. The Aleut Sea Otter Hunt in the Late Nineteenth Century. *Anthropological Papers of the University of Alaska* 8(2):131–5

Federal Subsistence Board. 1999. *Subsistence Management Regulations for the Harvest of Fish and Shellfish on Federal Public Lands and Waters in*

Alaska. Effective 1 October 1999 – 28 February, 2001. Anchorage, AK: US Fish & Wildlife Service, Office of Subsistence Management

– 2001. *Subsistence Management Regulations for the Harvest of Fish and Shellfish on Federal Public Lands and Waters in Alaska.* Effective 1 October 2001. Anchorage, AK: US Fish & Wildlife Service, Office of Subsistence Management

– 2003. *Subsistence Management Regulations for the Harvest of Fish and Shellfish on Federal Public Lands and Waters in Alaska.* Effective 1 March 2003 – 29 February 2004. Anchorage, AK: US Fish & Wildlife Service, Office of Subsistence Management

Ferguson, James. 1999. *Expectations of Modernity: Myths and Meanings of Urban Life in the Zambian Copperbelt.* Berkeley: University of California Press

Fields, Leslie Leyland. 1997. *The Entangling Net: Alaska's Commercial Fishing Women Tell Their Lives.* Urbana: University of Illinois Press

Fienup-Riordan, Ann. 1983a. *The Effects of Renewable Resource Disruption on the Socioeconomic and Socio-cultural Systems of the Yukon Delta.* Anchorage: Alaska Council on Science and Technology

– 1983b. *The Nelson Island Eskimo: Social Structure and Ritual Distribution.* Anchorage: Alaska Pacific University Press

– 1990a. *Eskimo Essays: Yup'ik Lives and How We See Them.* New Brunswick, NJ: Rutgers University Press

– 1990b. Yup'ik Warfare and the Myth of the Peaceful Eskimo. In *Eskimo Essays: Yup'ik Lives and How We See Them,* 146–66. New Brunswick, NJ: Rutgers University Press

– 1994. *Boundaries and Passages: Rule and Ritual in Yup'ik Eskimo Oral Tradition.* Norman: University of Oklahoma Press

– 2000. *Hunting Tradition in a Changing World: Yup'ik Lives in Alaska.* New Brunswick, NJ: Rutgers University Press

– 2002. The World Contains No Others, Only Our Human Selves: Yup'ik Views of Self and Other. Paper presented at the 9th International Conferenced on Hunting-Gathering Societies, September 2002, in Edinburgh

Finney, Bruce. 1998. Long-Term Variability of Alaskan Sockeye Salmon Abundance Determined by Analysis of Sediment Cores. *North Pacific Anadromous Fish Commission Bulletin* 1:388–95

Finney, Bruce, Irene Gregory-Eaves, Jon Sweetman, Marianne S.V. Douglas, and John P. Smol. 2000. Impacts of Climate Change and Fishing on Pacific Salmon Abundance over the Past 300 Years. *Science* 290:795–9

Firth, Raymond. 1939. *Primitive Polynesian Economy.* London: Routledge

Fischer, Frank. 2000. *Citizens, Experts, and the Environment: The Politics of Local Knowledge.* Durham, NC: Duke University Press.

Fiske, Jo-Anne. 1987. Fishing Is Women's Business: Changing Economic Roles of Carrier Women and Men. In *Native People, Native Lands*, ed. B.A. Cox, 186–98. Ottawa: Carleton University Press

Flanders, Nicholas. 1989. The Alaska Native Corporation as Conglomerate: The Problem of Profitability. *Human Organization* 48(4):299–312

Ford, Corey. 1966. *Where the Sea Breaks Its Back: The Epic Story of Early Naturalist Georg Steller and the Russian Exploration of Alaska.* Anchorage: Alaska Northwest Books

Fortuine, Robert. 1992. *Chills and Fever: Health and Disease in the Early History of Alaska.* Fairbanks: University of Alaska Press

Foucault, Michel. 1972. *The Archaeology of Knowledge.* Translated from French by A.M. Sheridan Smith. New York: Pantheon Books

– 1977. *Discipline and Punish: The Birth of the Prison.* First American edition. New York: Pantheon Books.

– 1979a. On Governmentality. *Ideology and Consciousness* 6:5–26

– 1979b. *Power, Truth, Strategy.* Sydney: Feral Publications

Fraser, Jerry. 2002. A Movement Without a Soul. Editor's log, *National Fisherman*, May, p. 4.

Fraser, Jr, Thomas. 1966. *Fishermen of South Thailand: The Malay Villagers.* New York: Holt, Rinehart, and Winston

Freeman, Milton M.R. 1993. The International Whaling Commission, Small-Type Whaling, and Coming to Terms with Subsistence. *Human Organization* 52(3):243–51

– 1997. Issues Affecting Subsistence Security in Arctic Societies. *Arctic Anthropology* 34(1):7–17

– 1998. *Inuit, Whaling, and Sustainability.* Contemporary Native American Communities, paper 1. Altamira Press

– ed. 2000. *Endangered Peoples of the Arctic.* Westport, CT: Greenwood Press

Freeman, Milton M.R., and Urs P. Kreuter, eds. 1995. *Elephants and Whales: Resources for Whom?* New York: Gordon and Breach

Free-Sloan, N., and C. Tide. 2007. Changes in the Distribution of Alaska's Commercial Fisheries Entry Permits, 1975–2006. CFEC Report 07-5N. Juneau: Alaska Commercial Fisheries Entry Commission

Fricke, Peter, ed. 1973. *Seafarer and Community.* London: Croom Helm

Fried, Morton. 1967. *Evolution of Political Society: An Essay in Political Anthropology.* New York: New York: Random House

Friedl, Ernestine. 1975. *Women and Men: An Anthropologist's View.* New York: Holt, Rinehart, and Winston

Friedman, J. 1992. The Past in the Future: History and the Politics of Identity. *American Anthropologist* 94(4):837–59

– 1994. *Cultural Identity and Global Process.* London: Thousand Oaks

Frost, O.W. 1992. *Bering and Chirikov: The American Voyages and Their Impact.* Anchorage: Alaska Historical Society

Gatewood, John B. 1983. Deciding Where to Fish: The Skipper's Dilemma in Southeast Alaskan Salmon Seining. *Coastal Zone Management Journal* 10(4):347–67

– 1984. Cooperation, Competition, and Synergy: Information-Sharing Groups among Southeast Alaskan Salmon Seiners. *American Ethnologist* 11:350–70

Geertz, Clifford. 1973. Deep Play: Notes on the Balinese Cockfight. In *Interpretation of Cultures: Selected Essays,* 412–56. New York: Basic Books

– 1980. *Negara: The Theater-State in Nineteenth-Century Bali.* Princeton: Princeton University Press

– 1983. Common Sense as a Cultural System. In *Local Knowledge: Further Essays in Interpretive Anthropology,* 73–93. New York: Basic Books

– 1998. Deep Hanging Out. *New York Review of Books,* 22 October p. 70

Giddens, Anthony. 1979. *Central Problems in Social Theory.* London: Macmillan

– 1984. *The Constitution of Society: Outline of a Theory of Structuration.* Berkeley: University of California Press

– 2002. *Runaway World: How Globalisation Is Reshaping Our Lives.* London: Profile Books

Gilbertsen, Neal. 1993. Chaos on the Commons: Salmon and Such. *Maritime Anthropological Studies* 6(1,2):74–91

Gluckman, Max. 1965. *Politics, Law, and Ritual in Tribal Society.* Oxford: Blackwell

Glushankov, I.V. 1973. The Aleutian Expedition of Krenitsyn and Levashov. *Alaska Journal* 3(4):204–10. Trans. M. Sadouski and R.A. Pierce. Juneau: Alaska Northwest Publishing Company

Golder, F.A. 1963a. Aleutian Stories. *Journal of American Folklore* 18(70):215–22

– 1963b. The Songs and Stories of the Aleuts, with Translations from Veniaminov. *Journal of American Folklore* 20(76):132–42

Goldschmidt, Walter. 1991. *The Human Career: The Self in the Symbolic World*. Cambridge, MA: Blackwell

Goldsmith, Scott. 1979. *Man-in-the-Arctic Series* Documentation. Anchorage: Institute of Social and Economic Research, University of Alaska (341 pp.)

Golovin, Pavel N. 1979. *The End of Russian America: Captain P.N. Golovin's Last Report, 1862*. Translated with introduction and notes by B. Dmytryshyn and E.A.P. Crownhart-Vaughan. Portland: Oregon Historical Society

‒ 1983. *Civil and Savage Encounters: The Worldly Travel Letters of an Imperial Russian Navy Officer 1860-1*. Trans. B. Dmytryshyn and E.A.P. Crownhart-Vaughan. Portland: Western Imprints, Press of the Oregon Historical Society

www.greenpeace.org. See archive.greenpeace.org/~oceans/stoppiratefishing/. *Pirate Fishing Plundering the Oceans. Greenpeace International Campaign against Pirate Fishing*. February 2001. Written by Helene Bours, Matthew Gianni, Desley Mather. Edited by Luisa Colasimone, Angela Congedo, and Sara Holden

Gustafson, Bob. 2001. Shots Fired at Mi'kmaq during "Peaceful Protest." *National Fisherman* 82(8):17

Hackenberg, B.H. 1972. Social Mobility in a Tribal Society: The Case of Papago Indian Veterans [Spanish and French summaries illus., bibliogr.] *Human Organization* 31(2):201-9

Haddon, Alfred C. 1898. *The Study of Man*. London: Murray

Haedrich, Richard, and Lawrence Hamilton. 2000. The Fall and Future of Newfoundland's Cod Fishery. *Society and Natural Resources* 13:359-72

Hall, Andy. 1999. A Village Out of Time? *Alaska Magazine* 65(6):26-31

Hall, S. 1988. *The Fourth World: The Heritage of the Arctic and Its Destruction*. Toronto: Vintage Books

Hamilton, Lawrence, Peter Lyster, and Oddmund Otterstad. 2000. Social Change, Ecology, and Climate in Twentieth-Century Greenland. *Climate Change* 47:193-211

Hamilton, Lawrence, and Carole Seyfrit. 1994a. Coming out of the Country: Community Size and Gender Balance among Alaska Natives. *Arctic Anthropology* 31(1):16-25

‒ 1994b. Female Flight? Gender Balance and Outmigration by Native Alaska Villagers. *Arctic Medical Research* 53 (supplement 2):189-93

Hamilton, W.D. 1964. The Genetical Evolution of Social Behaviour. *Journal of Theoretical Biology* 7:1-52

Hardin, Garrett. 1968. The Tragedy of the Commons. *Science* 162:1243-8

Harper, A.B. 1976. Aleut Life Expectancy and Adaptation. *American Journal of Physical Anthropology* 44(1):183

Harris, Marvin. 1968. *The Rise of Anthropological Theory*. New York: Crowell

Harrison, S. 1993. *The Mask of War: Violence, Ritual, and the Self in Melanesia*. Manchester: Manchester University Press

Hawkes, Kristen. 1993. Why Hunter-Gatherers Work. *Current Anthropology* 34(4):341–61

Hennigh, Lawrence. 1972. You Have to Be a Good Lawyer to be an Eskimo. In *Alliance in Eskimo Society*, ed. L. Guemple, 89–109. Proceedings of the American Ethnological Society (1971). Seattle: University of Washington Press

Hensel, Chase. 1996. *Telling Our Selves: Ethnicity and Discourse in Southwestern Alaska*. Oxford: Oxford University Press

– 2001. Yup'ik Identity and Subsistence Discourse: Social Resources in Interaction. *Etudes/Inuit/Studies* 25(1–2):217–27

Hensel, Chase, and Phyllis Morrow. 1998. Co-Management and Co-Optation: Alaska Native Participation in Regulatory Processes. *Cultural Survival Quarterly*. Fall: 69–71

Herzfeld, Michael. 1996. *Cultural Intimacy: Social Poetics in the Nation-State*. New York: Routledge

Hill, Kim, and Ana Magdalena Hurtado. 1996. *Ache Life History*. Hawthorne, NY: Aldine de Gruyter

Hill, Kim, and Hillard Kaplan. 1994. On Why Male Foragers Hunt and Share Food. *Current Anthropology* 34:701–6

Hisnanick, John. 1994. Comparative Analysis of Violent Deaths in American Indians and Alaska Natives. *Social Biology* 41(1–2):96–109

Hobsbawm, E., and T. Ranger, eds. 1983. *The Invention of Tradition*. Cambridge: Cambridge University Press

Hodgson, B. 1992. Hard Harvest on the Bering Sea. *National Geographic* 182(4):72–103

Hodgson, Dorothy. 2002. Introduction: Comparative Perspectives on the Indigenous Rights Movement in Africa and the Americas. *American Anthropologist* 104(4):1037–49

Hoffman, Brian. 1999. Agayadan Village: Household Archaeology on Unimak Island, Alaska. *Journal of Field Archaeology* 26: 147–2

Hooper, C.L. 1897. Report on the Sea-Otter Banks of Alaska. *Treasury Department Document 1977*. Washington, DC: Government Printing Office

Hrdlicka, A. 1945. *The Aleutian and Commander Islands and Their Inhabitants.* Philadelphia: Wistar Institute of Anatomy and Biology Press

Hrdy, Sarah Blaffer. 1999. *Mother Nature.* London: Chatto and Windus

Hubbard, Father Bernard R. 1935. *Cradle of Storms.* New York: Dodd, Mead

Hudson, Ray. 1998. *Moments Rightly Placed: An Aleutian Memoir.* Fairbanks: Epicenter Press

Huelsman, M. 1983. Violence on Anchorage's Fourth Avenue from the Perspective of Street People. *Alaska Medicine* 25(2):39–44

Huntington, Henry. 1989. The Alaska Eskimo Whaling Commission: Efficient Local Management of a Subsistence Resource. Unpublished MPHIL thesis, Scott Polar Research Institute, University of Cambridge

– 1992. *Wildlife Management and Subsistence Hunting in Alaska.* Seattle: University of Washington Press

Hutchinson, Sharon. 1996. *Nuer Dilemmas: Coping with Money, War, and the State.* Berkeley: University of California Press

Irons, William. 1979. Cultural and Biological Success. In *Evolutionary Biology and Human Social Behavior: An Anthropological Perspective*, ed. N. Chagnon and W. Irons, 257–72. North Scituate, MA: Duxbury Press

Iudicello, Suzanne, Michael Weber, and Robert Wieland. 1999. *Fish, Markets, and Fishermen: The Economics of Overfishing.* Washington, DC: Island Press

Iverson, Kurt, and Patrick Malecha. 2000. *Characteristics of Vessels Participating in the Alaska Peninsula Salmon Purse Seine and Drift Gillnet Fisheries, 1978 to 1999.* Report 00–10N. Juneau: Commercial Fisheries Entry Commission

Jacka, Jerry. 1999. Fishing. In *The History and Ethnohistory of the Aleutians East Borough.* ed. Lydia Black, Sarah McGowan, Jerry Jacka, Natalia Taksami, and Miranda Wright, 213–42. Fairbanks: University of Alaska Press

Jankowski, Martin Sanchez. 1991. *Islands in the Street: Gangs and American Urban Society.* Berkeley: University of California Press

J.L.S. 1776. *Neue nachrichten von denen neuentdekten insuln in der see zwischen Asien und Amerika; aus mitgetheilten urkunden und auszügen verfasset von J.L.S.* Hamburg and Leipzig: F.L. Gleditsch. (173 pp.)

Jochelson, W. 1925. *Archaeological Investigations in the Aleutian Islands.* Washington, DC: Carnegie Institute of Washington

– 1928. People of the Foggy Seas: The Aleut and Their Islands. *Journal of the Museum of Natural History* 28

– 1933. *History, Ethnology, and Anthropology of the Aleut*. Netherlands: Oosterhout, NB: Carnegie Institution of Washington. Publication 432

Johnson, Charles. 1997. The Role of Indigenous Peoples in Forming Environmental Policies. In *Contested Arctic*, ed. E.A. Smith and J. McCarter, 1–12. Seattle: University of Washington Press

Jolles, Carol Zane. 2002. *Faith, Food, and Family in a Yupik Whaling Community*. Seattle: University of Washington Press

Jonaitis, Aldona. 1991. *Chiefly Feasts: The Enduring Kwakiutl Potlatch*. Seattle: University of Washington Press

Jones, D.K. 1980. *A Century of Servitude: Pribilof Aleuts under U.S. Rule*. Lanham, MD: University Press of America

Jones, D.M. 1969a. A Study of Social and Economic Problems in Unalaska: An Aleut Village. PHD dissertation in Anthropology, University of California, Berkeley

– 1969b. Child Welfare Problems in an Alaskan Native Village. *Social Science Review* 43(3):297–309

– 1972. Adaptation of Whites in an Alaska Native Village. *Anthropologica* 14(2):119–218

– 1973a. *Patterns of Village Growth and Decline in the Aleutians*. Occasional Paper 11. Fairbanks: Institute of Social, Economic, and Government Research, University of Alaska

– 1973b. Race Relations in an Alaska Native Village. *Anthropologica* 15(2):167–90

– 1976. *Aleuts in Transition: A Comparison of Two Villages*. Seattle: University of Washington Press

Jones, D.M., and J.R. Wood. 1975. *An Aleut Bibliography*. Report 44. Fairbanks: Institute of Social, Economic, and Government Research, University of Alaska

Jordan, J.W., and H.D.G. Maschner. 2000. Coastal Paleogeography and Human Occupation of the Lower Alaska Peninsula. *Geoarchaeology: An International Journal* 15(5):385–414

Jorion, Paul. 1976. To Be a Good Fisherman You Do Not Need Any Fish. *Cambridge Anthropology* 3(1):1–12

– 1982. All Brother Crews in the North Atlantic. *Canadian Review of Sociology and Anthropology* 19(4):513–26

Kari, James, and James Fall. 2003. *Shem Pete's Alaska: The Territory of the Upper Cook Inlet Dena'ina*. 2nd edn. Fairbanks: University of Alaska Press

Keiser, Lincoln. 1979. *The Vice Lords: Warriors of the Street*. New York: Holt, Rinehart, and Winston

Kelly, Robert. 1995. *The Foraging Spectrum: Diversity in Hunter-Gatherer Lifeways.* Washington, DC: Smithsonian Institution Press

Khlebnikov. 1994. *Notes on Russian America.* Parts 2–5: *Kad'iak, Unalashka, Atkha, the Pribylovs.* Compiled by R.G. Liapunova and S.G. Fedorova. Trans. M. Ramsay, ed. R.A. Pierce. Kingston, ON: Limestone Press (originally published in 1979 in Russian)

King, Thomas. 1997. Folk Management among Belizean Lobster Fishermen: Success and Resilience or Decline and Depletion? *Human Organization* 56(4):418–26

Kirtland, John C. 1981. *The Relocation and Internment of the Aleut People during World War II: A Case in Law and Equity for Compensation.* Anchorage: Aleutian/Pribilof Islands Association

Kizzia, Tom. 1999. Town Defends Its Rights to Fishery. *Anchorage Daily News*, 27 June

Kleinfeld, J. 1971. Sources of Parental Ambivalence toward Education in an Aleut Community. *Journal of American Indian Education* 10(2):8–14

Knapp, Gunnar. 2000. The Future of the Alaska Seafood Industry. *Alaska Business Monthly* 16(11):20–4

Knapp, Gunnar, Darla Siver, Pat Deroche, and Alexandra Hill. 2002. *Effects of the 2002 Chignik Salmon Cooperative: A Survey of Chignik Salmon Permit Holders.* December. Anchorage: Institute of Social and Economic Research, University of Alaska

Knowles, Governor Tony. 2000a. Declaration of Disaster. 19 July. www.state.ak.us

– 2000b. Letter to Alaska Board of Fisheries Chairman Dan Coffey. 9 August. www.state.ak.us

Knudson, Tom. 2002. Environment, Inc. *Sacramento Bee* (five-part series), 22–26 April. www.sacbee.com/static/archive/news /projects/environment/20010422.html

Kohlhoff, Dean. 1995. *When the Wind Was a River: Aleut Evacuation in World War II.* Seattle: University of Washington Press

Krech III, Shephard. 1999. *The Ecological Indian.* New York: W.W. Norton

Krivoshapkin, Vladimir. 1996. Who Will Help the Aleuts of the Commander Islands? *Arctic Voice* 12:21–2

Kruse, John. 1991. Alaska Inupiat Subsistence and Wage Employment Patterns: Understanding Individual Choice. *Human Organization* 50(4):317–26

Kurlansky, M. 1997. *Cod: A Biography of the Fish That Changed the World.* Toronto: Knopf

Langdon, Stephen J. 1980. *Transfer Patterns in Alaskan Limited Entry Fisheries*. Final Report for the Limited Entry Study Group of the Alaska State Legislature

– 1982. *Alaska Peninsula Socioeconomic and Sociocultural Systems Analysis*. US Bureau of Land Management, Alaska Outer Continental Shelf Office, Technical Report 71. Springfield, VA: National Technical Information Service

– 1989. From Communal Property to Common Property to Limited Entry: Historical Ironies in the Management of Southeast Alaska Salmon. In *A Sea of Small Boats*, ed. J. Cordell, 304–32. Cambridge, MA: Cultural Survival

– 1991. The Integration of Cash and Subsistence in Southwest Alaskan Yup'ik Eskimo Communities. *Senri Ethnological Studies* 30:269–91

– ed. 1986. *Contemporary Alaska Native Economies*. Lanham, MD: University Press of America

Langsdorff, Georg H. von. 1813–14. *Voyages and Travels in Various Parts of the World during the Years 1803, 1804, 1805, 1806, and 1807*. 2 vols. London: H. Colburn

Lantis, Margaret. 1940. Note on the Alaskan Whale Cult and Its Affinities. *American Anthropologist* 42:336–69

– 1960. *Eskimo Childhood and Interpersonal Relationships: Nunivak Biographies and Genealogies*. Seattle: University of Washington Press

– 1970. The Aleut Social System, 1750 to 1810, from Early Historic Sources. In *Ethnohistory in Southwestern Alaska and the Southern Yukon: Method and Content*. ed. M. Lantis. Studies in Anthropology 7. Lexington: University Press of Kentucky

– 1984. Aleut. In *Handbook of North American Indians*, vol. 5, *Arctic*, ed. David Damas, 161–84. Washington, DC: Smithsonian Institution Press

Laughlin, W.S. 1963. Eskimos and Aleuts: Their Origins and Evolution. *Science* 142(3591): 633–45

– 1980. *Aleuts: Survivors of the Bering Land Bridge*. New York: Holt, Rinehart, and Winston

Laughlin, W.S., and J.S. Aigner. 1975. Aleut Adaptation and Evolution. In *Prehistoric Maritime Adaptations of the Circumpolar Zone*, ed. W. Fitzhugh. Paris: Mouton

Layton, Robert. 1997. *An Introduction to Theory in Anthropology*. Cambridge: Cambridge University Press

Leach, E.R. 1954. *Political Systems of Highland Burma*. Cambridge, MA: Harvard University Press

Leacock, Eleanor. 1981. *Myths of Male Dominance.* New York: Monthly Review Press

Leacock, Eleanor, and Richard Lee, eds. 1982. *Politics and History in Band Societies.* Cambridge: Cambridge University Press

Lebedeva, Janna. 1993. The Aleuts' Culture on the Komandorskie Islands May Disappear. *Northern News* 8(55):1–3

Lee, Nella. 1995. Culture Conflict and Crime in Alaskan Native Villages. *Journal of Criminal Justice* 23(2):177–89

– 2000. *Crime and Culture in Yup'ik Villages: An Exploratory Study.* Criminology Studies, vol. 10. Lewiston, NY: Edwin Mellen Press

Lee, Richard. 1969. Eating Christmas in the Kalahari. *Natural History*, December

– 1979. *The !Kung San: Men, Women and Work in a Foraging Society.* New York: Cambridge University Press

– 1984. *The Dobe !Kung.* New York: Holt, Rinehart, and Winston

– 1988. Reflections on Primitive Communism. In *Hunters and Gatherers,* vol. 1, *History, Evolution, and Social Change.* ed. T. Ingold, D. Riches, and J. Woodburn, 252–68. Explorations in Anthropology Series. Oxford: BERG

Lee, Richard, and Richard Daly, eds. 1999. *The Cambridge Encyclopedia of Hunters and Gatherers.* Cambridge: Cambridge University Press

Lepowsky, Maria. 1993. *Fruit of the Motherland: Gender in an Egalitarian Society.* New York: Columbia University Press

Lévi-Strauss, Claude. 1966. *The Savage Mind.* Chicago: University of Chicago Press

– 1969. *The Elementary Structures of Kinship.* Boston: Beacon Press

Lewis, David, Geoffrey Wood, and Rick Gregory. 1996. *Trading the Silver Seed: Local Knowledge and Market Moralities in Aquaculture Development.* London: ITDG Publishing

Liapunova, R.G. 1996. *Essays on the Ethnography of the Aleuts (at the End of the Eighteenth and the First Half of the Nineteenth Century).* Trans. J. Shelest, ed. W. Workman and L. Black. Rasmuson Library Historical Translation Series, vol. 9. Fairbanks: University of Alaska Press

Lisianskii, I.F. 1814. *A Voyage Round the World in the Years 1803, 4, 5, & 6: Performed by Order of His Imperial Majesty Alexander First, Emperor of Russia, in the Ship Neva.* London: Printed for J. Booth

Litke, Fedor Pretrovich (alias Frederic). 1987. *A Voyage around the World, 1826–1829.* Vol. 1, *To Russian America and Siberia.* Ed. R.A. Pierce. Kingston, ON: Limestone Press

Llewelyn-Davies, Melissa. 1981. Women, Warriors, and Patriarchs. In *Sexual Meanings: The Cultural Construction of Gender and Sexuality,* ed. S. Ortner and H. Whitehead, 330–58. Cambridge: Cambridge University Press

Lord, Nancy. 1997. *Fishcamp: Life on an Alaskan Shore.* Washington, DC: Counterpoint

Lowe, Marie. 2008. Crab Rationalization and Potential Community Impacts of Vertical Integration in Alaska's Fisheries. In *Enclosing the Fisheries: People, Places, and Power,* ed. Marie Lowe and Courtney Carothers, 119–53. American Fisheries Society Symposium 60. Bethesda, MD: American Fisheries Society

Lurie, Nancy. 1971. The World's Oldest On-Going Protest Demonstration: North American Indian Drinking Patterns. *Pacific Historical Review* 40:311–32

Lynge, Finn. 1992. *Arctic Wars: Animal Rights, Endangered Peoples.* Biddeford, ME: University Press of New England

McCartney, Allen. 1974. Prehistoric Cultural Integration along the Alaska Peninsula. *Anthropological Papers of the University of Alaska* 16(1):59–84

– 1984. Prehistory of the Aleutian region. In *Handbook of North American Indians,* vol. 5, *Arctic,* ed. D. Damas, 119–35. Washington, DC: Smithsonian Institution Press

McCay, Bonnie. 1984. The Pirates of Piscary: Ethnohistory of Illegal Fishing in New Jersey. *Ethnohistory* 31:17–37

McCay, Bonnie J., and James M. Acheson, eds. 1987. *The Question of the Commons: The Culture and Ecology of Communal Resources.* Tucson: University of Arizona Press

McCloskey, William. 1998. *Their Fathers' Work: Casting Nets with the World's Fishermen.* New York: McGraw-Hill

MacCormack, Carol, and Marilyn Strathern, eds. 1981. *Nature, Culture, and Gender.* Cambridge: Cambridge: University of Cambridge Press

McDaniel, Josh. 1997. Communal Fisheries Management in the Peruvian Amazon. *Human Organization* 56(2):147–52

McDiarmid, G. Williamson. 1983. Community and Competence: A Study of an Indigenous Primary Prevention Organization in an Alaskan Village. *White Cloud Journal* 3(1):53–74

McGoodwin, James R. 1990. *Crisis in the World's Fisheries: People, Problems, and Policies.* Stanford: Stanford University Press

McGowan, Sarah. 1999a. Fox Farming: A History of the Industry in the American Period. In *The History and Ethnohistory of the Aleutians*

East Borough, ed. L. Black et al., 243–51. Kingston, ON: Limestone
. Press

– 1999b. Commercial Whaling at Akutan. In *The History and Ethnohistory of the Aleutians East Borough*, ed. L. Black et al., 265–78. Kingston,
ON: Limestone Press

MacLeish, Sumner. 1997. *Seven Words for Wind: Essays and Field Notes
from Alaska's Pribilof Islands*. Seattle: Epicenter Press

McNabb, Steven. 1985. A Final Comment on the Measurement of the
"Skipper Effect." *American Ethnologist* 12:543–4

– 1988. Impacts of Federal Policy Decisions on Alaska Natives. *Journal of
Ethnic Studies* 18(1):111–26

Madden, R. 1992. The Forgotten People: The Relocation and Internment
of Aleuts during World War II. *American Indian Culture and Research
Journal* 16(4):55–76

Makarova, Raisa. 1975. *Russians on the Pacific, 1743–1799*. Ed. R.A.
Pierce and A.S. Donnelly. Kingston, ON: Limestone Press.

Malecha, Patrick, Al Tingley, and Kurt Iverson. 2000. *Changes in the Dis-
tribution of Alaska's Commercial Fisheries Entry Permits, 1975–1999*.
CFEC Report no. 00–3N. August. Juneau: Commercial Fisheries Entry
Commission

Malinowski, Bronislaw. 1922. *Argonauts of the Western Pacific*. New
York: Dutton

– 1926. *Crime and Custom in Savage Society*. London: Routledge and
Kegan Paul

Marcus, George. 1998. *Ethnography through Thick and Thin*. Princeton:
Princeton University Press

Marenin, Otwin. 1992. Explaining Patterns of Crime in the Native Villages of Alaska. *Canadian Journal of Criminology* 34(July/Oct.):339–68

Marsh, Gordon. 1954. A Comparative Survey of Eskimo-Aleut Religion.
Anthropological Papers of the University of Alaska 3(1):21–36

Marsh, Gordon, and William Laughlin. 1956. Human Anatomical Knowledge among the Aleutian Islanders. *Southwestern Journal of Anthropology* 12(1):38–78

Mary-Rousselière, Guy. 1984. Iglulik. In *Handbook of North American
Indians*, vol. 5, *Arctic*, ed. D. Damas, 431–46. Washington, DC: Smithsonian Institution Press

Maschner, Herbert. 1996. Mobile, Egalitarian and Peaceful: Hunter-
Gatherer Archaeo-mythology in Western North America. Depart-
mental colloquium, Department of Anthropology, University of
Wisconsin-Madison

– 1998. Salmon Run Volatility, Subsistence, and the Development of
North Pacific Societies. *Proceedings of the 12th International Abashiri
Symposium: Salmon Fishery in the North and Its Change through Time.*
Edited by the Hokkaido Museum of Northern Peoples, 11–28. Abashiri,
Hokkaido, Japan: Association for the Promotion of Northern Cultures

– 1999a. Prologue to the Prehistory of the Lower Alaska Peninsula. *Arctic
Anthropology* 36(1–2):84–102

– 1999b. Sedentism, Settlement, and Village Organization on the Lower
Alaska Peninsula: A Preliminary Assessment. In *Settlement Pattern Studies in the Americas: Fifty Years since Viru*, ed. B. Billman and G. Feinman,
56–76. Washington, DC: Smithsonian Institution Press

– 2000. Catastrophic Change and Regional Interaction: The Southern
Bering Sea in a Dynamic World System. In *Identities and Cultural Con-
tacts in the Arctic*, ed. Martin Appelt, Joel Berglund, and Hans Christian
Gulløv, 252–65. Proceedings of a conference held 30 November to 2
December 1999 at the Danish National Museum, Copenhagen

Maschner, H.D.G., and B. Hoffman. 2003. The Development of Large
Corporate Households along the North Pacific Rim. *Alaska Journal of
Anthropology* 1(2):41–63

Maschner, Herbert, and Katherine Reedy-Maschner. 1998. Raid, Retreat,
Defend (Repeat): The Archaeology and Ethnohistory of Warfare on the
North Pacific Rim. *Journal of Anthropological Archaeology* 17:19–51

– 2005. Aleuts and the Sea. *Archaeology Magazine*, March/April, pp.
63–70

Maschner, Herbert, James Jordan, Brian Hoffman, and Tina Dochat. 1997.
The Archaeology of the Lower Alaska Peninsula. Report 4 of the Lab-
oratory of Arctic and North Pacific Archaeology. Madison: University
of Wisconsin

Masterson, James, and Helen Brower. 1948. *Bering's Successors, 1745–
1780: Contributions of Peter Simon Pallas to the History of Russian
Exploration toward Alaska.* Seattle: University of Washington Press

Maurstad, Anita. 2000. To Fish or Not to Fish: Small-Scale Fishing and
Changing Regulations of the Cod Fishery in Northern Norway. *Human
Organization* 59(1):37–47

Maynard-Smith, John. 1964. Group Selection and Kin Selection. *Nature*
20:1145–7

Menzies, Charles, ed. 2006. *Traditional Ecological Knowledge and Natural Resource Management.* Lincoln: University of Nebraska Press

Merck, C.H. 1980. *Siberia and Northwestern America, 1785–1795. The
Journal of Carl Heinrich Merck, Naturalist with the Russian Scientific*

Expedition Led by Captain Joseph Billings. Translated from the 1937 German manuscript by F. Jaensch. Kingston, ON: Limestone Press

Merculieff, Ilarion. 1994. Western Society's Linear Systems and Aboriginal Cultures: The Need for Two-Way Exchanges for the Sake of Survival. In *Key Issues in Hunter-Gatherer Research*, ed. E.S. Burch and L. Ellanna, 405–15. Explorations in Anthropology Series. Oxford: BERG

– 1997. Eco-tourism Development on St Paul Island, the Pribilofs, Alaska. In *Arctic Ecology and Identity*, ed. S.A. Mousalimas, 133–41. ISTOR Books 8. Los Angelas: International Society for Trans-Oceanic Research

Milan, L.C. 1974. Ethnohistory of Disease and Medical Care among the Aleut. *Anthropological Papers of the University of Alaska* 16(2):15–40

Miller, Pam, and Norman Buske. 1996. *Nuclear Flashback: Report of a Greenpeace Scientific Expedition to Amchitka Island, Alaska – Site of the Largest Underground Nuclear Test in U.S. History.* A Greenpeace Report. 30 October

Milton, Kay. 1993. *Environmentalism: A View from Anthropology.* New York: Routledge

– 1996. *Environmentalism and Cultural Theory: Explaining the Role of Anthropology in Environmental Discourse.* New York: Routledge

Minnegal, Monica, Tanya King, Roger Just, and Peter Dwyer. 2003. Deep Identity, Shallow Time: Sustaining a Future in Victorian Fishing Communities. *Australian Journal of Anthropology* 14(1):53–71

Mishler, Craig, and Rachel Mason. 1996. Alutiiq Vikings: Kinship and Fishing in Old Harbor, Alaska. *Human Organization* 55(3):263–9

Montaigne, Fen. 2003. Everybody Loves Atlantic Salmon, Here's the Catch ... *National Geographic*, July, pp. 100–23

Morgan, Lael. 1976. Anchorage and Fairbanks – the Biggest Native Villages of Them All. *Alaska* 42(3):33–7, 77–9

– ed. 1980. The Aleutians. *Alaska Geographic* 7(3)

Morrow, Phyllis. 1992. Culture and Communication in the Alaskan Courtroom: A Place to Be Made to Talk. *Arctic Research of the United States* 6:65–70. Washington, DC: National Science Foundation

– 1993. Sociolinguistic Mismatch: Central Alaskan Yup'iks and the Legal System. *Alaska Justice Forum* 10(2):1

– 1994. Legal Interpreting in Alaska. *Alaska Justice Forum* 10(4):1, 3–6

Morrow, Phyllis, and Chase Hensel. 1992. Hidden Dissension: Minority-Majority Relationships and the Use of Contested Terminology. *Arctic Anthropology* 29(1):38–53

Mousalimas, Soter A. 1990. "... If reports can be believed, Russian priests destroyed all the masks they could find ..." [Aleutian Islands; French summary] *Etudes/Inuit/Studies* 14(1/2):1–208

– 1995. *The Transition from Shamanism to Russian Orthodoxy in Alaska*. Oxford: Berghahn Books

Moyer, Sharon. 1992. Race, Gender, and Homicide: Comparisons between Aboriginals and Other Canadians. *Canadian Journal of Criminology*, July–October, pp. 387–402

Mulcahy, Joanne B. 2001. *Birth and Rebirth on an Alaskan Island: The Life of an Alutiiq Healer*. Athens: University of Georgia Press

Myers, Fred. 1988. Critical Trends in the Study of Hunter-Gatherers. *Annual Review of Anthropology* 17:261–82

– 1994. Culture-Making: Performing Aboriginality in the Asia Society Gallery. *American Ethnologist* 21(4):679–99

Nadasdy, Paul. 1999. The Politics of TEK: Power and the "Integration" of Knowledge. *Arctic Anthropology* 36(1–2):1–18

Nadel, Jane. 1984. Stigma and Separation: Pariah Status and Community Persistence in a Scottish Fishing Village. *Ethnology* 23(2):101–15

Nadel-Klein, Jane. 2003. *Fishing for Heritage: Modernity and Loss along the Scottish Coast*. Oxford: BERG

Nadel-Klein, Jane, and Dona Lee Davis, eds. 1988. *To Work and To Weep: Women in Fishing Economies*. Social and Economic Paper no. 18, St John's, NF: Institute of Social and Economic Research, Memorial University of Newfoundland

www.narf.org. 1999. Native American Rights Fund. *Native Village of Elim, Nome Eskimo Community, and Kawerak, Inc. v. State of Alaska, Frank Rue in his official capacity as Commissioner of Fish & Game, and Peninsula Marketing Association*. 15 October. See also www.touchngo.com/sp/html/sp-5192.htm

National Research Council. 2003. *Decline of the Steller Sea Lion in Alaskan Waters: Untangling Food Webs and Fishing Nets*. National Research Council of the National Academies. Ocean Studies Board and Polar Research Board. Washington, DC: National Academies Press

Netsvetov, Iakov. 1980. *The Journals of Iakov Netsvetov*. Vol. 1, *The Atkha Years, 1828–1844*. Trans. L. Black. Kingston, ON: Limestone Press

Northern Economics, Inc. 2000. *Importance of Salmon to the Aleutians East Borough*. Parts 1 and 2. Prepared for the Aleutians East Borough. January. Anchorage: Northern Economics

– 2001. *Relative Importance of Groundfish, Salmon, and Crab to Communities in Southwest Alaska* (draft). Prepared for the Southwest Alaska Municipal Conference. November (84 pp.)

Nuttall, Mark. 1992. *Arctic Homeland: Kinship, Community and Development in Northwest Greenland.* Toronto: University of Toronto Press

– 1998. *Protecting the Arctic: Indigenous Peoples and Cultural Survival.* Studies in Environmental Anthropology, Vol. 3. Amsterdam: Harwood Academic Publishers

– 2000. Choosing Kin in a Greenlandic Community. In *Dividends of Kinship: Meanings and Uses of Social Relatedness,* ed. P. Schweitzer, 33–60. London: Routledge

Oceana. 2003. *Coral Report – Deep Sea Corals: Out of Sight but Not Out of Mind.* www.oceana.org. Access date: November 2003

Oceana and The Ocean Conservancy. 2003. *Aleutian Archipelago: Cradle of Life in Alaska's Seas.* Pamphlet on preserving cold water corals in the Aleutians. www.oceana.org. Access date: November 2003

O'Leary, Matthew. 1995. Geography and Chronology of Central Yupiit Warrior Traditions. Paper presented at the annual meeting of the Alaska Anthropological Association, 1995, in Anchorage

– 2002. Estimating Casualties for the Aleut Resistance, 1763–1775. Paper presented at the annual meeting of the Alaska Anthropological Association, April 2002, in Anchorage

O'Neill, Theresa. 1999. "Coming Home" among Northern Plains Vietnam Veterans: Psychological Transformations in Pragmatic Perspective [in issue "The Pragmatic Turn in Psychological Anthropology"]. *Ethos.* 27(4):441–65.

Orth, Geoffrey. 1986. Fishing Strategies among Southeast Alaskan Salmon Seiners. MA thesis, University of Alaska, Fairbanks

Ortner, Sherry. 1981. Gender and Sexuality in Hierarchical Societies: The Case of Polynesia and Some Comparative Implications. In *Sexual Meanings: The Cultural Construction of Gender and Sexuality,* ed. Sherry Ortner and Harriet Whitehead, 359–409. Cambridege: Cambridge University Press

– 1984. Theory and Anthropology since the Sixties. In *Comparative Studies in Society and History* 26(1):126–66

– 1989. *High Religion: A Cultural and Political History of Sherpa Buddhism.* Princeton: Princeton University Press

– 1996. *Making Gender: The Politics and Erotics of Culture.* Boston: Beacon Press

Ortner, Sherry, and Harriet Whitehead. 1981. Introduction: Accounting for Sexual Meanings. In *Sexual Meanings: The Cultural Construction of Gender and Sexuality*, ed. Ortner and Whitehead, 1–27. Cambridge: Cambridge University Press

Osherenko, Gail, and Oran Young. 1989. *The Age of the Arctic: Hot Conflicts and Cold Realities*. Cambridge University Press

Palinkas, Lawrence A. 1987. Points of Stress and Modes of Adjustment in Southwest Alaska. *Human Organization* 46(4):292–304

Pálsson, Gísli. 1988. Hunters and Gatherers of the Sea. In *Hunters and Gatherers*, vol. 1, *History, Evolution, and Social Change*, ed. T. Ingold, D. Riches, and J. Woodburn, 189–204. Explorations in Anthropology Series. Oxford: BERG

– 1991. *Coastal Economies, Cultural Accounts: Human Ecology and Icelandic Discourse*. Manchester: Manchester University Press

– 1993. Household Words: Attention, Agency and the Ethnography of Fishing. In *Beyond Boundaries: Understanding, Translation and Anthropological Discourse*, ed. G. Pálsson, 117–39. Oxford: BERG

– 1994. Enskilment at Sea. *Journal of the Royal Anthropological Institute* 29(4):901–27

Pálsson, Gísli, and E. Paul Durrenberger. 1990. Systems of Production and Social Discourse: The Skipper Effect Revisited. *American Anthropologist* 92(1):130–41

Pallas, Peter Simon. 1802/1803. *Travels through the Southern Provinces of the Russian Empire, in the Years 1793 and 1794*. Translated from the German by the author. London: Printed by A. Strahan

Paulin, Jim. 2000. Fishermen Deny Allegations of Chucking Chum Overboard. *Dutch Harbor Fisherman*, 29 June, p. 4

Pentikäinen, Juha. 1983. Voluntary Death and Single Battle: Suicidal Behavior and Arctic World Views. *Psychiatria Fennica* (suppl.), 123–36

Perry, Richard. 1996. *From Time Immemorial: Indigenous Peoples and State Systems*. Austin: University of Texas Press

Pérusse, Daniel. 1993. Cultural and Biological Success in Industrial Societies. *Behavioural and Brain Sciences* 9:267–322

Peterson, Nicolas. 1993. Demand Sharing: Reciprocity and the Pressure for Generosity among Foragers. *American Anthropologist* 95(4):860–74

Petrivelli, Alice. 1991. A View from the Aleutian Islands [in English and Inuktitut] *Inuktitut* 73:14–29

Petrivelli, Patricia. 1997. Comment, Alaska Humanities Forum. *Frame of Reference* 8(1):10

Petterson, John. 1983. Policy and Culture: The Bristol Bay Case. *Coastal Zone Management Journal* 10(4):313–30

Philemonof, Dimitri. 2001. Improving Aleutian/Pribilof and Yukon Kuskokwim Tribal Relations. *Aang Angagin, Aang Angaginas* 20(1):2–3

Pierce, R.A., ed. 1978. *The Russian Orthodox Religious Mission in America, 1794–1837: With Materials Concerning the Life and Works of the Monk German, and Ethnographic Notes by the Hieromonk Gedeon.* Translated from the 1894 Russian edition by C. Bearne. Kingston, ON: Limestone Press

Pilcher, W.W. 1972. *The Portland Longshoremen: A Dispersed Urban Community.* New York: Holt, Rinehart, and Winston

Playfair, Susan. 2003. *Vanishing Species: Saving the Fish, Sacrificing the Fisherman.* Hanover: University Press of New England

Poggie, John, and Richard Pollnac. 1988. Danger and Rituals of Avoidance among New England Fishermen. *Maritime Anthropological Studies* 1(1):66–78

Polanyi, Karl. 1945. *Origins of Our Time: The Great Transformation.* 2nd edn. London: Gollancz

Porter, Robert A. 1890. *Report on the Population and Resources of Alaska at the Eleventh Census: 1890.* Department of Interior. Washington, DC: US Government Printing Office

Price, David. 2003. Un-American Anthropological Thought: The Opler-Meggers Exchange. *Journal of Anthropological Research* 59(2):183–203

Price, T.D., and J.A. Brown, eds. 1985. *Prehistoric Hunter-Gatherers: The Emergence of Cultural Complexity.* New York: Academic Press

Pullar, Gordon L. 1992. Ethnic Identity, Cultural Pride, and Generations of Baggage: A Personal Experience. *Arctic Anthropology* 29(2):182–91

Quimby, George. 1944. *Aleutian Islanders: Eskimos of the North Pacific.* Anthropology leaflet no. 35. Chicago: Chicago Natural History Museum

Rabinowitz, Daniel. 1997. *Overlooking Nazareth: The Ethnography of Exclusion Galilee.* Cambridge: Cambridge University Press

Ransom, Jay Ellis. 1946. Aleut Natural-Food Economy. *American Anthropologist* 48(4):607–23

Rasing, W.C.E. 1994. *"Too Many People": Order and Nonconformity in Iglulingmiut Social Process.* Reeks Recht & Samenleving no. 8. Den Haag: Cip-Gegevens Koninklijke Bibliotheek

Reedy-Maschner, Katherine. 2001. Aleut Identity and Indigenous Commercial Economies: Local Responses under Global Pressures in the Eastern Aleutians. *Alaska Journal of Anthropology* 1(1):62–82

Reimer, Catherine S. 1999. *Counseling the Inupiat Eskimo*. Westport, CT: Greenwood Press

Renouf, M.A.P. 1984. Northern Coastal Hunter-Fishers: An Archaeological Model. *World Archaeology* 16:18–27

Riches, David. 1982. *Northern Nomadic Hunter-Gatherers: A Humanistic Approach*. London: Academic Press

– ed. 1986. *The Anthropology of Violence*. Oxford: Blackwell

Ridley, Matt. 1993. *The Red Queen: Sex and the Evolution of Human Nature*. London: Viking

– 1996. *The Origins of Virtue: Human Instincts and the Evolution of Cooperation*. London: Viking

Robarchek, Clayton, and Carole Robarchek. 1998. *Waorani: The Contexts of Violence and War*. Fort Worth: Harcourt Brace

Robert-Lamblin, Joëlle. 1982a. An Historical and Contemporary Demography of Akutan, an Aleutian Village. *Etudes/Inuit/Studies* 6(1):99–126

– 1982b. Woman's Role and Power within the Traditional Aleut Society. *Folk* 24–197–202

Rogers, D. 1990. Stock Composition and Timing of Sockeye Salmon in the False Pass Fishery. University of Washington School of Fisheries, Fisheries Research Institute, FRI–UW–9006

Rogers, D., C. Boatright, and R. Hilborn. 2000. Alaska Peninsula Salmon, 1999. School of Fisheries SOF-UW-2004. May (21 pp.)

Rosaldo, Michelle, and Louise Lamphere, eds. 1974. *Women, Culture, and Society*. Stanford: Stanford University Press

Rosaldo, Renato. 1979. Utter Savages of Scientific Value. In *Politics and History in Band Societies*, ed. Eleanor Leacock and Richard Lee, 309–25. Cambridge: Cambridge University Press

– 1993. *Culture and Truth: The Remaking of Social Analysis*. London: Routledge

Rosman, Abraham, and Paula Rubel. 1971. *Feasting with Mine Enemy: Rank and Exchange among Northwest Coast Societies*. New York: Columbia University

Rubel, Arthur J. 1961. Partnership and Wife-Exchange among the Eskimo and Aleut of Northern North America. *Anthropological Papers of the University of Alaska* 10(1):59–72

Sacks, Karen. 1979. *Sisters and Wives: The Past and Future of Sexual Equality*. Contributions in Women's Studies, no. 10. Westport, CT: Greenwood Press

Sahlins, Marshall. 1972. *Stone Age Economics*. New York: Aldine

- 1976. *Culture and Practical Reason*. Chicago: University of Chicago Press
- 1985. *Islands of History*. Chicago: Chicago University Press
- 1995. *How "Natives" Think (about Captain Cook, for example)*. Chicago: University of Chicago Press

Sarafin, W.L. 1977. Smallpox Strikes the Aleuts. *Alaska Journal* 7(1):46–9

Sauer, Martin. 1972 [1802] *Expedition to the Northern Parts of Russia. [Account of a Geographical and Astronomical Expedition to the Northern Parts of Russia]*. Surrey: Richmond Publishing

Schafer, N.E., Richard W. Curtis, and Cassie Atwell. 1997. Disproportionate Representation of Minorities in the Alaska Juvenile Justice System: Phase I Report. September. Anchorage: Justice Center, University of Alaska

Schweitzer, Peter, ed. 2000. *Dividends of Kinship: Meanings and Uses of Social Relatedness*. London: Routledge

Seeb, L.W., and P.A. Crane. 1999. Allozymes and Mitochondrial DNA Discriminate Asian and North American Populations of Chum Salmon in Mixed-Stock Fisheries along the South Coast of the Alaska Peninsula. *Transactions American Fisheries Society* 128:88–103

Seeb, L.W., P.A. Crane, and E.M. Debevec. 1998. *Genetic Analysis of Chum Salmon Harvested in the South Unimak and Shumagin Islands June Fisheries, 1993–1996*. Regional Information Report no. 5J97–17. Anchorage: Alaska Department of Fish & Game

Seyfrit, C.L, L.C. Hamilton, and C.M. Duncan. 1998. Ethnic Identity and Aspirations among Rural Alaska Youth. *Sociological Perspectives* 41(2):343–65

Shelikhov, G.I. 1981. *A Voyage to America, 1783–1786*. Trans. M. Ramsay, ed. R.A. Pierce. Kingston, ON: Limestone Press

Shields, Captain Ed. 2001. *Salt of the Sea: The Pacific Coast Cod Fishery and the Last Days of Sail*. Lopez Island, WA: Pacific Heritage Press

Shinkwin, Anne, and Mary Pete. 1982. Alaskan Villagers' Views on Problem Drinking: "Those Who Forget." *Human Organization* 41(4):315–22

- 1983. *Homes in Disruption: Spouse Abuse in Yup'ik Eskimo Society*. Fairbanks: University of Alaska

Shirley, Susan. 1996. *Area M Purse Seine Vessels: Report to the Alaska Board of Fisheries*. CFEC Report 96–1N. Juneau: Commercial Fisheries Entry Commission

Shore, Bradd. 1996. *Culture in Mind: Cognition, Culture, and the Problem of Meaning*. Oxford: Oxford University Press

Sider, Gerald. 1986. *Culture and Class in Anthropology and History: Newfoundland Illustration*. New York: Cambridge University Press

Sikes, Gina. 1998. *Eight Ball Chicks: A Year in the Violent World of Girl Gangsters*. New York: Doubleday

Smith, Anthony. 1981. *The Ethnic Revival in the Modern World*. Cambridge: Cambridge University Press

Smith, Barbara Sweetland, and Patricia Petrivelli. 1994. *A Sure Foundation: Aleut Churches in World War II*. Anchorage: Aleutian/Pribilof Islands Association

Smith, Courtland. 1981. Satisfaction Bonus from Salmon Fishing: Implications for Economic Evaluation. *Land Economics* 57(2):181–96

Smith, Eric Alden, and Joan McCarter, eds. 1997. *Contested Arctic: Indigenous Peoples, Industrial States, and the Circumpolar Environment*. Seattle: University of Washington Press

Snigaroff, Cedor. 1979. *Niigugis maqaxtazaqangis: Atkan Historical Traditions Told in 1952*. 2nd edn., ed. K. Bergsland. Fairbanks: Alaska Native Language Center

Sökefeld, Martin. 1999. Debating Self, Identity, and Culture in Anthropology. *Current Anthropology* 40(4):417–47

Spaulding, Philip. 1955. An Ethnohistorical Study of Akutan: An Aleut Community. MA thesis, University of Oregon, Eugene

Spencer, R.F. 1959. *The North Alaskan Eskimo: A Study in Ecology and Society*. Washington, DC: Bureau of American Ethnology

Sprott, Julie E. 1997. Christmas, Basketball, and Sled Dog Races: Common and Uncommon Themes in the New Seasonal Round in an Inupiaq Village. *Arctic Anthropology* 34(1):68–85

www.state.ak.us. State of Alaska's official website

Stæhlin, Jakob von. 1774. *An Account of the New Northern Archipelago, Lately Discovered by the Russians in the Seas of Kamtschatka and Anadir*. Trans. from the German original. London: Printed for C. Heydinger

Steller, Georg Wilhelm. 1988 [1743]. *Journal of a Voyage with Bering, 1741–1742*. Ed. O. Frost. Stanford: Stanford University Press

Stevens, Stan, ed. 1997. *Conservation through Cultural Survival: Indigenous Peoples and Protected Areas*. Washington, DC: Island Press

Steward, Julian. 1955. *The Theory of Culture Change: The Methodology of Multilinear Evolution*. Urbana: University of Illinois Press

Stoller, Gary. 2003. Despite Law, Fishermen Face Deadliest Job Risks. *USA Today*, 12 March

Strathern, Marilyn. 1988. *The Gender of the Gift: Problems with Women and Problems with Society in Melanesia*. Berkeley: University of California Press

Stump, Ken, and Dave Baker. 1996. *Sinking Fast: How Factory Trawlers Are Destroying U.S. Fisheries and Marine Ecosystems*. Washington, DC: Greenpeace

Swift, Jeremy, ed. 1978. Marginal Peoples at the Modern Frontier in Asia and the Arctic. *Development and Change* 9(1):3–20

Symons, Donald. 1979. *The Evolution of Human Sexuality*. New York: Oxford University Press

Taksami, Natalia. 1999. Unga Coal and Gold Mining. In *The History and Ethnohistory of the Aleutians East Borough*, ed. Lydia Black, Sarah McGowan, Jerry Jacka, Natalia Taksami, and Miranda Wright, 279–86. Fairbanks: University of Alaska Press

Tango-Lowy, Torene, and Robert Robertson. 2002. Predisposition toward Adoption of Open Ocean Aquaculture by Northern New England's Inshore Commercial Fishermen. *Human Organization* 61(3):240–51

Taylor, Lawrence. 1981. "Man The Fisher": Salmon Fishing and the Expression of Community in a Rural Irish Settlement. *American Ethnologist* 8(4):774–88

Tennberg, Monica. 1996. Indigenous Peoples' Involvement in the Arctic Council. *Northern Notes* 4 (December):21–32

Tooby, John, and Leda Cosmides. 1992. The Psychological Foundations of Culture. In *The Adapted Mind*, ed. J. Barkow, L. Cosmides, and J. Tooby, 19–136. New York: Oxford University Press

Townsend, J.B. 1980. Ranked Societies of the Alaskan Pacific Rim. *Senri Ethnological Studies* 4:123–56

– 1983. Pre-contact Political Organization and Slavery in Aleut Societies. In *The Development of Political Organization in Native North America*, ed. E. Tooker, 120–32. Washington DC: Proceedings of the American Ethnological Society, 1979

Trivers, R.L. 1971. The Evolution of Reciprocal Altruism. *Quarterly Review of Biology* 46:35–57

Turner, Victor. 1967. *The Forest of Symbols: Aspects of Ndembu Ritual*. New York: Cornell University Press

U.S. Fish & Wildlife Service. 2001. *Sea Otter Declines in Southwest Alaska: A Growing Concern*. November. Anchorage: Marine Mammals Management Office

Van Gennep, Arnold. 1960. *Rites of Passage.* Chicago: University of
Chicago Press

Vansina, Jan. 1985. *Oral Tradition as History.* Madison: University of
Wisconsin Press

VanStone, James. 1960.A Successful Combination of Subsistence and
Wage Economies on the Village Level. *Economic Development and
Cultural Change* 8(2):174–91

Veltre, Douglas W., and Allen P. McCartney. 2002. Russian Exploitation
of Aleuts and Fur Seal: The Archaeology of Eighteenth- and Early-Nine-
teenth-Century Settlements in the Pribilof Islands, Alaska. *Historical
Archaeology* 36(3):8–17

Veltre, Douglas W., and Mary J. Veltre. 1987. The Northern Fur Seal:
A Subsistence and Commercial Resource for Aleuts of the Aleutian
and Pribilof Islands, Alaska [French summary]. *Etudes/Inuit/Studies*
11:51–72

Veniaminov, I. 1840. *Notes on the Islands of the Unalashka District.* Vols.
1, 2, 3. St Petersburg, Russia: Russian-American Company

– 1984. *Notes on the Islands of the Unalashka District [1840].* Trans. L.
Black and R.H. Goeghega, ed. R.A. Pierce. Alaska History 27. Kingston,
ON: Limestone Press

– 1993. *Journals of the Priest Ioann Veniaminov in Alaska, 1823 to 1836.*
The Rasmuson Library Historical Translation Series. Vol. 7. Trans. J.
Kisslinger. Introduction and commentary by S.A. Mousalimas. Fair-
banks: University of Alaska Press

Wachowich, Nancy. 2001. Making a Living, Making a Life: Subsistence
and the Reenactment of Iglulingmiut Cultural Practices (Nunavut). PHD
dissertation, University of British Columbia

Walker, Monica, ed. 1997. *Interpreting Crime Statistics.* Oxford:
Clarendon Press

Waller, David. 1996. Friendly Fire: When Environmentalists Dehumanize American Indians. *American Indian Culture and Research Journal*
20(2):107–26

Waxell, Sven. 1952 [1743] *The American Expedition.* Translation, introduction, and notes by M.A. Michael. London: William Hodge

Weber, Max. 1947. Social Stratification and Class Structure. In *Max
Weber: The Theory of Social and Economic Organization,* trans. A.M.
Henderson and Talcott Parsons, 424–9. New York: Free Press.

– 1948. Class, Status, Party. In *From Max Weber: Essays in Sociology,*
trans. and ed. H.H. Gerth and C. Wright Mills, 180–95. London: Routledge & Kegan Paul

Weibust, Knut. 1958. *The Crew as a Social System*. Oslo: Norsk Sjøfarts-museum, Båtgransking.

Wenzel, George. 1991. *Animal Rights, Human Rights: Ecology, Economy, and Ideology in the Canadian Arctic*. Toronto: University of Toronto Press

Wheeler, Patricia C. 1998. The Role of Cash in Northern Economies: A Case Study of Four Alaskan Athabascan Villages. PHD dissertation. University of Alberta.

Wiessner, Polly, and Wulf Shiefenhövel, eds. 1996. *Food and the Status Quest: An Interdisciplinary Perspective*. Providence: Berghahn Books

Wilson, Margo, and Martin Daly. 1985. Competitiveness, Risk Taking, and Violence: The Young Male Syndrome. *Ethology and Sociobiology* 6:59–73

Wolfe, Robert J. 1984. Commercial Fishing in the Hunting-Gathering Economy of Yukon River Yup'ik Society. *Etudes/Inuit/Studies* 8:159–83

Wolfe, Robert J., and Robert J. Walker. 1987. Subsistence Economies in Alaska: Productivity, Geography, and Development Impacts. *Arctic Anthropology* 24:56–81

Wolfe, R.J., J.J. Gross, S.J. Langdon, J.M. Wright, G.K. Sherrod, L.J. Ellanna, V. Sumida, and P.J. Usher. 1984. *Subsistence-Based Economies in Coastal Communities of Southwest Alaska*. Technical Paper no. 89. Juneau: Division of Subsistence, Alaska Department of Fish & Game

Wood, Darryl. 1997. Violent Crime and Characteristics of Twelve Inuit Communities in the Baffin Region, NWT. PHD dissertation, Simon Fraser University, British Columbia

– 1999a. Patterns of Crime in the Circumpolar North. Paper presented at the annual meeting of the Academy of Criminal Justice Sciences, March 1999, in Orlando, Florida

– 1999b. Job Attrition among Alaska Village Public Safety Officers: Preliminary Findings from a Survey of Current and Former Officers. Paper presented at the annual meeting of the Academy of Criminal Justice Sciences, March 1999, Orlando

– 2000. Officer Turnover in the Village Public Safety Officer Program. *Alaska Justice Forum* 17(2):1, 4–7

Wood, Darryl, and Lawrence Trostle. 1997. The Nonenforcement Role of Police in Western Alaska and the Eastern Canadian Arctic: An Analysis of Police Tasks in Remote Arctic Communities. *Journal of Criminal Justice* 25(5):367–79

Woodburn, James. 1982. Egalitarian Societies. *Man* 17:431–51

- 1988. African Hunter-Gatherer Social Organization: Is It Best Understood as a Product of Encapsulation? In *Hunters and Gatherers*, vol. 1, *History, Evolution and Social Change*, ed. T. Ingold, D. Riches, and J. Woodburn, 31–64. Oxford: BERG

Woodward, Kathryn, ed. 1997. *Identity and Difference*. London: Sage
- 2000. *Questioning Identity: Gender, Class, Nation*. London: Routledge

Worl, Rosita. 1980. The North Slope Inupiat Whaling Complex. *Senri Ethnological Studies* 4:305–20

Worl, Rosita, and Charles Smythe. 1986. *Barrow: A Decade of Modernization*. Minerals Management Services Technical Report no. 125. Anchorage: US Department of Interior, Alaska Outer Continental Shelf Region

Wrangham, Richard, and Dale Peterson. 1996. *Demonic Males: Apes and the Origins of Human Violence*. Boston: Houghton Mifflin

Wright, Robert. 1994. *The Moral Animal: Evolutionary Psychology and Everyday Life*. New York: Vintage Books

Index

access: to crew members, 127; to fisheries, 5, 22, 66, 70–2, 79, 109–10; to food, 45; to goods and services, 153; to labour, 153; and male status and prestige, 26, 30, 69, 128, 239–41; as measurement of well-being, 245; to money, 94, 132; to political positions, 159, 161, 166; to resources, 30–2, 103, 132, 206–7, 239; to sexual partners, 27, 147–8; to traditional way of life, 108

acculturation, 19, 33, 55

Adak Island, 11, 40, 260n3

Agattu, 259n3

Agdaagux Tribal Council, xxi, 16, 76, 158, 162

adoption, 87

adornment, 22, 49, 51, 190

agency, 25; and intentionality, 28; and practice, 32

aggrandizement, 26, 29–30, 123

Akutan, 12, 23, 62, 69, 83, 263n3

Alaska Beluga Whale Commission (ABWC), 193

Alaska Commercial Company (ACC), 56–7

Alaska Department of Fish and Game (ADF&G), 74, 94–5, 106, 109, 116–17, 157, 181–3, 192, 225, 245, 262n8, 266n16

Alaska Eskimo Whaling Commission (AEWC), 193

Alaska Federation of Natives (AFN), 60, 197

Alaska Fishermen's Union, 66

Alaska Maritime National Wildlife Refuge, 60

Alaska National Interest Lands Conservation Act (ANILCA), 73, 262n2

Alaska Native Claims Settlement Act (ANCSA), 16, 61, 258n8

Alaska Natives, 3, 5, 38, 249; and commercial economy, 81; as commercial fishermen, 75, 127; competition and conflict within community, 187; ethnic revival, 203–4; and imagined principles of sustainability, 196; in justice system, 220–1; "levelling out" of standard of living, 174; life expectancy, 150, 237, 264n9; out-migration of, 35; self-government of, 58, 220; status, 186; subject to federal Indian law, 61; and subsistence, 8–9; subsistence use of salmon, 168, 186; variability of economic exchange, 243

Alaska Peninsula Coastal Fishermen's Association (APCFA), 66